AF352609

The Question of the Other

Selected Studies in Phenomenology
and Existential Philosophy 15

The Question of the Other

Essays in Contemporary Continental Philosophy

edited by
Arleen B. Dallery and Charles E. Scott

State University of New York Press

Published by
State University of New York Press, Albany

For information, address State University of New York
Press, State University Plaza, Albany, N.Y., 12246

Library of Congress Cataloging-in-Publication Data

The Question of the other: essays in contemporary continental philosophy /
    edited by Arleen B. Dallery and Charles E. Scott.
        p.   cm. — (Selected studies in phenomenology and existential
    philosophy; 15)
    Includes index.
    ISBN 0-7914-0032-8. — ISBN 0-7914-0033-6
    1. Philosophy, Modern—20th century. 2. Philosophy, European—History—
20th century. I. Dallery, Arleen B. II. Scott, Charles E. III. Series.
B804.Q47   1989
190—dc19   88-39152
                                                                CIP

10 9 8 7 6 5 4 3 2 1

Contents

VI. *Foucault: Theory and the Destabilized Subject*

I

Levinas: The Face of the Other

— 1 —

From Intentionality to Responsibility:
On Levinas's Philosophy of Language

Adriaan Peperzak

In this paper I would like to show how Emmanuel Levinas, in close affinity with Martin Heidegger, but at the same time in sharp opposition to him, has developed his understanding of language into a radical transformation of "first philosophy." The way along which this transformation becomes possible includes an original interpretation of what we habitually call "Western philosophy." By giving a critical diagnosis of this 2600-year-long epoch of Greek and European thought, Levinas tries to determine its leading orientation and the perspective from which it developed into a philosophy that—notwithstanding its unique greatness—neglected and distorted some all-important, simple, and obvious elements of human existence.

Among the issues taken up by Levinas in order to guide his readers from the Western tradition to a new perspective (which, in fact, is a very old and very common one) is the basic concept of Husserlian phenomenology: *intentionality.* (Since we will, in this paper, give some attention to the relationships connecting as well as separating Levinas from Heidegger, it may be good to remember that for Heidegger, too, meditation on the status and meaning of intentionality was one of the major paths from the tradition to a new origin, as can be seen, for example, from his course of the summer of 1925 on the history of the concept of time, published as *Prolegomena zur Geschichte des Zeitbegriffs.*)[1] Levinas's meditation on language has been presented by him as a central part of his persistent reflection on Edmund Husserl's principle of intentionality. By systematizing somewhat the elements of a theory of language that can be found mainly in *Otherwise than Being; or, Beyond Essence*[2] and the essay "Language and Proximity,"[3] I shall try to give a succinct picture of Levinas's critical retrieval of that principle and his passing beyond it towards a trans- or pre-intentional origin, which, in fact, is not an *arche* but an *anarchical* "beginning."

The Principle of Phenomenology

Let us follow the main line of Levinas's argument in "Language and Proximity" and start from intuition, "the principle of principles," as Husserl calls it in *Ideas I*, § 24:

> Every originarily given intuition is a source for the legitimation of knowledge; everything that presents itself originarily to us (so to say in bodily actuality), must be simply accepted as that as what it gives itself, but only within the limits within which it therein gives itself. . . . Every enunciation (*Aussage*) that does not do anything else than to give expression to such givens (*Gegebenheiten*) through mere explication and adequately corresponding significations, is therefore actually . . . an absolute beginning (*Anfang*), that is, in a true sense, called to be a foundation (*Grundlegung*), *principium*.[4]

Many questions may arise from the reading of this text. An important one concerns the expressions "originarily present" and "given." If, for this moment, we grant Husserl that the search for an absolute foundation of knowledge does not rest on dogmatic or false assumptions, we might ask: Where do we find a given that has the character of an origin and can function as foundation? We know Husserl's answer: It is the intuition of some x that presents itself as though it were a living body there in front of our eyes. Intuition is claimed to assure a firm ground on which we can build other layers of a solid construction called "true and ascertained knowledge." This answer, however, provokes the following critical question: Is the metaphor of an eye seeing bodies an adequate or even the most adequate rendering of a primordial evidence that is able to function as an origin?

Plato is the original authority for the seeing metaphor. In *Republic* 507d–509c he stated that a truthful contact between eye and phenomenon would not be possible without a specific mediation that accords light to both the phenomenon and the looking eye. His meditation on this necessary medium resulted in a metaphysics that proclaimed light itself to be more eminent and more originary than either the world of phenomena or the seeing psyche recognizing them as phenomena.

There are other possibilities of making contact with reality. The mediation on which the hearing of a sound depends is less obvious, and the distance between the hearer and the heard is smaller than that of visual perceptions, but distance and mediation cannot be abolished altogether. Feeling, however, seems to be the most immediate way of being in touch with phenomena or their primordial constituents.

The most elementary sensation is the most immediate contact between a sensing and a sensed, so immediate that we may call it a fusion or confusion. If there is no experience of any distance at all, the feeling and the felt are not given as distinct elements. Can we, in this case, speak of anything given? To whom, to what, *as* what, then, would it be given? If this immediacy were the most radical and the all-encompassing dimension of human existence, the origin would be the unity of a pure confusion without contours or relations; a chaotic and "formless void" before the emergence of any profile (AE 40–43, OB 32–34).

In AE 41–43 (OB 32–34) Levinas observes that when Husserl introduces the notion of an arch-impression (*Ur-impression*) as the absolute start of all experience—a sort of first creation—he hints at a sort of timeless presence "before" all possible modifications and before the scission that splits consciousness and being. If consciousness and being have not yet separated, the 'presentation' or 'giving' of something to, for, or by consciousness is, however, impossible. And since consciousness is understood by Husserl as 'having present before' or as 'presenting or representing something to itself', there is, at this level of first creation or *archi-presence,* neither consciousness nor givenness. Intentionality and phenomenality have not yet emerged.

In order to be presented or given, that is, in order to appear or become phenomenal, a being must deploy itself *in time.* A being becomes a phenomenon (or an element thereof), the hidden becomes perceptible, a timeless presence becomes a given presence, by unfolding itself within the openness of temporality. The exhibition of something before consciousness is conditioned by the temporal ekstases of its unrolling itself from a past to a future, while the ekstases through retention (memory) and protention (expectation) are gathered into the horizon of a concrete presentation or representation.[5] Intuition, the principle of principles, is conditioned by temporal modifications that do not alter the content of the given. Disclosedness implies, or rather *is,* the deployment of time. The phenomenality of all phenomena presupposes and essentially implies temporality. Time is the light without whose mediation perceptibility would be impossible (AE 33–38, OB 26–30).

For the experience and the concept of presence, this insight involves, as a consequence, that "the present" is *either* that which, as a moment of the primitive flow of time, is never present—one comes always too late to capture it—*or* something that comes "after" the originary gathering of temporal ekstases: something captured and arrested—for example, as a theme, by an identifying gesture. To become conscious of an *x* as "this-here-and-now," one must come back onto that which already has passed or is being passed. By a most elementary sort of *anamnesis* (recollection), one must remember what already has escaped. Without time, consciousness would not awaken from its immersion in the indistinct confusion (ED 222–

23, CP 113–15). The "bodily presence" of a phenomenon is constituted by the gathering of its temporal ekstases; it presupposes a presentification, and this is, as we will see, possible only as an active identification.

Indeed, the presentification to which a phenomenon owes its possibility of appearing before consciousness demands more than temporality alone. To appear as a phenomenon, being must also be identified *as this or that*. Through identification the confusion-before-creation receives its first possibility of showing shapes and figures. In the absence of any identification, there would be only the rustling of a totally anonymous and shapeless "there is" (*il y a*) in which everything gets confused with everything else.

The identification of a phenomenon as this or that is its *thematization:* "Being manifests itself by becoming a theme," that is, by being gathered, centered, and posited as . . . . The identity of a phenomenon is *thetic* in virtue of its being 'seen' or 'thought of' *as* an issue taken and stated as this or that. To 'see' or 'conceive' of a given as this or that is not a form of pure receptivity, but a specific way of looking at or 'taking' and positing as. Consciousness "takes" or "*means*" the given as . . . . Identification is a *Meinen* and *Vermeinen*. The *as-structure* indicates the position achieved by consciousness in every possible intuition to lay hands on a phenomenon.[6] Intentionality implies the capturing of givens through the recollection of their sensible multiplicity by taking or positing them as thetic realities. There is a sort of sovereignty in this way of getting in touch with the given. Consciousness leads the game and determines the positions of the pawns. (See ED 218–219, CP 110–111.)

By taking a phenomenon as a theme, I perceive it in the light of a specific meaning expressed by the "as" of the as-structure. To use Husserlian terms: I impose an ideality on a given. Being cannot become phenomenal if it does not appear as having this or that meaning. This meaning, however, is not given immediately before any temporal synchronization and thematic recollection. The given must be meant in order to have a meaning. In a way, its meaning is not given, but rather imposed. To mean this *as* this, is a claim or allegiance (*prétention*) through which consciousness *intends*, or even—in a pre-behavioral sense—'wills' the given as an appearance. To make this constitutive moment of phenomenality and perception understandable, Levinas uses the ambiguity of the German word *meinen,* which means 'to have the impression, the belief, or the conviction that' as well as 'to intend', 'to aim', or 'to have the purpose', and of the French *entendre,* which means 'to understand' as well as 'to want' or 'to will'.[7] The original understanding of a phenomenon is not a purely passive reception through which it would produce a corresponding "idea" in the perceiving consciousness, but an *intention* in the strong sense of an intending (*entendre*) that is a claim, a pretending (*prétendre*) or pretension (*prétention*), which may be justifiable or not. The difference between the immediately given and the meaning claimed or "pretended" by consciousness cannot be abolished by any evidence. This difference does not lie in the distance between the emptiness of a signative act and the originary given of a bodily present phenomenon—a distance that could be bridged progressively, at least in part, by a series of new experiences; it is the difference of two different dimensions (ED 218, CP 110). The meaning is neither given nor not-given; it is meant, claimed, pretended. The fulfillment of the empty signative act is therefore necessarily delayed. For the presence of a phenomenon it is essential that consciousness subsumes, gathers, and synchronizes the given multiplicity under a theme. The intending or meaning of a phenomenon as a present this or that achieves a *synopsis*. Without such a synopsis, no intuition would be possible. The authority of Husserl's "principle of all principles," thus, rests upon the meaning or "intention" (including a "pretention") by which a synthetic and synchronic, thematizing and identifying consciousness presents and—as temporal consciousness—represents the given.

Meaning and Language

If the identification of a being presupposes its thematization in the light of an ideal meaning, the imposition of this ideality on the given—its being taken and claimed as . . .—presupposes its being illuminated and consecrated by a sort of *doxa:* a 'word' or 'fore-word', for which Levinas uses the expressions *epos* and *fable*.

From the outset a given is perceived, taken as . . . , thematized, and identified in light of and as an instance of something that goes beyond the given as simply received: a sort of "already said" (*déjà-dit*) that is not yet heard or spoken, but is already more than a perceptual grasping of the given (AE 45–46, OB 35–36). If Levinas uses the word *fable* to indicate this *verbum mentis* or fore-word,[8] he probably alludes to the character of an exemplary story that can be illustrated by many cases. The word *epos* (AE 46, 48, OB 34, 36) stresses the narrative context of our thematizing of phenomena as meaningful, as well as the (pre)linguistic aspect of our "meaning" them as meaningful. The "already said" of this doxa or epos precedes, however, all particular languages of history.[9]

In going beyond mere givenness, the ideal meaning is a universal, but its universality cannot be understood as that of a genus or species of which the phenomena of human experience would be the individual realizations. The identification of this as this does not proceed by individualization or exemplification of a universal idea that would be present as an a priori.

Even the very first phenomenon that strikes us is necessarily seen as the appearance of a meaning that is not exhausted by this appearance. But neither is it a case of a general idea remaining equal to itself in all the instances concretizing it. Even a *singulare tantum* like Socrates is perceived as an instance of a certain way of being that could be called 'Socratizing' (AE 53, OB 41).

Although the ontological status of the prelinguistic epos or fable is not easy to determine, there must be such a sort of fore-word preceding actual speech or writing, because the thematizing identification, by which a phenomenon is constituted as such, would not be possible, if it were not guided by an affirmation or affirmative gesture, which normally expresses itself in linguistic discourse. The affirmative character of identification is *kerygmatic:* to identify a being is to pronounce a kerygma or proclamation; consciousness proclaims this phenomenon to be this and such. The most explicit form of such a proclamation is a philosophical judgment, but the same structure can be found in any narration, myth, tale, or story. All of them gather things, events, and relations into the synchronic unity of a whole, in which the fluency of time is punctuated by the identification of knots and relations. Predication, as contained in a philosophical theory, is an explicit form of kerygmatic identification by which immediate experience is laid open as a world of phenomena. The overcoming of the prephenomenal chaos and the emergence of an order from the anonymous grumbling of being before "creation" is conditioned by the *logos* of a saying or writing, which—in its turn—is conditioned by the emergence of givens from the persistent flow of time.

The appearance of a phenomenon implies, thus, the essential structure of *phenomenology.* Intentionality is a specific union of consciousness and being, made possible by a thematic way of saying (*Dire*). Every phenomenon is (a) said (*Dit*). The exhibition of being, its disclosure or manifestation, the very idea of phenomenality presupposes *and* conditions a particular mode of language: the *apophantic* language of gathering identification and thematic presentification of a said; kerygmatic proclamation; phenomenology.

Language and Being

We remain within the dimension of the phenomenologically said when we reflect, with Levinas, upon the "amphibology of being." As with the French *être* the English word *being* can, indeed, be used to *name* a single being or the totality of all beings, but also used as a *verb,* to indicate the being process, which—as Heidegger showed—must be understood as the active and transitive essence, or *essance,* thanks to which beings are, in various ways, what they are. Without entering, at this moment, into a discussion of the ontological difference as understood by Heidegger and reinterpreted by Levinas, I would like to dwell a little while on the linguistic difference through which the ontological difference is said.[10]

If Levinas is right in pointing out that the identification of phenomenal being implies a kerygmatic proclamation, which is the core of apophantic language, then being and language are so intimately connected that an adequate distinction between them is impossible. Being is inseparable from its spoken meaning. Then, also, the ways in which beings appear or "are" can be heard in language.

The designation of a being by a *noun* identifies it as a characteristic unit emerging from the constant flow of time. It is fixed and, to a certain extent, immobilized. By denomination one takes a being from the anonymous "there is" (*il y a*) of confused and chaotic sensation. Designation by nouns presupposes a preceding epos or fable: the speaker must already have heard a fore-word; he obeys a pro-phetic doxa when he tries to name the being that happens to him. To capture a being by a noun is a sort of consecration of it, without which it would not be what it is.

The said is, however, not exhausted by *nouns* alone; *verbs,* too, belong to its possibilities of proclamation. Verbs do not immobilize beings; thanks to them the fluency and the modifications of beings' being as a process of temporalization becomes apparent and audible. In a verb we can hear the vibration of sensibility, the modes of essence, the adverbiality of beings, the ways in which things and events pass as modifications of the ongoing deployment of disclosure. A noun does not suffice to say what happens or what is the case. The being of what there is—that is, the temporal essence of things, relations, and events—needs apophantic predication to become perceptible. There is no essence or appearance behind the said; the verbally said *is* the ostension and disclosure of being. In the predicative proposition the verb "exposes the silent resonance of the essence" (AE 51, OB 40). In a verb, being is meant and heard as time. Temporality is the verbality of being.

The power of verbality is best expressed in contemporary art. This is not only an example, but the very expression of the secret of the said and its attractive realm. Instead of fixing figures and profiles, or telling tales about events, today's art celebrates the ways in which essence and temporality pass, appearing and resounding in their modifications. As mere ostension of modalities of being, art is absolute exhibition without fixed quiddities. All representations of things are liquified in order to show colors, contrasts, timbres, rhythms, sounds, qualities. Everything must sing. The modalities of essence must beam and dance before the eye. This demands a continuous renewal. Conformity to once-accepted standards and iconographic codes would result in the withdrawal of Being's modalities. In art the language of words, forms, and sounds has become a "pure how" ("un pur comment," AE 52, OB 40). Not only music and architecture but all sorts of art show the adverbiality of being, which is forgotten if we concentrate on nouns and substantives.

It is, perhaps, not fortuitous that in philosophy, too, art has become more important than morality since Hegel dedicated much of his courses to aesthetics, whereas moral philosophy was made a subordinate part of his theory of law, economy, and the state. Heidegger, too, thought that he could delay indefinitely the questions of ethics, whereas poetics and visual arts were as important as philosophy itself for him. As we will see, for Levinas morality is as important and originary as the questions of metaphysics and more important than ontology. In order to understand why this does not represent a simple backsliding into the pre-Heideggerian tradition of philosophy, we must continue our analysis of language.

To conclude the first stage of this analysis, we may state that the amphibology of being belongs to the dimension of the Said. The hesitation of language between nouns and verbs, its switching from beings to Being and the other way around, characterizes it as *logos, apophansis,* Said (*le Dit*). Language is, however, more than that which is or can be said; it is more than the resounding essence of beings and their essance, more than an epos, myth, or *Sage,* more than the disclosure of a difference that would be restricted to the realm of ontology.

Saying

Perception and language have been described so far as belonging to the realm of the Said (*le Dit*). By this expression Levinas does not want to suggest an opposition between spoken and written language—on the contrary, written texts are the clearest examples of the Said. As opposed to the Saying (*le Dire*), the Said encompasses all discourses or narratives in which beings are identified and essence verbalized. The opposition between Saying and Said is neither a difference of two species belonging to one genus nor a dialectical contradiction like that between being and nonbeing. It is simultaneously a separation and an intimate relation between two dimensions that cannot be synthesized or integrated into a totality. (See for this and the following explication AE 55–61, OB 43–48.)

According to Levinas, the whole history of Western philosophy has been dominated by the idea that the philosophical problem of language can be identified as a problem of texts in which beings and Being show themselves by being worded in speech or writing. The whole of philosophy would coincide with *phenomenology,* and since the phenomena cannot show themselves as meaningful, that is, they cannot "speak," if they are not worded, philosophy would also necessarily be a *logology.* Heidegger has awakened our consciousness to the ontological difference, but, in Levinas's interpretation, Heidegger's diagnosis of our civilization and his search for a more originary origin have remained captive to the phenomenological and logological intentions of Greek-Western philosophy. Without minimizing the importance of the ontological difference and its oblivion, Levinas indicates a more radical oblivion when he points at a very simple fact, which surprisingly never has been taken into serious account by philosophy: *the fact that a discourse or epos (or Sage) always is said by someone to one or more others (or to oneself as listener or reader).*

The saying of a said is certainly one of the most ordinary and basic events of everybody's everyday life, as well as a root of the whole enterprise of civilization, unfolding itself in communication, social institutions, moral codes, skills, science, philosophy, religion, etc. Why, then, has the saying as such never become a theme of philosophical reflection? Why has this always concentrated exclusively on the said, without thematizing the saying through and "in" which the said exists?

The first answer is that saying resists becoming a theme. As we have seen, the very structure of thematization makes every being into a said, that is, a being that is identified as a phenomenon within the context of a story or discourse. Saying a said is not an element of such a context; it signifies a text and a context, but stays out of them by preceding all saids.

If, however, it is true that saying cannot be treated as a special sort or case of said, how, then, can we describe and analyze it? Descriptions, analyses, characterizations, theories, etc., are, indeed, ways of identification and thematization. If saying is not a phenomenon, that is, if it is neither a being nor Being as such, and if it is not a structure or form that can be identified as an element of being, how can we, then, give it a place in philosophy?

Levinas uses the Husserlian word *reduction* to indicate a way of writing and speaking philosophically about saying without simply reducing it to a variety of the said. When we try to give a description and an analysis of saying, the theme from which our reflection takes its departure is the said. But in a retrogressive and backward-thinking way we must, then, hint at the otherness by which the saying, prior to all saids, differs from any theme. The difficulties met here are analogous to those of Heidegger's attempt to name Being itself in its difference from the universe of beings and to those of Neoplatonic thought in trying to transcend the realm of *noèta* towards the One that cannot be treated as a subject of apophantic language. In a way somewhat similar to but also different from the Pseudo-Dionysian negative theology, Levinas tries to solve the paradox of a discourse on that which precedes but cannot enter into any discourse, by defending the necessity of alternately saying (*dire* in the sense of stating) and unsaying (*dédire* in the sense of denying) all that ought to be said about saying. But before we draw our attention to this apology for his texts about saying, let us first concentrate on their content.

Language is not only and not primarily enunciation, apophansis, or expression, but *communication*. In talking or writing I always address my words—and myself!—to someone: I speak to another person who I suppose hears me. Even if I speak or write to myself, I, the listener or reader of my words, differ from myself as writer or speaker. Speaking or writing, thus, includes necessarily a relation between someone and some other. This relation is the fact or event forgotten by Western philosophy.

One way to obscure it or leave it unnoticed is by simply not talking about it, as if it were self-evident that and how we can communicate, whereas everybody's relationships to world, society, Being, and oneself are considered to be problematic and worthwhile to be reflected upon.

Another way of hiding the peculiarity of saying is to distort it by treating it as a phenomenon comparable to other phenomena. To speak to someone is, however, radically different from treating somebody as the noema of an intention of mine. The other to whom I speak is not there before me as a phenomenon that I can observe, study, analyze, reflect upon, but as someone to whom I offer something that I have observed, felt, heard, studied, reflected upon, written, or said. Of course, I can take the measures of someone's body, look at the color of human eyes, appreciate the beauty of somebody's nose, but these intentions are separated by an unbridgeable abyss from the relation constituted by speaking to—or also by facing—another. The phenomenon seen by looking at the color of someone's eyes or the peculiarities of a human individual's anatomy belong to the universe of beings that can and must be described by an overall phenomenology, but the other to whom I speak is not such a phenomenon, and my relation to him or her does not have the structure of intentionality. By treating or observing another in a way that would be appropriate to a phenomenon in the normal sense of the word, I prevent myself from having an encounter with this person. In facing a face that looks at me and in speaking to someone, I separate myself from the identifying and thematizing attitude that is characteristic of a theoretical and technical and even of an aesthetic approach. By seeing another as an interesting variety of phenomenal being I reduce the other's otherness to an element of the thematic universe or context over which I preside by giving a place and function to all beings, relations, and events. By describing another as someone with green eyes, an elegant mouth, a sportive suit, a sweet voice, brilliant ideas, great erudition, and a pleasant character, I miss exactly the element that makes it possible that this person can face me and that I can speak to her or him. The one to whom I address myself in speaking or writing is not an element of any context; as long as we think in terms of phenomenal beings that have a place and function in texts and contexts, the other is a hole or absence: in contrast to the phenomena that I can observe, the other whom I meet as other is *invisible*.

According to Levinas, to whom phenomenality, as we have seen, is equivalent with the possibility of being identified and thematized, the other is not a phenomenon at all.

The Western fascination with theory and thematization has neglected or repressed the truth of the other's emergence from the context of noematic beings. This is the second answer to the question why saying and facing, and, in general, the relation between one human and the other, have been hidden in the traditions of our civilization. The theoretical intention is essentially inapt to take this most trivial experience of everyday life seriously; it cannot do justice to the fact that words are *addressed to someone*. The problem with philosophy is that, as soon as we want to concentrate on this experience, we make it into a theme and in so doing betray its truth: by becoming a theme, an address hides or loses the very moment of saying and, therefore, that by which its "signification" is communicative or signifying. By reducing it to a theme we cut the saying off from its orientation toward an actual or possible hearer and thus kill it as saying. The "to" has changed into the "in front of" or "before" of a noema that is present before consciousness or a *"with"* by which we can express our similarity or equality as co-human participants in a collective *we*.

A *third* way of forgetting or repressing the otherness of saying is to identify the problem of communication from the outset as a question of participation. If communication can be understood as a way of sharing common views or arguments, the relation of speaker to listener can be reduced to the universality and fundamental sameness of all human beings who recognize one another as participants in a common culture or *ethos*. This is the way followed by Heidegger when he treats communication as a form of *Mitteilung* and analyzes it as a particular mode of the existential *Mitsein* (SZ 214–21, GA 2: 161–66).

In *Sein und Zeit,* section 34, language is defined as the being-spoken-out of discourse (*Rede*), and discourse as the "signifying" articulation of the understandability of being-in-the-world. *Mitteilung,* sharing-with or the communicative aspect of language, comes to the fore if we notice that being-with (*Mitsein*) belongs as an existential constituent to being-in-the-world and that this always exists in a determinate mode of being-with-others (*Miteinandersein*). Among the constitutive moments of discourse (*Rede*), sharing-with (*Mitteilung*) must, therefore, be listed with the "what about" (das *Worüber*), the articulated (*das Geredete*), and the announcement (*die Bekundung*, SZ 216). In a strict parallelism with the relation between *Dasein* in general and its constituent *Mitsein*, which in sections 25–26 was introduced briefly as an introduction to and for the sake of the analysis of *das Man* in section 27, Heidegger treats *Mitteilung* in section 34 as a moment of language that comes after its primary essence, which is the articulation of *Dasein's* understanding of its being-in-the-world. Apophantic communication is a special case of the fundamental communication that is contained in the existential being-with. On this fundamental level there is already a sharing of disposedness (*Befindlichkeit*) and understanding (*Verstehen*) of being-in-the-world and being-with-others. Before any linguistic communication these existential structures are already revealed to those who share those structures as well as their being revealed and understood. The newness of the *Mitteilung* lies *only* in the explicit sharing (*Teilung*) of the *with* (*Mit*) by which they are joined in *Dasein* (SZ 215).

Hearing is analyzed by Heidegger in a similar way (SZ 217–18). The most original *Hören* is the existential openness of *Dasein* to its own capability of being. It is a belonging (*Hörigkeit*), made possible by the understanding in which Dasein as being-in-the-world-with-others hears and listens (is *hörig* with regard) to itself and belongs (is *zugehörig*) to itself. Speaking and hearing are considered exclusively as explicitations of the structure *Dasein*-with-others-near-innerworldly-beings. "With" (*mit*) and "near" (*bei*) specify the "*in*" of the "being-in." The relation to other humans is reduced to the "with" or the side-by-side of common participation, and this is subordinated to the overall relation of *Dasein* and *world*. No attention at all is given to the confrontation of two persons who speak to one another or to the encounter of two facing faces. The exchange of words, the alternation of addressing and responding essential to *all* speech—even if an answer is not given actually, but only expected—is not even mentioned, except, perhaps, in one place, where its importance is denied rather bluntly: "A denial as answer, too, results at first directly from the understanding of the 'shared' what about (*Worüber*) of speech."[11]

Our conclusion must be that Heidegger was not interested in that aspect of communication which is *not* reducible to a preceding and already present understanding common to people who meet and speak. For Heidegger there is nothing radically new in a speech I listen to or in the face that looks at me; communication is primarily, even exclusively, sharing and explicitation.

In his essay, *The Origin of the Work of Art*,[12] Heidegger is still more explicit when he states that—notwithstanding the current opinion, according to which the essence of language is a sort of communication (*Mit-*

teilung)—"language is not only and not primarily an expression by sounds or writing of that which ought to be communicated." Its primary essence is its "bringing the being as a being into the open." In the absence of language there is no openness of being. In naming beings language, by proclamation, "brings them from their being to their being" (GA 5: 61). Here, all Heidegger's attention is directed toward the triangle Language-Dasein-Being, as in *Sein und Zeit* it was concentrated on Dasein-Rede-World. The possibility of transcending myself and the world by addressing them to another who is not contained in them, is hidden by the caricature of "a transport of experiences, e.g., opinions and desires, from the interiority of one subject into the interiority of another subject" (SZ 215). However, according to Levinas, the alternative presented before the reader—either to vote for this caricature or to accept a description that reduces all intersubjectivity to shared participation in an anonymous instance fully present in *Dasein* as such—distorts the actuality of speaking and the human face-to-face. Although our speaking depends to a very large extent on the sagas and myths, the literary traditions and current sayings of the contexts in which we have become what we are, it is *not* true that language, understood as an anonymous power, speaks. The sentence telling us that language speaks[13] may be a rhetorically justified provocation meant to awaken our thought to a forgotten truth, but exaggerations like "the death of the subject," the repression of all individuality, and the indefinite delay of ethics are refuted by the simple fact that all saids and texts are addressed by someone to some other. There is always a vocative in our language; the irreducible relation to the addressee is clearly expressed not only in greetings that do not contain any message ("Hello!" or "Hi!"), but also in very informative sentences, since they are always spoken *to* or written *for* someone, who thereby is provoked to an answer. The fact that both the provocation and the answer, as to their content and form, can be understood as variations on the traditional patterns of a shared culture and *ethos,* does not abolish their being uttered and addressed by a saying that does not enter, as a contextual or intertextual element, into any said.

Whereas Heidegger's search is dominated by the quest of Being itself, Levinas points to another Beyond: the other who faces me, awakens me to a "dimension" beyond the universe of beings and their Being. In speaking to somebody I transcend the realm of Being by accepting my being meant to be there for the other.

Responsibility

In saying something to you, I not only present a text, but I expose, discover, present, and offer myself to you, who happens to hear me. You surprise me by coming to me. Even if I invited you, I must face a disturbance of my world. Indeed, your entering into my dwelling place interrupts the coherence of my world; you disarrange my order in which all things familiar to me have their proper place, function, and time. Your emergence makes holes in the walls of my house. If I could see and treat you as a being amidst other beings, like a knot in the all-encompassing time flow or as an element of a universe unfolding its riches before my mental eye, you would have been bereft of everything that justifies my calling you by the pronoun ''you.'' You would be a peculiar part of my realm.

To speak is not a special sort of intention that would be comparable to other noetico-noematic correlations; it is *transcendence*—the happening of a relation that ''precedes'' and conditions all sorts of intentions by offering the *whole* of my identifying and verbalizing acts, that is, the whole of my world, to someone who is not a part or moment or event within that whole. You and I are not to be found ''*in*'' the world, because you come from afar and, in speaking to you, I do not coincide with my being-in-the-world. The relation by which you and I are connected, as well as separated, is not a constituent of our being-in-the-world; you cannot be seen as a worldly being, whereas my subjectivity, as response to your facing me, precedes any nestling in the domain of phenomenal beings. Your being you is your invisibility; my being me is the origin of all responsibility: responsibility for you, for others, for all the others, and also for me.[14]

If we understand ''*Mitsein*'' as an expression of our coparticipation in a common culture, it is an existential constituent of our being-in-the-world, but neither ''mineness'' nor ''yourness'' can enter into this concept, except, perhaps, to indicate the characteristic style of your and my works and words. If, however, we take ''*Mitsein*'' to mean the originary—or, as Levinas calls it, the pre-original—relation from which all intersubjective and social contacts between humans spring, we must say that it does not belong, as a constitutive element, to the world and our being-in-it. The totality of our being-in-the-world (its *Ganzheit,* as Heidegger persistently calls it in *Sein und Zeit* and in the courses of the late twenties[15]) either forbids the entrance of another or is broken by it. The other who looks at me is not a phenomenon; a face is invisible, because it cannot be identified as a theme; it is not the noema of an intention in the sense that was described before. The ''epiphany'' of a visage cannot become familiar as a piece of my surroundings or a part of my social context; the other pierces the skin of my world when she or he visits me as an absolute stranger coming from Beyond.[16]

My speech, too, comes from a ''Beyond'' insofar as it precedes everything which is or can be said thematically. Saying is and remains exterior to the totality of texts that can be presented by it. The exteriority, which, according to its subtitle "*Essai sur l'extériorité*," is the subject of *Totality and Infinity*, is an Otherwise than the being of phenomena, and, if phenomenality is synonymous with Being, it "is" an *Otherwise than* or a "Beyond" of *Being*.

Even if my saying is a thematizing one, it cannot enter, as an element, into the discourse offered by it. It cannot be interpreted or appropriated because it precedes all contents and forms or structures. In its contentless and nondiscursive repetition it is always new, it has always already passed when its message is heard. It comes from a past that never can become a present. Its originality consists in the fact that it cannot be treated as a cause or ground, an *arche* or origin within the horizons of phenomenology and ontology. This is the reason why Levinas does not call saying an origin of the said, but rather the pre-original past from which the said comes—a past that never can become a graspable or identifiable present.

The subject of my speaking to another is the I who is responding to the stranger who visits me. Finding myself facing another awakens me to *responsibility:* an infinite responsibility for the other, who is in need of everything that is necessary for a human life. By addressing myself to another I practice this responsibility, be it reluctantly or not. A total refusal of it would express itself through murder. Total acceptance would coincide with perfect love.

Speaking can never become a theme or noema because its structure is radically different: it establishes a *contact* and a *proximity* which are neither forms of knowledge nor possible themes of a theory. The relation between speaker and listener is not a theoretical or thetic intention; it precedes the scission of theory and practice but includes an ethical moment. The pretheoretical responsibility practiced in proximity is analyzed extensively by Levinas as *substitution, obsession, accusation, election,* and *persecution.* The existential structure of "the one-for-the-other" marks every human life as a "me" in the accusative (the accusative of my responding to an appeal by the words "*Me voici*"—"See me, here and now"). The subjectivity of this "me" is being the one—the unique and only one—who is responsible for any other who arises in front of me. Affected by the defenseless nudity of another's face, I am exposed and inescapably delivered to an orientation that does not rest upon a choice of mine. The human subject is not dead, but it is not absolute autonomy either. Against the dogma of an original and originary liberty, and against its total abolition by some writers of today, Levinas shows that the obligations of my responsibility do not stem from any decision or contact or convention originating in my or our will. Before I even could think or choose or freely accept, I have become responsible. My responsibility for the others has begun before I became aware of my own being. Before my capacity to will, there is a more profound *passivity* in me. Human subjectivity has been determined by a past that never was and never will be a present. An immemorial and irretrievable past has chosen me as this individual here and now, who came from nowhere, to be responsible for these others.

Responsibility can be described as a pre-phenomenal and pre-ontological inspiration, but this should not lead us to the idea of an ethereal something, a soul or ghost that hides behind the skin of a human body. Against all forms of anthropological dualism Levinas's analyses show that human subjectivity exists as a sensible, affective, working, speaking, and suffering body, whose skin is the possibility of contact, proximity, and vulnerability and whose respiration is the dynamism of a moral inspiration and the expiration of someone who lives for others who may continue to live after one's death.

The human body with its sensibility is, however, not an exclusively altruistic possibility. As directed toward others it also enjoys earthly satisfactions and pleasures. The appeal to responsibility is heard by someone who already has been immersed in an ocean of lust and pains. Even after the discovery of other-directed responsibility, enjoyment still remains a necessity. Indeed, what could I offer the others, if it were not in any respect pleasant? Or what could I give, if I did not know by experience how good it feels to receive these gifts?

Signification

If speaking and writing are, first of all, responding to another's entrance into the world of the speaker or writer, the basic structure of language is the contact between one singularity indicating itself as "I" and another singularity called "you" by "me." The anonymous language of grammar and semantic theory comes after that. Language does not speak: it is the realm of all that has been or can be said; human subjects, however, speak, for example, when they greet each other without saying anything that has the character of a thesis or information. The realm of the Said is the realm of Western ontology. In it the truth of body, language, perception, culture, and subjectivity is confined to meanings that are perceptible from a phenomenological perspective. The individuality of speakers and listeners and the peculiarity of their relationships disappear behind the universality of the noematic correlates of the theoretical approach. This can be illustrated by an analysis of human *signature*.

If, in our reading of a text, we concentrate on that which therein is said, it will be difficult not to agree with those who state that every text is an exponent of—at the utmost a surprising variation on—a common heritage made up of ongoing myths and discursive practices that do not belong to anybody but can be appropriated by singular participants of such a common heritage. In this context a signature does not indicate more than an act of appropriation, which may still be justified to a certain extent, insofar as the author of this variation has marked the anonymous heritage by a more or less original style. From the perspective of the said a signature is the name of a work or style that differs from other works or styles in the history of a culture. The individuals behind the work are not interesting except insofar as the peculiarities of their texts and their affiliations, dependencies, etc., can be understood better through information about their life.

If language primarily is not an anonymous condition or source of saying, but saying itself, a signature is a gesture by which writers signal their responsibility for possible readers. By a sort of greeting they expose themselves as subjects who do not want to escape from their obligation to approach possible readers in a responsible way. Without having the pretention that we can originate or *possess* the content and the presuppositions of our texts, we still agree to our responsibility for them. Being the guardians of the language, the ethos, and the culture that have become ours through education and practice, we are "condemned" to give apologies for particular traditions. Nobody has invented the sources of our being human, but no individual, not even the most empty or stupid one, can be reduced to his or her work as if he or she were an event of language. For everybody's speaking or writing comes from a pre-original or anachronic past before culture and transcends the boundaries of any phenomenology.

Saying and Denying

The difference between the Saying and the Said cannot be the last word of a philosophy, because the relations by which they are connected demand reflection. However, such a reflection necessarily thematizes those relations and the two terms they relate, just as the foregoing and all possible reflection on transcendence betrays it in the very act of distinguishing it from intentionality. What is Levinas's answer to this paradox?

The program that must be executed in order to solve this paradox embraces three main questions: First, one must justify the enterprise of philosophically talking about a reality—transcendence, saying, substitution, subjectivity, and so on—that does not permit us to see, to think, or to treat it as a phenomenon, a noema, or a theme, and to which Levinas even denies the name of being. Once a philosophical discourse about a "beyond of being" has been justified, one ought, secondly, to show how the two incomparable dimensions of the said and the saying can be brought together in a philosophy of their difference and connectedness, that is, how phenomenology (or ontology) within one text can go together with non-phenomenological transcendence. Thirdly, a metatheoretical reflection is needed in order to determine the mode of thought by which this philosophy of both essance *and* transcendence can save itself from absurdity. Since it is impossible to treat here these questions in a satisfactory way, I will conclude by giving only a very succinct summary of Levinas's answer to the first question: How is it possible to treat philosophically the pre-original or *an-archical* Beyond that cannot be captured by the normal, reflective, and thematizing methods of our philosophical tradition?

Levinas agrees that his whole discourse on the other, saying, subjectivity, transcendence, etc., betrays these nonobjects by thematizing them. Although they are neither themes nor part of the Said, within philosophy they are necessarily treated as if they were. Still, Levinas could say, my work shows that one can thematize and (re)present these "non-phenomena" in a way that makes their radical difference from phenomenal beings understandable. Thematizing language apparently has two possibilities: besides the normal one, it is capable of pointing at, and somehow of determining, the borderlines of the thematizable as well as that which "is" beyond. Because such a determination necessarily involves a negation with regard to the essence of phenomenal, identifiable, and thematizable being, it involves a denial of whatever has been and must be said in a thematizing way. This denial cannot constitute a dialectical negation, which, according to Hegel, would lead to a synthetic concept. For if this were the adequate method, transcendence, saying, otherness, etc., would reveal themselves to be moments of a thought that has all the features of identifiable presence conceivable by a solitary Eye. The thetic treatment of transcendence and its subsequent denial, thus, create a tension that cannot be overcome by a straightforward discourse. A reconciliation within philosophy is not possible, if the concept of reconciliation implies a synthetic and synchronic view in which the two dimensions are understood as parts or moments of one whole. Stating and denying, saying (*dire*) and unsaying (*dédire*),[17] evoking and revoking are both necessary to bring our thought into a good relation with the transcendent. But since they cannot be thought simultaneously, their mode is alternation. Instead of the synchronic time of traditional philosophy, the *diachrony* of successive affirmations and denials is the only possibility of being true to "what there is and happens" and the conditions thereof. According to Levinas, all discourses must result in the undoing of the tissue they wove. Is Penelope, more than Parmenides, the patron of philosophy?

A repetitious and never-ending succession of saying and unsaying of the thematically said does not constitute a satisfactory theory. It seems to indicate a dead end, an "end" or frontier of philosophy itself. Levinas goes one step further when he states that the destination of apophantic language (the Said) is in its "ancillary or angelic" function (AE 7, OB 6). The subordination of all said to saying contains the germ of a metatheory of philosophy, in which there is, perhaps, more than the repetition of affirmations and negations without end. When Levinas, at the end of *Otherwise than Being*, explains the word "philosophy" as meaning an understanding on the basis of and from the perspective of love (σοψια της ψιλιας, "une sagesse de l'amour") (AE 207, OB 162), he points to a source beyond philosophy that might be approached more closely by a particular sort of life than by the profound reflections of ontology.

— 2 —

Rereading *Totality and Infinity*

Robert Bernasconi

It is now more than twenty-five years since the publication of Emmanuel Levinas's *Totality and Infinity*.[1] During that time certain habits of reading have been established. The focus has come to fall on the thirty pages that open its third part. In consequence, *Totality and Infinity* is known as a book about ethics, and it is often thought that if one wants to engage Levinas, it is sufficient to address the idea that the face-to-face relation provides the foundation for ethics.[2] How far that widespread impression is justified is too large a question for me to entertain today. I mention it only as a prelude to the question that has most preoccupied discussion about Levinas. The question is: what status is to be accorded the face-to-face relation? Here interpretations diverge. Some interpreters understand it as a concrete experience that we can recognize in our lives. Other commentators have understood the face-to-face relation to be the condition for the possibility of ethics and indeed of all economic existence and knowledge. If the first interpretation arises from what might be called an empirical reading, the second might be referred to as the transcendental reading. The puzzle is that Levinas himself seems unable to decide between these rival interpretations. Although in response to critics who have found his thought utopian he has insisted that the face-to-face relation can be experienced, he has also authorized the transcendental reading, as, for example, when in answer to a question put to him by the Dutch philosopher Theodore de Boer, he agreed that his thought was "a transcendentalism which starts with ethics."[3]

It should be noted, before accepting this division between an empirical and a transcendental reading of *Totality and Infinity,* that Levinas himself often hesitates before the very terms which characterize them. For example, in the preface to *Totality and Infinity,* the application of the word *experience* is put in question, so long as it is standardly understood: "The relation with infinity cannot, to be sure, be stated in terms of experience, for infinity overflows the thought that thinks it. . . . but if experience precisely means a relation with the absolutely other, that is, with what always overflows thought, the relation with infinity accomplishes experience in the fullest sense of the word" (TI 25; TeI xiii). Similarly, and on the very same

23

page, Levinas shows his uneasiness before the word *transcendental*, to which he nevertheless appeals: "The way we are describing to work back and remain this side of objective certitude *resembles* what has come to be called the transcendental method . . ." (emphasis added). The word *resembles* is the key here because by it Levinas attempts to distance himself from the common conception of the transcendental method. His reservations are explained some years later when, in the same place that Levinas gives his positive answer to de Boer's question about an ethical transcendentalism, he questions its association with the search for foundations (DVI 141). But then what is to be made of his claim that the face-to-face relation is the foundation of ethics?

There are further problems in supposing that Levinas is seeking to reconcile the motifs of transcendental philosophy with an appeal to experience. Levinas made it clear when he designated the face-to-face as an experience that this was possible only because the face of the Other ruptures what is ordinarily called experience. But can transcendental thinking survive such a rupture? Does not the very process of tracking the transcendental conditions of experience require that a continuous path be drawn between experience and its condition? In other words, can a transcendental thinking maintain the thought of transcendence? Levinas answers this question and shows the way in which his thought only *resembles* the transcendental method in the following passage: "We can proceed from the experience of totality back to a situation where totality breaks up, a situation that conditions the totality itself" (TI 24; TeI xiii). It might be said in consequence that the conditions for the possibility of the experience of totality are at the same time the conditions for the impossibility of the experience of totality, in the sense that the rupture with totality shows that there never was a totality. And the totality is ruptured by what Levinas calls *exteriority,* the transcendence in the face of the Other. Levinas follows the transcendental method to the point where it is halted and in order to sustain itself must draw on that which is radically exterior to it. This exteriority is itself therefore the condition both for that which had been revealed in transcendental thought and for transcendental thought itself.

This is what allows Levinas to say that the " 'beyond' the totality and objective experience . . . is reflected *within* the totality and history, *within* experience" (TI 23; TeI xi). And, at the risk of repeating what is already familiar, that is why the terms of the title *Totality and Infinity* are not opposed in such a way as to mean totality *versus* infinity. If the *infinite,* Levinas's word adopted from Descartes for that which breaks with the totality, was simply opposed to the totality, this would allow for their reintegration, according to a logic learned from Hegel, addressed by Levinas in *Totality and Infinity* (TI 53; TeI 23–24) and taken up again by Jacques Derrida in "Violence and Metaphysics."[4] Levinas elaborates on this path—insufficiently acknowledged by most commentators—in the following passage: "Between a philosophy of transcendence . . . and a philosophy of immanence . . . we propose to describe, within the unfolding of terrestrial existence, of economic existence (as we shall call it), a relationship with the other that does not result in a divine or human totality, that is not a totalization of history but the idea of infinity" (TI 52; TeI 23). The proposal underlies both the claim that the infinite in the finite is produced as desire (TI 50; TeI 21) and the claim that doing and labor are said to imply the relation with the transcendent (TI 109; TeI 81). But in what sense can it be said that labor implies a relation with the transcendent? As I shall try to show later, the attempt to answer that question occupies Levinas in section 2 of *Totality and Infinity,* under the title "Interiority and Economy."

The empirical and transcendental readings of *Totality and Infinity* provide the terms for almost every introduction to Levinas's thought, and I have so far discussed them only in their most elementary form; they also lie at the heart of more highly articulated readings. The empirical reading of *Totality and Infinity* need not just amount to an insistence that the face-to-face is a concrete experience. At the end of "Violence and Metaphysics," Derrida offers the verdict that there is in Levinas a renewal and inversion of empiricism "with an audacity, a profundity, and a resoluteness never before attained" (WD 151; ED 225). Levinas is said to have accomplished this by revealing empiricism to be also (what *he* calls) metaphysics. Derrida finds evidence for this complicity also in Kant, Husserl, Schelling, and Bergson, and this in spite of the fact that empiricism has always been determined by philosophy as philosophy's other, as nonphilosophy. And yet this empiricism, which appears to be opposed to philosophy, is, on closer examination, shown to call for it: "Nothing can so profoundly *solicit* the Greek logos—philosophy—than this irruption of the totally-other" (WD 152; ED 226). And so Derrida's admiration for Levinas turns to a questioning. This questioning focuses on the concept of experience itself and on Levinas's alleged attempt to break with Greek philosophy (and not simply to interrupt it). Early in the essay Derrida had suggested that Levinas appeals to experience against the Greek logos: Levinas's thought "by remaining faithful to the immediate, but buried nudity of experience itself, seeks to liberate itself from the Greek domination of the Same and the One . . . as if from oppression itself— . . . an ontological or transcendental oppression"[5] (WD 82–83; ED 122–23). But by the end of the essay Derrida was ready to pose at least as a question the possibility that the word *experience* had "always been determined by the metaphysics of presence," so that experience was "always an encountering of an irreducible presence" (WD 152; ED 225). It should be observed that these questions were not simply rhetorical. Derrida, unlike some of his followers, does not suppose that there is a language of metaphysics as such. In fact, earlier in the essay he had drawn on Levinas's recently published essays on the trace to acknowledge the possibility of an experience exceeding these limits: the beyond history is "present at the heart of experience," and yet it is "present not as a total presence but as a *trace*" (WD 95; ED 142).

At this point it ceases to be clear how Derrida conceives Levinas's renewal and inversion of empiricism. The uncertainty is fostered at least in part by the ambiguity of the word *metaphysics*. It is almost as though Derrida were suggesting that Levinas had accomplished the renewal of empiricism in spite of himself. Levinas had turned to a radical empiricism (which he also called "metaphysics") in an unsuccessful attempt to break with the tradition of Western philosophy, which he called *ontology* and which Derrida—following Heidegger—continued to call "metaphysics." Derrida, however, would find in the failure of this attempt an incidence of the law proposed throughout "Violence and Metaphysics," that it is necessary to lodge oneself within traditional conceptuality in order to destroy it (WD 111; ED 165). The complicity that Derrida finds between metaphysics and empiricism (as philosophy's other) exemplifies that law. The question is whether Levinas was as unsuspecting of it as Derrida, in places in the essay, seems to suggest. The interweaving of the transcendental and empirical motifs might offer some evidence that he was not.

The main proponent of the transcendental reading is de Boer in his important essay, "An Ethical Transcendental Philosophy."[6] De Boer specifies the dangers to which this characterization might give rise: for example, the suspicion that such a philosophy must be based on the indubitable certainty of the *ego cogito* (FFL 83). Instead he proposes to model his account of the "transcendental" relation of the same to the other on Levinas's reading of the Cartesian idea of infinity (FFL 95). I shall question this attempt to separate the Cartesian *cogito* from the Cartesian idea of the infinite later. De Boer is on more solid ground when he explains that by an ethical transcendental philosophy he does not mean "a universal, impersonal, and necessary structure, which can be reconstructed out of the phenomena," in line with traditional transcendental philosophy (FFL 100). The transcendental condition is "not a necessary ontological structure that can be reconstructed from the empirical phenomena." But can the face as the object of transcendental cognition be designated "an unrecoverable contingent or ontic incidence that intersects the ontological order," as de Boer suggests (FFL 108)? Levinas had always sought to distance himself from Heidegger's determination of the ontological difference and the related distinction between the existential and the existentiell, because he saw in them "an insidious form of the impersonal neuter" (TI 272; TeI 250). Their reintroduction here is therefore problematic. Furthermore, they represent an empirical moment at the heart of de Boer's attempt to sustain the transcendental reading. So at one point de Boer writes that "the transcendental condition is an ethical experience enacted in discourse" (FFL 97). And yet de Boer holds back from the conclusion to which this interpretation appears to lead, when he adds that "the condition for the possibility of experience is not experience itself" (FFL 105). De Boer, having at one point hinted at the conjunction of the transcendental and empirical readings, leaves their interrelation unclear. The difficulty in which de Boer finds himself is not accidental, as I shall try to show.

Unlike many commentators on Levinas, de Boer does not ignore the section of *Totality and Infinity* entitled "Interiority and Economy," but it has even more significance for the question at hand than perhaps even he recognizes. It is in the second part of *Totality and Infinity* that Levinas specifically addresses the interrelation between the transcendental and the empirical. I shall devote the remainder of my paper to this section. As a result I will be unable to give a direct answer to the question I raised earlier about the status Levinas gives to his account of the face-to-face. But I would claim that only through an examination of this second section are we in a position to understand how Levinas prepares his answer.

The second part of *Totality and Infinity* is concerned with labor and objectifying thought as relations *analogous* to transcendence (TI 109; TeI 81). And yet these relations analogous to transcendence "already imply the relation with the transcendent," the relation to the other. Levinas must therefore pursue the twofold task of, first, showing the difference between transcendent relations and relations analogous to transcendence and, secondly, showing the former to be reflected within the latter. Levinas is quite explicit that this can be accomplished in conformity with neither the classical logic of noncontradiction, "where the other of A is the negation of A," nor the dialectical logic, "where the same participates in and is reconciled with the other in the unity of a system" (TI 150; TeI 124). In both cases the transcendent relation cannot be maintained. What Levinas finds in his analyses is the "interval of separation." The notion of separation breaks with the ordinary understanding of relation. Whereas we ordinarily understand by *relation* "a simultaneity of distance between the terms and their union," in separation "the being that is in relation absolves itself from the relation, is absolute within the relationship" (TI 110; TeI 82). Separation as inner life, as psychism, the interiority of a presence at home with oneself, habitation and economy, already exhibits the distance that resists totalization.

Throughout this discussion Levinas uses Husserl and Heidegger as foils. More specifically, and it is confirmed by the opening sentences of the section, Husserl is characterized as being concerned primarily with the intentional relation as a thematic or objectifying relation with an object, whereas Heidegger is understood primarily in terms of the account of Being-in-the-world to be found in the first division of *Being and Time*. Levinas is not unaware that he oversimplifies these two thinkers and that he could have found other resources in their writings which might have been closer to his own concerns. He was, for example, in the course of publishing a series of articles in which he showed Husserl to have gone far beyond intentionality in its classic sense, but in these sections he is content to confine himself to Husserl's ''obsession'' with representation (TI 122; TeI 95). Similar reservations could be expressed about his treatment of Heidegger, but again the distortion must be judged with reference to its underlying purpose.

In the first instance, Levinas's question is whether the structures that Husserl and Heidegger employ do justice to the character of enjoyment. Levinas suggests that neither the primacy of the representational act as proposed by Husserl, nor the dominance of the ''in-order-to'' which Heidegger developed in *Being and Time* in the course of his discussion of equipmentality, can account for what Levinas analyzes under the name *vivre de* or ''living from.'' Enjoyment is not something added on to life subsequently, like the addition of an attribute to a substance. Rather ''life is *love of life*'' (TI 112; TeI 84). As a polemical reply to Heidegger's conception of *Sorge* as care, this would amount to no more than the substitution of one ideal of existence for another. But Levinas's aim extends further. He claims that ''the reality of life . . . is beyond ontology'' (TI 112; TeI 84); or, in the same vein, ''To be I is to exist in such a way as to be already beyond being, in happiness'' (TI 120; TeI 92). That happiness is beyond being and not an accident of being is shown, he suggests, by the fact that being is risked for happiness (TI 112; TeI 84). And in spite of the distinction between need and desire with which the first part began, the realm of needs—to which happiness belongs—already transports us ''outside the categories of being'' (TI 115; TeI 87), categories such as activity and passivity, means and ends. Need, by virtue of *having* time and postponing dependence, is thus found to rest on desire. The unicity, solitude, isolation, and withdrawal of happiness and need already rupture the totality (TI 118; TeI 90). Needs ''constitute a being independent of the world, a veritable subject'' (TI 116; TeI 89).

If the first section of part 2 serves largely to introduce the notion of enjoyment, it is in the second section, ''Enjoyment and Separation,'' that it is put to work. In this section Levinas examines, in isolation from each other, first representation and then enjoyment, before proceeding to exhibit their interdependency. "Detached from its sources," "taken in itself, as it were uprooted" (TI 123; TeI 96), the exteriority of the object appears to be a meaning ascribed by the representing subject. That is to say, reflection reveals the object as a work of thought (TI 125; TeI 97). Alterity disappears in the same. "The distinction between me and the object, between interior and exterior, is effaced" (TI 124; TeI 96).

By contrast, the intentionality of enjoyment maintains the exteriority that representation suspends. It thus follows a different structure. Whereas in representation "the same is in relation with the other but in such a way that the other does not determine the same" (TI 124; TeI 97), in enjoyment "the same determines the other while being determined by it" (TI 128; TeI 101). Whereas representation conforms to the model of adequation, enjoyment overflows its meaning. The maintenance of the exteriority characteristic of enjoyment is accomplished by the body, which is the reversion of representation into life. The needs of the body "affirm 'exteriority' as nonconstituted, prior to all affirmation" (TI 127; TeI 100). The structure of enjoyment is therefore an offense against the transcendental method, which in Levinas's mind is closely tied to representation. The language of transcendental conditions is turned upside down: "The aliment conditions the very thought that would think it as a condition" (TI 128; TeI 101). The constituted becomes the condition of the constituting. Corporeity as both affirmation of exteriority and position on the earth contests the transcendental method and its reliance on the universality of representation and the directionality of constitution. "The world I constitute nourishes me and bathes me. It is aliment and 'medium' ('*milieu*'). The intentionality aiming at the exterior changes direction in the course of its very aim by becoming interior to the exteriority it constitutes, somehow comes from the point to which it goes, recognizing itself past in its future, lives from what it thinks" (TI 129; TeI 102). In a formulation that anticipates the notion of the trace, Levinas writes:

> A movement radically different from thought is manifested when the constitution by thought finds its condition in what it has freely welcomed or refused, when the represented turns into a past that had not traversed the *present* of representation, as an absolute past not receiving its meaning from memory. (TI 130; TeI 103)

The represented, the present, already belongs to the past as a fact.

The subsequent paragraphs of the second section of part 2 are devoted to making more explicit what it is that challenges representation in this way. Levinas refers to the element or medium from which things come to representation (TI 130; TeI 103). To understand things as emerging from and returning to the elemental is, Levinas maintains, to challenge the attempt to absorb things into a system of operational references, the "technical finality" of the Heideggerian world. This he does without reference to Heidegger's interpretation of *phusis* to which it more closely approximates. Indeed, in *Otherwise than Being; or, Beyond Essence* Levinas collapses the differences between the Husserlian and Heideggerian accounts and accuses Heidegger of maintaining a commitment to "the founding primacy of cognition."[7] Levinas thus locates a latent representationalism in Heidegger's account of projection. And he does so in spite of Heidegger's challenge to the priority of knowledge in section 13 of *Being and Time*. Levinas was not unaware of this discussion. It had provided him in his 1930 dissertation, *The Theory of Intuition in Husserl's Phenomenology*, with the basis of his criticism of Husserl's thesis on the priority of presentifying acts.[8] But meanwhile he had come to believe that the "ancient thesis that puts representation at the basis of every practical behavior" is "too hastily discredited" (TI 94; TeI 67).

When Levinas complains that Heidegger does not take enjoyment into account, when he observes that *Dasein* is never hungry and that an ontology which classifies food as an implement is true only for a world of exploitation (TI 134; TeI 108), he is not primarily confronting Heidegger at the level of description. At the level of description, there will be times when exploitation is indeed dominant. Levinas is rather recalling a discussion in *Existence and Existents,* where the notions of both intentionality and of ontological finality were judged insufficiently penetrating. In *Existence and Existents,* the notion of the 'sincerity' of intentions is prominent. Levinas drew attention to an absorption in the desirable from which the care for existence is absent. Levinas commented, "It is not really true to say that we eat in order to live, we eat because we are hungry."[9] In *Totality and Infinity,* the focus shifts to the notion of enjoyment, but it is only a matter of emphasis: "If I eat my bread in order to labor and to live, I live *from* my labor and *from* my bread" (TI 111; TeI 83). The essential point remains the same: "The need for food does not have existence as its goal, but food" (TI 134; TeI 107). That is to say, the Heideggerian analysis overlooks that which fills our life (whether in sadness or delight). And in an effort to disarm the Heideggerian response that this seems to be a retreat into fallenness, Levinas makes the point that this absorption in the desirable is not a diversion from the bare fact of existence in the Pascalian sense (TI 111; TeI 83). Levinas continues, as if he were answering the opening of Aristotle's *Nicomachean Ethics:* "Activity does not derive its meaning and its value from an ultimate and unique goal, as though the world formed one system of use-references whose term touches our very existence. The world answers to a set of autonomous finalities which ignore one another" (TI

133; TeI 106–7). But even if he regards Heidegger's rejection of representation as too hasty, Levinas continues to contest the privilege traditionally accorded to representation. How could representation serve as the founding act? "How would the tension and care of a life arise from impassive representation?" (TI 168; TeI 143). It might seem that Levinas is going round in circles in his effort to do justice to representation without according it that priority which it finds in the tradition.

Representation is understood by intellectualism as constitutive, and yet it is also found to be conditioned, "already implanted" in the being it claims to constitute. That is its "transcendental pretension" (TI 169; TeI 143). Representation performs a kind of reversal by accounting for that which in fact underlies it. But I have only to open my eyes—or one might say, reinhabit naive perceptual faith, for here Levinas is in total agreement with Merleau-Ponty—and the reversal is undone. "The 'turning' of the constituted into a condition is accomplished as soon as I open my eyes: I but open my eyes and already enjoy the spectacle" (TI 130; TeI 103). I have only to eat and my body has already begun to contest representation: "In 'living from . . .' the process of constitution which comes into play wherever there is representation is reversed" (TI 128; TeI 101; see also TI 129; TeI 102). But Levinas does not side with the body here against representation; rather he examines the structure to which they both give rise.

The Husserlian privileging of representation and the Heideggerian privileging of care are both questioned on the grounds that "the interval of separation," the distance between the I and its object, their opposition, is denied (TI 110; TeI 82). Whereas "representation consists in the possibility of accounting for the object as though it were constituted by a thought" (TI 128; TeI 101), in the enjoyment of, for example, eating, the condition supports and nourishes the constituting I. We find here a radical difference which does not allow us to assimilate enjoyment to the model of representation. The reverting of representation into life (TI 127; TeI 100), the turning of ecstatic representation into enjoyment in every instant restores the antecedence of what I constitute to this very constitution (TI 147; TeI 121). "The represented turns into a past that had not traversed the *present* of representation, as an absolute past not receiving its meaning from memory" (TI 130; TeI 103). The represented, the present, as a *fact,* already belongs to the past prior to its representation.

The empirical and the transcendental have their place in Levinas's *Totality and Infinity* in the discussion of the intentionality of enjoyment and of representation. Transcendental thought is under investigation with representation, just as concretization (corresponding to empiricism) is at issue in the theme of enjoyment. Levinas does not choose between them or attempt to reconcile them. They remain irreducible moments of the logically absurd structure of the *anterior posteriori* (TI 170; TeI 144). The a priori constitution of the object as performed by the idealist subject takes place only after the event, that is to say, a posteriori (TI 153; TeI 126).

When Levinas says that not only knowing but also doing and labor imply the relation of transcendence, he continues the transcendental enterprise behind the I, beneath representation, to the point where the I is called into question by the Other. This is the sense in which the method Levinas adopts "resembles" the transcendental method, but is nevertheless to be differentiated from it. Indeed, representation and enjoyment do not only imply transcendence, they are analogous to transcendence. They are analogous to transcendence in the sense that they also exhibit the anterior posteriori of the relation of the infinite to the cogito. The double origin of the I and the element from which it lives is analogous to the double origin of the I and the radically exterior Other. The blind spot in most discussions of Levinas, whether Levinas's account of the face-to-face is given a transcendental or an empirical status, is that they maintain the absolute priority of the face-to-face, something which Levinas's analyses constantly question. What is "analogous to transcendence" in the discussion of "Interiority and Economy" is the double origin. Just as representation and enjoyment are each found to presuppose each other, "the alleged scandal of alterity presupposes the tranquil identity of the same" (TI 203; TeI 178), while at the same time making it possible. In his attempt to secure a transcendental reading of Levinas, de Boer rejects reference to the Cartesian *cogito* (FFL 85) in favor of the model afforded by the Cartesian infinite, so that the other "functions as the transcendental foundation of the same" (FFL 95). But this is to neglect the way in which Levinas had insisted in the first part of *Totality and Infinity* that the *cogito* and the infinite are both absolute starting points for Descartes.[10]

There is a paragraph near the end of the second part of *Totality and Infinity* in which Levinas attempts to clarify the way in which he understands the transcendental and the empirical or concrete in their interrelation:

> Our work in all its developments strives to free itself from the conception that seeks to unite events of existence affected with opposite signs in an ambivalent condition which alone would have ontological dignity, while the events themselves proceeding in one direction [*sens*] or in another would remain empirical, articulating nothing ontologically new. The method practiced here does indeed consist in seeking the condition of empirical situations, but it leaves to the developments called empirical, in which the conditioning possibility is accomplished—it leaves to the *concretization*—an ontological role that specifies the meaning [*sens*] of the fundamental possibility, a meaning invisible in that condition. (TI 173; TeI 148).

This difficult passage can be understood to be nothing more than the return of the problem of the ontological versus the ontic, of the formal or the abstract versus the concrete, as we found it in de Boer's account. The first sentence contains a reference to Heidegger's concept of deficient modes, whereby leaving undone is a deficient mode of concern, Being-alone is a deficient mode of Being-with, and passing another by is an indifferent mode of solicitude.[11] In each case the reader is told not to understand the latter term—concern, Being-with, and passing another by—with its ordinary connotations but ontologically, although the suspicion prevails that Heidegger is himself aware that the neutralization of this ethically charged language can rarely, if ever, be accomplished. Setting himself against Heidegger's philosophy once more, Levinas in this passage doubts the efficacy of a procedure that remains viable only so long as the existential is kept safe from contamination by the existentiell. But must the second sentence of the paragraph then come to be understood to say that the meaning given to the formal structures by concretization equip them with an irreducible cultural specificity? The face-to-face, for example, would always be colored by the concrete situation in which it always finds itself. It has to be said that time and time again Levinas has opposed formulations of this kind. Hence the thrust of the passage in question is not to deny the possibility of attaining a realm of meaning prior to or independent of culture and history. The passage is rather Levinas's acknowledgment that although his method is transcendental (at least by resemblance), the sense of the fundamental possibility it reveals is given concretely. It is given not as an injunction imposing a specific ethical act, but as specifying a direction [*sens*], the ethical direction, which neutralization would have eradicated.[12] Levinas's transcendentalism may formally resemble that of Descartes, but in the latter, formal structures hold sway. Descartes's procedure, in common with all transcendental philosophy hitherto, renders invisible the *sens* of the condition it reveals by withdrawing from the empirical or concrete.

That is why in the first part of *Totality and Infinity* Levinas emphasizes that the face of the Other is a concretization which deformalizes the Cartesian structure of the idea of infinity (TI 50; TeI 21). Levinas may on occasion call the face abstract, but he does so only in the sense that it is a disturbance which breaks with cultural meaning and calls into question the horizons of the world. The face is also the most concrete in that the face cannot be approached with empty hands but only from within society. "The transcendence of the face is not enacted outside of the world"—outside of economic life (TI 172; TeI 147). This is how Levinas himself distinguishes the face-to-face from the I-Thou relation of Buber, as de Boer properly acknowledges (FFl 109). The I-Thou relation amounts to a formalism that does not determine any concrete structure (TI 68; TeI 40). "No face can be approached with empty hands and closed home,'' is Levinas's way of saying that the relation with the absolutely Other who paralyzes possession presupposes economic existence and the Other who welcomes me in the home (TI 172; TeI 147). Thus in a movement parallel to that found in the account of representation and enjoyment, Levinas reverses the movement by which it seemed that the face of the Other was being made an ultimate ground. Hence the intimacy of the home is the ''first concretization'' (TI 153; TeI 126).

It seems to me that Levinas is using the language of transcendental philosophy and the language of empiricism not in order to draw them together into a transcendental empiricism, but in an effort to find a way between these twin options given to us by the philosophical—and nonphilosophical—language that we have inherited. Only by employing both languages and drawing them into contradiction as he does in the notion of the anterior posteriori can he hope to introduce us to a way of thinking which rests on neither. Early in *Totality and Infinity* Levinas wrote that ''the term welcome of the Other expresses a simultaneity of activity and passivity which places the relation with the other outside of the dichotomies valid for things: the a priori and the a posteriori, activity and passivity'' (TI 89; TeI 62). If the disputes among the readers of Levinas have largely been a matter of contesting which limb of the dichotomy should be uppermost— the transcendental or the empirical—then we are still a long way from negotiating his language, which operates by a displacement of their disjunction. Neither a transcendental nor an empirical discourse can be maintained in isolation from the other. Their complicity therefore parallels the complicity which Derrida found between empiricism and metaphysics and exhibits the proximity between these two thinkers.

— **3** —

Absolute Positivity and Ultrapositivity: Husserl and Levinas

Richard A. Cohen

The Radical Positivity of Phenomena

In *Ideas I* Edmund Husserl speaks of phenomenology as a positivism, a positivism based on direct intuition and thus a positivism even more positive than the natural sciences which base themselves on experience:

> If *"positivism"* is tantamount to an absolutely unprejudiced grounding of all sciences on the "positive," that is to say, on what can be seized upon originaliter, then *we* are the genuine positivists . . . .

> We take our start from what lies *prior to* all standpoints: from the total realm of whatever is itself given intuitionally and prior to all theorizing, from everything that one can immediately see and seize upon.[1]

The famous "principle of all principles" of Husserl's phenomenology combines the broadest possible definition of phenomena with the most radical care to cast off all extra-phenomenal presuppositions. It says that to count as truth a truth claim must be supported by nothing but the evidence of a direct intuition into the phenomenon proper to the truth claim. Truths about perception must be backed by perceptions; truths about imagination must be backed by imaginings; truths about memory must be backed by memories; etc. Intuition of the thing itself is the ultimate justification of all knowledge. Extra-intuitive notions of what counts as real, notions which because they are not rooted in intuition are laden with unexamined theoretical baggage, the famous "thesis of the natural attitude," must be rigorously put aside, bracketed out of consideration, excluded, reduced.

> Deductive theorizings are excluded from phenomenology. *Mediate inferences* are not exactly denied to it; but, since all its cognitions ought to be descriptive, purely befitting the immanental sphere, inferences, non-intuitive modes of procedure of any kind, only have the methodic function of leading us to the matters in question upon which a subsequent direct seeing of essences

35

> must make given. Analogies which emerge may suggest presumed likeli-
> hoods about concatenations of essences prior to actual intuition, and conclu-
> sions may be drawn from them; but ultimately an actual seeing of the
> concatenations of essences must redeem the presumed likelihoods. As long
> as that has not occurred, we have no phenomenological result. . . . It is
> now completely clear to us that nothing of value for the establishing of phe-
> nomenology can be gained by proceeding according to analogy.
>
> Phenomenology . . . like any other descriptive, non-substructing and non-
> idealizing discipline, has its inherent legitimacy.[2]

"The great manifesto *Ideas I*," Alphonso Lingis has recently written of the
above texts and of Husserl's positivism,

> declares heroically that what will be built is a philosophical discourse which
> from one end to the other will be grounded in immediate insight, the direct
> observation of what is given in evidence, and will consist nowhere of argu-
> mentation, nowhere of deduction, nowhere of induction, will not advance
> one sole statement that is not guaranteed by direct intuition ever available,
> ever repeatable.[3]

If Parmenides's theogony is the inaugural and founding statement of
the Western thought that is scientific, then surely Husserl's phenomenology
is its concluding statement. Parmenides's dual insight that "thinking and
the object of thought are the same," and that "never shall it be proven that
non-being is"—a dual insight he sums up and justifies in the modal terms
of necessity and possibility: "It is necessary both to say and to think that
being is. For to be is possible and not-to-be is impossible"[4]—is a pre-
scription for scientific positivity. By extending the positivity of scientific
evidence beyond the confines of experience as defined by empiricism, experience as sensuous experience, to include all the evidences available
to intuition, even and especially the evidence of intellectual intuition into
essences, Husserl in Freiburg concludes the long journey from myth to
science that began with Parmenides in Elea.

It is fairly easy to confirm the positivity of Husserl's principle of principles in such areas as perception, imagination, and memory, where judgments about perceiving and the perceived, or imagining and the imagined,
or remembering and the remembered, are confirmed or denied on the evidence of actual perceptions, imaginations, and memories, evoked and carried through by the practicing phenomenologist, and described for
repeatable intersubjective verification. Perceptual claims about the Statue of
Liberty, for example, are ultimately validated by perceptions of the Statue
of Liberty in New York harbor. The only hitch in these areas seems to come

from the necessity to use language to describe or report on perception, imagination, memory, etc., or on any other area open to phenomenological investigation. Is there a phenomenological theory of judgment, one must ask, whose positivity supports the positivity of all of phenomenology's other descriptive claims? Or, more simply, does the necessary use of language introduce a negativity into phenomenology that undermines its full positivity and hence undermines phenomenology's claim to scientific status?

A look at Husserl's *Formal and Transcendental Logic*, where these sorts of questions are addressed, confirms the view that for Husserl phenomenology is to be grounded in absolutely positive evidence, even in the realm of judgment.[5] First, at the least determinate, most formal level of judgment ("theory of forms"), what makes any judgment a judgment in the widest sense, and hence a judgment ultimately though not immediately capable of conveying truth scientifically, is its *distinctness*. And this distinctness, at the morphological base of any and all judgments, is or can be known through direct intuition. For example, one intuits that a cluster of words joined together, such as "the is cat brown" is confused in meaning, and that the cluster of words "the cat is brown" is distinct in meaning. When a judgment does have a morphologically correct form, that is, is a distinct judgment, a second positive intuition must still be possible before the judgment's candidacy as a knowledge claim can be registered. For Husserl, one must intuit, in an anticipatory intuition, that the distinct judgment does not and will not contradict other distinct judgments ("logic of noncontradiction"). The criterion of noncontradiction or coherency is not given a priori or imposed a posteriori in the Husserlian analysis. It must be intuited, in an intuition Husserl calls an intuition of "clarity." Finally, before entering the body of established scientific knowledge, a distinct and clear judgment must be subject to fulfillment or lack of fulfillment in a further intuition to determine its truth claim ("logic of truth").

Thus even when one turns to the area most likely to be non-intuitive, to the area most likely to introduce negativity into phenomenological positivity, one must at every point return to the positivity of intuition, to evidence as an immediate presence to consciousness. We can understand, then, what one contemporary Husserl scholar means when he writes that "the distinctions between the different levels of logic are grounded on or founded in, at least in the final analysis, the distinctions between the different manners of intention and fulfillment."[6] The propositions of scientific knowledge, as well as the propositions that may be candidates for scientific knowledge, are accepted and confirmed through the positivity of intuitions whose fulfillment or lack of fulfillment weeds out falsehood as well as vagueness and confusion.

The Superlative Positivity of the Other Person

It seems incredible, therefore, that in response to the most radical positivity conceivable, the positivity of the Husserlian phenomenology, Emmanuel Levinas launches an attack on phenomenology not in the name of an irreducible negativity, as do Sartre and Adorno, nor in the name of a deferral of sense, as do Heidegger and Derrida, but precisely in the name of an immediacy and a concreteness, a positivity, *greater* than phenomenological positivity, an immediacy and a concreteness not only hidden to phenomenological positivity, despite its all-embracing egology and the infinity of its fields of investigation, but precisely hidden *by* phenomenological positivity. How does Levinas make good on this extravagant claim?

Rather than simply quoting texts from Levinas's many writings to show that he makes this claim and how he justifies this claim, let us be guided by Husserl's call to return to the things themselves, in conjunction with the special attention Levinas pays to the face of the other person. Let us "do" a phenomenology of the face. Presumably a phenomenology of the face is a subset of a phenomenology of perception. The face serves as our guiding clue, not just as an instance of a perceived object or a perceptual phenomenon, but as an object or phenomenon in its own right. The phenomenologist might begin with a painting of a face, a photograph of a face, a marble bust, a death mask, or, even better, the phenomenologist's own face as seen in a mirror. But because we are guided in this investigation both by Husserl's call to the things themselves and by Levinas's directive that we attend to the face of the other person, the best—i.e., the most positive—phenomenological evidence for a phenomenology of the face of the other person is nothing other than the flesh-and-blood face of another person.

So the phenomenologist, in search of the intuitionally most positive evidence, faces a face which faces the phenomenologist. The first step in doing any phenomenology is to get into contact with the phenomena. In order to get into contact with the *phenomenon* of the face of the other person the phenomenologist must first bracket his or her own doxic thesis of the natural attitude. That is to say, the phenomenologist must put out of play or disconnect any naive believings in the *reality* of the face of the other person, in order to be in the presence of the phenomenon of another's face. This reduction is meant to put out of play historically determined presuppositions about such things as appropriate behaviors, or good manners, but even more importantly, it puts out of play presuppositions about the reality or ontological status of the other's face.

But here already, with the very first step in the phenomenological procedure, a dilemma emerges that makes the investigation not merely difficult, or impossible, but, depending on how the phenomenologist responds, a dilemma emerges that puts the phenomenological investigation into ethical jeopardy. I think it is fair to say that the dilemma the phenomenologist encounters when investigating the face of the other person is the one summed up in the description of the biologist who in his research must kill to dissect. To disconnect the thesis of the natural attitude when facing the face of the other person is to treat the other person as nonreal, as a presentation to the consciousness of the investigator, as a perceptual phenomenon constitutionally correlated to perceiving. There is no doubt that the face is a perceptual phenomenon and that it can be treated as such. But is it not also more than a phenomenon? Why is there a gnawing sense that something more than an unreflected doxic thesis is disconnected when the face of the other person is reduced to its phenomenality? Why does it seem that the face of the other person is not merely the ultimate positive basis for fulfilling judgments about portraits, busts, masks, and the like, but is somehow, in addition, or otherwise, something else altogether different, something more important?

Let us look more closely at the dilemma the "phenomenon" of the face seems to present for phenomenology. Anything in the natural attitude—a stone, a dish, or an elephant's trunk—becomes "something else" when reduced to the phenomenological domain. This transformation is expected and deliberate. It is the very point of phenomenological science. When treated as a phenomenon rather than as a real being, when treated as the noema of a noesis rather than as an object valued and used in everyday practice, the phenomenologist, unlike the ordinary person, can uncover the truth about the thing, can articulate its proper intentional sense, and the origin of sense in consciousness. Again, this is the point of phenomenological science. What, then, makes the face any different? The difference is that in facing the face of the other person in the natural attitude there is already more at play than a doxic thesis and unreflected intentional correlations of sense. This "more," it must be said straightaway, refers to a qualitative difference rather than to a quantitative difference. The other person is not merely one real entity among others in the world of real things, a real entity with specific defining attributes, whether objective or subjective; nor is the other person a concatenation of sense, of meanings, even when constituted across associative syntheses as "another myself"; rather, beyond these characteristics, *the other person is someone who always already has a claim on me.*

This all seems so simple and obvious that one wonders why it leads to an attack on phenomenology. The reason the other's excessive alterity poses a problem for phenomenology is that the other person, which is what Levinas means by "the face," cannot be brought to full intuitive presence, and this precisely because the "presence" of the other person overwhelms subjectivity, overloads the subject, burdens the ego with more than its own abilities, more than its own active and passive syntheses can handle. The other, in sum, is too much for phenomenology. This is so because the face is not only present but is *already present* (has already passed) *and* is *yet to come* (has not yet arrived into the present), such that the other cannot, in principle—and especially in principle—be brought to presence. The face facing, prior to the phenomenological reduction and after the phenomenological reduction, defies the constituting ego's synthesizing abilities, defies the ego's self-definition, defies the ownness of the ego's sphere of ownness. No matter how present the phenomenon of the face becomes to the consciousness of the phenomenologist, the face "itself" has always already been present, and "at the same time" the face comes to phenomenality from an inexhaustibility that always has yet to appear. The language of science, even the broad descriptive language of phenomenological science, is simply and *essentially* inadequate to "account for" this overload. That is to say, the other person, from the first and prior to the constitution of meaning, puts the self into a posture of debt that can best be characterized in terms of ethical debt, obligation to the other, rather than in terms of ontological or phenomenological depth and horizons of sense. To face the face of the other is to be made to assume the posture of being for-the-other prior to being for-oneself. This structure of already-being-beholden to the other person, this being put into debt, is neither necessary nor possible nor meaningful in the phenomenological senses of these terms, yet it is the very heart or subjectivity of the subject.

To be obligated by the other person is not necessary, as can be seen very simply in the fact that the phenomenologist *can* treat the face of the other person as a phenomenon, *can* simply apprehend a perceiving of the other as a perceived entity, even as an entity with a certain value and randomness. One does not *have* to face up to the prior claims of the other person; one *can refuse* the alterity of the other person. To some degree this very refusal is necessary for phenomenological inquiry. Phenomenological reduction, then, far from being the neutral instrument of a positive science, is an act which must be set within an ethical context. Phenomenological reduction is the always more or less justified act of the phenomenologist who more or less refuses the prior claims of the other person. Given the disinterest required of the phenomenologist in order to do scientific work scientifically, and given that the world which the phenomenologist investigates is an as yet unredeemed world, i.e., a morally imperfect world, phenomenological disinterest is local, temporary, artificial, and as such stands in general conflict with a broader context of ethical demands, which latter demands may require the suspension of the phenomenological reductions.

That these conflicting exigencies must be balanced is doubtlessly not specific to phenomenology. Ethical necessity always claims priority over epistemological necessity. It is this ethical priority that "constitutes" the face which faces the phenomenologist beyond the face apprehended phenomenologically. It occurs in an elicitation rather than an elucidation.

To be beholden to the other person is not a possibility, either, because unlike all possibilities, it is neither structured by sense conferral nor is it a condition of phenomenality. Heidegger articulates a similarly peculiar conditionality when he distinguishes existential analysis from categorical analysis, where the former involves a hermeneutic circularity hidden to the latter. The face, however, does not overload the abstract possibilities of mundane or transcendental reflection with the concrete possibilities of hermeneutic reflexivity, as in Heidegger; it overloads phenomenological reflexivity with an impossible but obligating ethical straightforwardness, a devotion and not a condition. The face of the other presents what is not necessary and what is im-possible, from the phenomenological point of view, by overloading manifestation with more than an abstract or concrete essence.

But why insist on the term *more* rather than on the term *less*? Why not simply revert to negatives, to the face *not* being a phenomenon, rather than the face being *more* than a phenomenon? In a sense we have already answered this question by establishing the absolute positivity of Husserlian phenomenology. If Husserlian phenomenology is absolute, then whatever overloads its grasp—not an unfulfilled, indistinct, vague, or empty intuition—must be more than a positivity. It is what Levinas, following Franz Rosenzweig, thinks of in terms of *emphasis* or hyperbole. The face of the other is an emphatic positivity, an excessive positivity, an ultrapositivity. The priority of the other person is a priority of *greater—more glorious— concreteness and significance* than the priority of scientific a prioris.

The constituting ego can constitute the signification "other person," by placing the other person within quotation marks. These marks—so dear to Husserl—remind us, or rather warn us, that a phenomenological reduction is in effect. To flesh out this signification is what we meant earlier by "doing" a phenomenology of the face. But the disturbance of the ego effected by the alterity of the other person is not constituted by the constituting ego. The other person is not merely a signification in the sense of a sign signifying within a system of signs and referents, verifiable in an intuition now or later. The other person signifies signification. This is not to say that the other person is the origin or source of meaning in the same way that for Husserl the transcendental ego is the origin and source of all meaning. It is not a question of relocating the constituting ego, giving it a new address, as if by placing the origin of constitution in the other person rather than in me or in a transpersonal transcendental ego to which I have access, the alterity of the other person could be brought into phenomenology. In such a perspective, one would still have to account for the constituting ego's location in this particular other rather than in another particular other. No, Levinas is not suggesting a simple relocation of the transcendental ego; he is contesting the originariness of the transcendental ego altogether.

In the face of the other person one finds that meaning requires the reception of meaning. Actually, one does not find this out, one suffers it, one undergoes it. To say something true, words must be morphologically organized in a distinct and clear way and open to intuitional confirmation. But prior to this "originary" constitution of meaning, words are meaningful because they are addressed to someone. This sense of *meaningful* is the ethical sense, one person obligated to another person, rather than the semantic or semiotic senses of *meaningful,* signs organized within systems of signs grounded at some point in intuitional confirmation. Prior to *what* is said, the alterity of the other person already has a claim on meaning, whether in the saying or in the responding. The dative disrupts the pure positivity of the nominative with an ever greater positivity. Subjectivity, even transcendental subjectivity, even when it constitutes all meaning, does not at all constitute the alterity of the other person *to whom* all meaning is given. Rather, the ego presupposes the alterity or the other person in a presupposition or devotion that can never be given up without some degree of ethical lapse, even if that lapse is justified in the name of a phenomenological science dedicated to pure truth, and even if that truth is dedicated to the noble purposes of social justice. In our historical times interpersonal ethics and social justice do not yet coincide. Thus the realm of truth, and the phenomenological science dedicated to that truth, still compromises the ethical presupposition, which is nonetheless its ultimate standard. All meanings are already subject to the other person, are already for-the-other, and thus are subjected to a meaningfulness greater, of greater significance, of more importance—in the ethical sense—than any and all meanings constituted or fulfilled.

In seeking for the *essence* "this face here and now facing" (in quotes), the face is necessarily reduced to being an instance of "faceness" (in quotes), or reduced to being the intuitional evidence for an essence. Yet the face is more concrete than the species of a genus, or the instance of an essence, or the case of a generality, or anything else whereby the phenomenologist qua phenomenologist "grasps" the face. The concreteness of the face is not a uniqueness derived from exceptional attributes, for example, the length of this particular nose, the shape of this particular cheek, the curve of these lips, although every face—like everything else spatial and temporal—is particular, unique. Particularity always eludes thought, always opens out onto a bad infinite, an infinitely microscopic empiricism. Every perceptual thing is particular in this way, yet not every perceptual thing is a face. The face of the other person is unique insofar as it makes claims on me that cannot be shirked without moral fault. The other person rivets the me to its place—irreplaceably beholden to the other, at the other's service. The face cannot be grasped, either intellectually or otherwise, without doing violence to the nonmediated claim it makes, the putting into question it effects, on the self of the investigating ego.

The ethical self underlies the investigating ego, not as one world lying beneath another, nor as one constitutive layer lying beneath and founding another, but as the rupture of the egoism of the ego. The alterity of the other person is already closer to the self, to the me, paradoxically, than is the transcendental ego which is the origin of all meaning. This is what Levinas means when he speaks of the subjection of subjectivity subject to the alterity of the other, in terms of a "passivity more passive than any receptivity."

The mushroom in the grass, the grass, the sky above, the stars beyond, do not make claims on me, nor question me, nor hold me to my place, vigilant, obligated, in the disturbing way that the face of the other does.[7] They are near and far, but the other is nearer and further, too near and too far, too close and too distant. The concreteness and immediacy of the face—the alterity of the other person—plunges an exceptional hold or vigilance so deep into the self, endlessly, that the self is better than the ego, is more alert, more ready for the other, before thinking of or for itself. Such a "hold" is not the grasp of consciousness, whether empirical or transcendental; its grip is ethical, the very orientation of myself toward the other person, myself beholden to, obligated to, in debt to, the other person, prior to any contracts or agreements about who owes what to whom.

The self finds its inexhaustible resources when and only when it is without reserve in the service of the other. Only in this way, by default as it were, can the phenomenologist "account for" the greater positivity, the ultrapositivity, that is the extraordinary irruption of the other's face.

II

The Question of the Other's Claim

— 4 —

Derrida and the Ethics of the Ear

Diane Michelfelder

If we open up our ears to the voice of Soren Kierkegaard's aesthete, we would be able to hear all sorts of quips and clever remarks—and not only clever remarks, but many kinds of other things as well: good jokes, speeches of once-upon-a-time, panegyrics on love, pointed wit, and ironic comments, and, if we ask for it, sincere, handy advice in the shape of "whatever you do now, you will regret it afterwards." Many forms of speech, but no stories, no narratives focused around an existing "I" or a real "subject." And why not? We know how Judge William will answer this question in writing to the aesthete: "The talent your soul lacks is memory." It all looks obvious enough: no memory, no narrative. And this because of fear, fear of continuity, which in the judge's mind sentences the aesthete to a despair-saturated life which only the choice for choice itself, the choice of the ethical, can overcome.

In the encounter between Jacques Derrida and Hans-Georg Gadamer that took place in Paris in 1981, the figure of Judge William appears in the context of Gadamer's ongoing response to Derrida, specifically in the letter he wrote as a response to Fred Dallmayr's extended review and critique of their meeting: "In him [Judge William] ethical continuity stands over against aesthetic immediacy,"[1] Gadamer writes, not to remind us of this well-known fact but to stress his own indebtedness to Kierkegaard for giving him the foundation for his "hermeneutical option for continuity." With this phrase Gadamer places hermeneutics squarely on the side of ethics, an association we can see as well in a philological observation that Gadamer has drawn on more than once since the encounter in talking about Derrida. Consider, he says, the literal meaning of understanding, *Ver-stehen:* to stand in the place of the other directly, as advocate, not amanuensis, telling the other's story within a courtroom, defending him or her in front of the judicial ear, representing the unique, particular other before the universality of the law.[2]

And what does Derrida have to do with any of this? "I have never known how to tell a story," he admits, at the outset of what would certainly seem to be a story-telling situation, his *Mémoires: For Paul de Man.*[3]

47

Not to be able to tell a story—this means not to be able to put oneself in the location of the other, to be always "dis-located" from the other, outside of the range of his or her hearing. No continuity and no narrative. And if one falls back into the dimensions of Kierkegaard's language to describe the situation, what would one say? Derrida does not know how to tell a story—what are the consequences of this? Does it imply that his thinking moves in a realm completely separated from the category of ethics? This is Dallmayr's reaction, for instance, when he takes note of Derrida's apparent unwillingness, on the occasion of his meeting with Gadamer, to carry on a philosophical discussion, to engage Gadamer in conversation and dialogue. What troubles Dallmayr about this unwillingness is that it seems to be a sign of a more general "celebration of indifference, non-engagement, and indecision"—attitudes that serve to determine where he situates Derrida in relation to ethical understanding. "The neglect (if not disparagement) of the ethical dimension is particularly evident in Derrida's stress on non-judgment or 'undecidability'."[4] A similar noninvolvement, Dallmayr goes on to say, characterizes Derrida's politics. Kierkegaard's aesthete, we might recall here, is likewise no stranger to political apathy. What does Judge William imagine hearing him say, when asked if he will sign a petition or get involved with a cause? "I am not in the game at all, I am outside like a tiny Spanish 's'." So it is not surprising that the name of Kierkegaard would come up in Dallmayr's critique. Derrida's indifference, he says, bears an uncomfortably close resemblance to Gadamer's concept of aesthetic consciousness which, following Kierkegaard, he identifies with sheer immediacy and discontinuity.

Now certainly it would be possible to show, contrary to this view, how the question of philosophy's relation to ethics and politics has taken on a more explicit, insistent role in Derrida's writings. We could follow its development from the position it occupied, for instance, in "The Ends of Man"—noteworthy but still peripheral—through its promotion to a more prominent place in recent texts, such as Derrida's contribution to *For Nelson Mandela*.[5] We could point to this development as evidence for the claim that Derrida's concerns go beyond the aesthetic thrill of mailing copies of the same postcard from destinations of all sorts to who knows what *destinée;* that he does address himself seriously and decisively to ethical topics and political issues.

Of course, to take such an approach to this question would be philosophically pedestrian. But aside from being pedestrian, it would also be philosophically unconvincing. There is no getting around either Derrida's own words to the effect that his thinking is not an ethics, or his warning that it would be a waste of time to try to derive an ethics from his thinking. In the light of this I want to approach the issue of the relation of Derrida's thinking to ethics from another angle altogether, one that does not depend on accumulating evidence of his interest in ethical topics. Toward the end of his reflections on the Gadamer-Derrida encounter, Dallmayr suggests a need to put Kierkegaard's concept of the relation between aesthetics and ethics behind us, to see them as intertwined, not separate. Following through on this suggestion would mean rethinking the temporality involved in ethical understanding. It is in the spirit of this suggestion that I want to take this other approach and to argue that Derrida has already taken some steps toward such a rethinking of ethics, toward a ''beyond'' of ethics that would still remain ethical in its dimensions. Dallmayr's point that the signs of noninvolvement and noncommittal in Derrida reveal a neglect of ethics is true—but true only up to a point. Derrida's thinking is not really ethics, at least not in the conventional sense of the search for a fundamental principle or value that one can hang on to and use as a basis for making certain sorts of decisions. Then again, it is not really *not* ethics, either. It is something like ethics, one might say. Within this ''something like ethics'' involvement, commitment, and responsibility come into play—or indeed something like them. As Derrida has put it with regard to responsibility:

> When I talk about responsibility, I don't reduce it only to an ethical or moral dimension, or to forms of responsibility implying the subject, consciousness, the ego, freedom, etc. All the same, there's a more radical responsibility before these questions.[6]

Hearing this totally different, radical sense of responsibility—this ''something like'' responsibility—puts a demand on our ears. With it in mind, I would like to go back to *Memoires* and to repeat a statement I mentioned earlier: ''I have never known how to tell a story.'' But then, in the very next line, a surprise: ''I love nothing better than remembering and Memory itself.'' Immediately we are thrust out of sync with Kierkegaard's aesthete. Memory takes us away from the present, away from immediacy, but toward what? It is a question that troubles Derrida himself, in remembering and telling (as the aesthete might do) not a narrative but a myth: itself told from memory by Socrates about Mnemosyne, who gives us the ''wax'' in which we can preserve the marks we want to keep, in order that we can, later on, as Derrida writes, ''speak of them and do them justice.'' So we can hear in the question Derrida raises on this occasion—''But what happens when the lover of Mnemosyne has not received the gift of narration?''—echoes of the question I am raising here about ethics: what of the relation one has to the other, if one's memory of the other does not follow the Socratic formula? What happens to ethics, if one cannot stand in for him and her and do them justice by speaking for them?

What happens, I want to say, is that although ethics in the conventional sense becomes impossible, it is still possible to have an ethical sensibility, connected to the role that memory plays in the structure of textuality itself. I am not thinking here of trying to derive this sensibility *from* the structure of textuality, but to see rather how it is implicated *in* this structure. And because this structure also implicates or involves the ear, we might think of this sensibility, this "something like ethics," as "an ethics of the ear." This phrase is inserted between quotation marks, a sign that what is being spoken about is not quite the real thing but, at the same time, not a simulacrum of the real thing either. I will try to make this "ethics of the ear" clearer by way of assembling a few points related to strategies of reading in both Gadamer and Derrida.

"It is the ear of the other that signs," Derrida will say, in the discussion following "Otobiographies." "The ear of the other says me to me. . . ."[7] We receive or inherit, as readers, not anonymous texts but ones whose signatures are still outstanding. This puts us into the awkward position of having to be responsible for what has been written—these texts in need of signatures that have been addressed to us, to our memories. Their inheritance is, in a sense, foisted upon us and we have no option but to confront it. Our responsibility to it is to what lies in our memories, having overtaken them: responsibility to what we have not chosen.

It is just in this kind of situation that Derrida believes those who currently participate in philosophical dialogue must find themselves. One inherits, in this situation, the question of the future of philosophy. Philosophy does not raise this question because it has decided to or because of the "internal maturation" of its history.[8] To be concerned with this question is basically *to be read into a conversation,* to be "overtaken by the dialogue of the question about itself and by itself." And even though this is a question whose meaning is still faint, its voice one we can barely hear; we have an inescapable responsibility to it, to maintain it as a question that perhaps, Derrida notes, "authorizes all inheritance and all pure memory."[9]

Still, our responsibility to what we inherit despite ourselves—the obligation to honor the signature of the other—does not mean that we are simply to repeat what we hear. When it comes to the name of Nietzsche, for instance, Derrida maintains that our hearing has to be especially talented, especially acute. Nietzsche himself recognized this talent as one of attunement to small differences. But despite how our inheritance of Nietzsche's texts puts us on the spot within the university, we are, as Derrida will point out, more than simply recipients of his voice. "To hear [Nietzsche's signature] and understand it, one must also produce it."[10] An active hearing or interpretation is called for here, one that would perform the act of signing Nietzsche's texts. So the matter of speaking the name of Nietzsche from out of one's memory is more than just a matter of repeating it. If it were simply that, it would tie the act of speaking from memory inseparably to the past and the telling of stories. The memory Derrida expresses as the object of his love is not, he states explicitly in *Mémoires,* turned toward what has already been.

But what happens if we go back to Gadamer's discussion of the resonances within *Verstehen*? Here we can see that for him as well the act of standing in for the other does not simply imply substituting for the other or acting as a proxy. Gadamer puts it like this in "Hermeneutics and Logocentrism": the person who stands in "does not just repeat what he has been told in advance or dictated; rather, he speaks for him." In this notion of a speaking for someone that goes beyond being his or her proxy, we can hear resonances of that definition of hermeneutics we have come to associate with the name of Gadamer—and we can find it in this lecture, too—"the art of grasping what the other has really wanted to say," so that one could make a stronger defense of the other than the other is capable of doing.[11]

Now of course if we have any interest in listening to someone speak so that we can hear precisely their silence, what they are *not* saying, we naturally have to keep our ears open. Just how much different is this from an obligation to honor the signature of the other by causing it to take place? It is very much, Gadamer believes, the same thing: "I too affirm that understanding is always understanding-differently."[12] For such understanding to happen at all, what one says, Gadamer notes in "Text and Interpretation," has to be "acoustically intelligible"—or legible, if we are dealing with written words.[13] But that is simply a precondition, since all reading, when it is paying attention to the unheard-of element in a text, exceeds the reproduction of meaning in recreating it.

Neither is there, one could add, an acoustic difference between Gadamer and Derrida when it comes to understanding what translation is. For Gadamer, translation also involves the re-creation of meaning, and thus a reading directed toward translation is only qualitatively different from other types of reading. Likewise, the message that comes from Derrida is that translation has nothing to do with reproducing an original language but with changing and adding to the original, even to the extent of changing the very language into which one is translating the original.

Now where, in all of the above, have we been able to hear the sound of "something like an ethics"? So far, it seems, we have not been able to get to an essential difference within the theoretical structures of hermeneutics and deconstruction that would allow the ethical sensibility within Derrida to be heard. Here one can either give up . . . or listen from another angle. Perhaps it might turn out that there is something *within* this structure of inheritance that would make a difference for deciding the question of the ethical relation in Derrida. As the "ear of the other," then, what is it that we are given to listen to?

When we sign the name of the other, we come in following the other, belatedly, not even as an eavesdropper—who knows when or how long after. This also belongs to the structure of textuality. No question about it, "the other will have spoken first,"[14] as Derrida says. The inheritance we have received is the trace of this speaking. Whenever we perform the signature of the other and make the other speak, we cannot forget this trace, which clings to our performance like a ghost, Derrida might say, or, more in keeping with my emphasis here, like a sound impossible for me to hear, beyond the range of my ears, silence itself. I hear and of course do not hear the silence of the other. It will precede any effort on my part to speak the name of the other, and so the more I speak, *the more the other will have already spoken*. No possibility here of a totalization, for my speaking to close the circle between myself and the other, or for it to allow the other to make good on what, in extending his signature to us, he has promised those who follow. But is there not in Gadamer, we could ask, also a recognition of this situation? In "Text and Interpretation" he affirms that "the text itself still remains the first point of relation over and against the questionality, arbitrariness, or at least multiplicity of the possibilities of interpretation that are directed towards the text."[15]

I would respond to that question by noting the following: In Derrida, the other always goes first as *Anspruch*—a word for which, in an essay on the condition of the university today, Derrida offers no less than six different meanings: "requirement, claim, request, demand, command, convocation."[16] The other generally does not go first in Derrida, as it does in Gadamer, as *Frage,* question—or when it does, it precedes as *Frage/Anspruch,* a question that at the same time is a kind of a command. And this seems to me to be of some significance. Even when the one who is asking questions is in a more authoritative position, the interplay between questioning and answering in Gadamer takes place on a homogeneous ground between its participants. In the dialogical relation as Gadamer conceives of it, questions are posed from within the same space as answers are given. But when in Derrida the other precedes as *Anspruch,* it is a different story. Questions that address us as imperatives come from a space that is not contiguous with our own.

To accept that the other precedes as a command or imperative would be to see that there is no *naming* of the other, no signing the signature of the other, without the recognition of the other's alterity and unnameability. The imperative to sign the text demands that we respond to the text not by *answering* it, but by *returning the text* to its author through our reading of it in such a way that we recognize his or her *irreducible particularity.* For example, if we are attempting a reading of one of Heidegger's texts, we should return the text to Heidegger in such a way that the reading would be *of* Heidegger—in the name of Heidegger—but at the same time not necessarily be *in defense* of Heidegger—as though one could step into Heidegger's place and plead his case.

Thus the structure of textuality in Derrida leads us (to revert to Kierkegaard's language) to a sense of ethical responsibility which has to do with the particular, which is an *affirmation* of the particular, over the universal. The obligation to sign the other's name is not a signing *for* the other; it involves a different justice. From *Truth and Method* on, Gadamer has recognized only two ways of speaking to the other: an unjust, sophistic way, where one's interest lies in winning an argument, and a just way where one attempts to strengthen the viewpoint of the other, speaking for the other and thus throwing oneself open to the possibility that the other might be right and one might be wrong. The "something like ethical responsibility" in Derrida, it seems to me, opens up another positive alternative, in that it is directed toward letting the other speak. In Gadamer, one has to make a choice—either monologue or dialogue—but in Derrida there is an alternative way of responding to the other that cuts through this either-or.

This alternative appears in their encounter in the shape of Derrida's apparent refusal to oppose himself to Gadamer in their Paris "encounter" and to play the role of "representative of deconstruction." We can perhaps hear the "yes, yes" of Nietzschean affirmation in Derrida's silence, an affirmation of both the *Destruktion* of metaphysical concepts and also of deconstruction, as though Derrida were, on the occasion of their meeting, enacting or performing a thought which he has already emphasized elsewhere in writing: that it is not a matter of choosing between these two ways of interpretation, between a kind of "Heideggerian deconstruction" and a "French deconstruction," as he says on one of these other occasions; not a matter of a choice between two languages.[17]

Now how does any of this translate into a sphere where one is not dealing with the names of Heidegger or Gadamer but with, for example, the names of Nelson Mandela or Winnie Mandela, or the names of sexual discrimination, computerized technology, and others? Can it even translate into this sphere, if Derrida's ethics—this "ethics of the ear"—does not give us a basis from which to act in particular situations, but at most seems to describe a certain orientation or attunement?

By way of a response to this, I would like to make the following suggestion; it relates to what Derrida has to say about the unique name of nuclear warfare in "No Apocalypse, Not Now."[18] This text is not without some parallel in Heidegger's remarks on the possibility of all-out nuclear warfare, which were given, we might recall, in the context of remembering a particular name, that of the composer Conradin Kreutzer.[19] Neither Heidegger nor Derrida focus on the object itself. They are neither concerned with describing the horrors of nuclear aggression nor with providing details on, say, the estimated quantity of nuclear bombs produced yearly. Not only does Heidegger not focus directly on nuclear warfare; he steers our attention away from it. For him, the critical problem is not nuclear warfare but the loss of our basic relatedness to the world. The issue, he says, is "keeping meditative thinking alive"—not the danger of nuclear destruction. Derrida, though, keeps our attention on the problem—not by looking directly at the possibility of nuclear warfare but by looking at the *discourse* about nuclear warfare, particularly the discourse in its defense. Those who would defend such warfare, Derrida points out, do so in the *name* of something that is more important than the name of life itself. But if all naming must wait until the other has arrived and opened his or her ears, who would sign for the other, if such an event were to occur? The name of this something, Derrida observes, has no promises to extend, nothing to inherit about it. In its name one would destroy the structures connected with the inheritance of the name—the rights of the author, the literary estate, the official "collected works," etc.—all part of what we hear, Derrida claims, when the word *literature* is spoken. So the name in which nuclear war is defended is a name in name only, not a name at all, really, only its simulacrum.

It is in the name of the name, then, that Derrida hopes to lengthen the time of that "long colloquy"—not a story or even a dialogue in the conventional sense but a colloquy—in which we are participants.[20] This desire is something like, although not identical with, a hope Gadamer expresses at the end of "*Destruktion* and Deconstruction":[21] that philosophical dialogue would expand to encompass radically different partners from a worldwide "heritage of humanity." Two hopes, two names—Gadamer and Derrida—and two ethical sensibilities, one attuned toward speaking for the other, and the other toward letting the other speak. This is a good deal for our ears to hear at once. Still, it is hard to imagine how we would have to—or want to—choose between the two.

— 5 —

Disseminating Originary Ethics and the Ethics of Dissemination

John D. Caputo

Disseminating Originary Ethics

Heidegger put metaphysical ethics in its place.* He produced a searching critique of the metaphysics of "values" by showing how it arises from the metaphysics of subjectivity. He showed the barrenness of any idea of Being that stands in need of supplementation by "value," and the hollowness of any imperative that is issued not by Being but by the subject. When Being is reduced to an object, values arise as the issue of the subject, so that values, by that very fact, have no binding power.

Now it is often and all too hastily concluded from Heidegger's critique of value-thinking that Heidegger thereby washed his hands of ethics, instead of seeing that he simply wanted nothing to do with what metaphysics calls ethics. The ethics which is not to be found in *Being and Time* is first and foremost what modernity calls ethics. There is no category of the "moral" there because the moral is a post-Cartesian notion that arises only if one conceives of Dasein as a worldless and solitary ego and then poses the problem of how to bind Dasein back to the world and to other persons, bonds which Heidegger refuses to sever in the first place. Modern ethics is a species of the metaphysics of subjectivity, which Heidegger regards as essentially decadent. In just the same way that Heidegger wants to undercut modern epistemology and return Dasein to its primordial ontological bond with the world, so also he undercuts modern moral theory and returns Dasein to its primordial engagement with the concrete world of historical action. Heidegger's objections to ethics are primarily objections to metaphysical ethics, to the ethics of rules, to the foundationalist project, to the fact-value distinction.

But it was not Heidegger's intention to cut himself off from every possible ethics, but rather to put in the place of the impoverished ethics of values a deeper thinking of the originary *ethos*. When the question was put to him, he said that all of his talk about the "truth of Being" had ethical

55

import. For the truth of Being means nothing less than the way a historical people "dwells" (*wohnt*); it refers to the constellation of art, science, and political institutions of a given historical form of life. The truth of Being means the way a historical people settles into an understanding of the world, of the gods, of itself. And so he rightly insisted that his "thinking" is a more originary ethics that is better prepared to think what is all around us today than any bankrupt theory of values.

That is the thrust of his response to the question about his ethics in the *Letter on Humanism*.[1] The relationship between the truth of Being and *ethos/Wohnen* goes all the way down. Talk about the truth of Being is ethical talk of a more radical, originary sort. It cuts across particular ethical differences in order to seize upon the basic shape of life in an epoch, the fundamental form according to which practices are organized from epoch to epoch. Thus the basic difference between *techne* and the *Gestell* of late modernity is not just a difference between two epochs of Being and truth, but also between two epochs of *ethos,* two different understandings of human life—one marked by a gentle letting-be and the other by ruinous control. In one, human life is conceived as the life of "mortals" who move in rhythm with the powers of the cosmos, in the other as the raw material of further control, of genetic engineering and behavioral technologies.

The *Gestell* provides the ontological setting for the endless ethical debates of philosophers and theologians, and nowadays of professionals of all sorts—health care professionals, lawyers, engineers, business managers, etc. It represents a kind of meta-ethical constellation within which particular ethical views are formed. "Ethics" in the usual sense is thus always one step removed from the level on which Heidegger is thinking.[2] Debates about the ethical use of life-supporting technologies, artificial insemination, and abortion take place within the hitherto unsuspected power to control human life which is provided by *Gestell*. Heidegger's more originary thinking in terms of the history of Being, which thinks the *Gestell* that frames our current ethical debate, penetrates more deeply into the question of *ethos* than any possible "value-thinking."

So it is a serious mistake to think that Heidegger has no ethics, and a serious underestimation of his work if we fail to take into account the salutary routing and deconstruction of value-thinking that occurs in his thinking. My brief remarks here are intended to extend this critique, to carry it further. I begin by taking my stand within the space opened up by this deconstruction of value-thinking. I want to radicalize what Heidegger has begun, not to undo it, and to do so I turn my attention to his "originary ethics." For if Heidegger displaces metaphysical ethics, he does so by putting an originary ethics in its place. He decenters by recentering, displaces by replacing. And it is this new center that I want to think.

Originary *ethos* turns on the originary truth of Being. But the "truth of Being" is but a pathmark along the path of thought, a milestone that his thinking finally passes by.[3] In my view Heidegger ends where he begins, by meditating the manifold senses of Being. He begins by asking, with Brentano, about the manifold sense (*mannigfache Bedeutung*) of Being and ends by thinking this manifold as a manifold, as a multiple unfolding of the many senses of Being. The meaning of Being ends up as the multiplicity of meanings—in the plural—which unfold in the history of the West. The manifold meaning is the meaning of the manifold, of the unfolding of irreducibly plural senses of Being. He begins by attempting a reduction of this plurality and ends by making a reduction to this plurality. In short, the search for the unitary meaning of Being culminates in the discovery of the *dissemination* of meanings, the pluralizing of its senses.

Heidegger's most radical thought lies beyond the truth of Being in the *Ereignis,* which is not the "meaning" or "truth" of Being ("Being as *Ereignis*") but that which gives Being, gives the manifold meaning*s* or truth*s* of Being. In the end we have to do only with the *manifold senses* of Being. The truth of Being is that there are many truths of Being, too many truths, playing themselves out in the history of the epochs. *A-letheia* does not mean the truth of Being granted to some historical people but the very process— of *a-lethe*—the a-lethic process by which whatever is granted to any historical people arises from the withdrawal of what is granting. We must learn to think *a-letheia* "over and beyond the Greeks"[4] as the epochal dispensation of the multiple and manifold truths of Being. *A-letheia* does not mean, cannot be translated as, truth, but points to that process by which Being and truth are granted, to that which produces Being and truth as effects, as historical, epochal effects, historical groupings and constellations of Being and truth within which a given people lives out its life. In the thought of the *Ereignis,* of the granting of the *es gibt,* of *a-letheia,* the meaning and truth of Being, the Being and meaning of truth, are subjected to a radical dissemination, a pluralizing, in which it gives because it gives, in which it plays because it plays—and always "without why."[5]

But if the originary *ethos* always comes back to the truth of Being, then there is no primordial *ethos* but only the manifold senses of *ethos,* of the various historical forms that dwelling takes. The dissemination of the truth of Being implies the dissemination of the truth of dwelling, of originary ethics. Fully radicalized, Heidegger's thought moves beyond all the nostalgia and hope clinging residually to the talk of the truth of Being. A metaphysical "eschatology" still clings to originary ethics. For it tells the story of a privileged and primordial *ethos* and the great beginning, prior to the subject-object split, and it looks ahead to a new dawn, which is to be an eschatological repetition and renewal of what began in the first dawn, before metaphysics and all metaphysical ethics. But the thought of the *Ereignis* has its doubts about primordial epochs and a coming new dawn and keeps a safe distance from nostalgia on the one hand and futurological hope on the other. Great beginnings are a mixed blessing. Ancient greatness looks better from a distance and is the result of blurring the *différance* by which it is inhabited. Every epoch is equally an epoch of withdrawal and *lethe*, which is indeed what *epoché* (suspension/withdrawal) means. Every epoch is equally resourceful in finding its own kind of violence.

The deconstruction of the metaphysics of values needs to be followed by the dissemination of originary ethics, by the deconstruction of the eschatology. Thinking means suspending the privileges of a privileged truth of Being, releasing the play of the epochs. And that entails the breakdown of a privileged *ethos* and releasing of the play of ethnological plurality, of the manifold sense of *ethos*. Every epoch is but a particular way we are granted to be and to dwell. The age of the early Greeks, of medieval towns and abbeys, of modernity: each is equally structured by granting and withdrawal. None can be privileged. Each has its own hazards. Each is inhabited in its own way by *différance* and *Unterschied*.

Nostalgia about ancient solidarity blinds us to deeper disruptions and rents in the garment of the ancient community. Eschatological tales are too simple, and the function of deconstruction is to complicate them, to unfold the plies and the folds in the manifold senses of Being. Things never are what they are, are never purely and unambiguously, never simply present. The Greek *polis*, as the scene of Greek history, is the place where the work of the poets and thinkers and statesmen is preserved.[6] It is the place of *techne*, of Greek jugs and craftsmen, of temples in rockcleft valleys, or on hilltops overlooking the Mediterranean, their white marble flesh gleaming in the sun, full of *phainesthai* and shining truth. Even so it also includes the slaves who dragged the stones up the hill. And we need to add "free man and slave, male and female, Greek and non-Greek" to the catalogue of binary oppositions whose paths intersect in the temple.

Slaves, women, and non-Greeks are also the place where the truth of the Greek world happens. The solidarity of the originary *ethos* is constituted by an act of exclusion—of whatever is not free, male, and Greek. Do the excluded also dwell in the clearing? How can they share in the "open" who have been closed off and excluded? Do slaves and women "intersect" in the Greek temple just as much as does the Fourfold? The ancient city was founded on hierarchical oppositions—between creator and created, sovereign and subject, free man and slave, male and female—the sociological embodiments of Derrida's binary, meta-physical presence/absence oppositions. And such a world deserved the undoing it received at the hands of the Enlightenment. Even if they are dead ends as foundationalist projects, the Cartesian experiment and the categorical imperative were strategically useful disruptions that paid off in lessons about universal freedom. If there is something to object to in the notion of autonomous reason, there is at least as much to object to in hierarchizing human worth in terms of gold, silver, and brass, or of occurrences along a divided line, or of freeman and slave, believer and infidel, and the rest of that intolerant world. Nothing is innocent.

The Ethics of Dissemination

But from whence are we to draw guidance and direction if we have put ''originary ethics'' into question and have allowed even it to tremble? Where do we stand, how can we have any standing at all, if we think in terms of the dissemination of the *Seinsgeschick,* of the letters delivered by Hermes? How are we to proceed after the breakdown of all hermeneutic privileges, after the loss of the master name and the primordial epoch?[7]

I would defend a notion of action that arises not from the security of metaphysical foundations but from a profound sense of the insecurity to which we are exposed. We act not on the basis of unshakeable grounds but in order to do what we can, taking what action as seems wise, and not without misgivings. We act, but we understand that we are not situated safely above the flux and that we do not have a view of the whole. We act, but with a heightened sense of the delimitation of subjectivity, not sure of this ''we,'' or of who or what acts within us, or what deeper impulses are at work on us. We act with fear and trembling, with a deep sense of the *ébranler,* whose tremors are all around us. We act because something has to be done. We act not on the basis of metaphysical schemes, nor on the more subtle basis of eschatological dreams, but on the other side of metaphysics and eschatology, after they have foundered, in the midst of (*inter-esse*) a condition of dissemination, which is also a condition of liberation.

I say liberation, for the loss of the master name seems to me not a loss but a liberation—from mastery of all sorts. We do not, after all, know who we are. *Quaestio mihi factus sum.*[8] This expression is not the metaphysical foundation of a new morals but a confession of the lack of foundation, which inspires trepidation about all our schemes and compassion for all of us, who must in any case take action. It is from a standpoint of Socratic ignorance that I speak of an ethics of dissemination and of *Gelassenheit,* an ethics after metaphysics. The dissemination of the master name makes us wary of power, of the will to impose schemes that we know to be no more than fictions which are sometimes useful and sometimes dangerous. It puts us on the alert to the exercise of power and sensitizes us to all those who are ground up by schemes and principles and metaphysical *archai.*

If the current epochality is to be described in terms of the metaphysics of power, control, and objectification, then it seems to me that the ethics needed to address the present time of need—the age of the *Gestell*—is just such an ethics of dissemination. For it is addressed to the sociology that is everywhere around us today, which instantiates the binary oppositional schemes of Western metaphysics: higher and lower, ruler and ruled, cause and effect, science and opinion, master and slave, same and different, male and female, rich and poor, privileged and unprivileged. The powers that be, the men (sic) of substance, of *ousia,* the man of means, the man of reason, the reason of men (males): these are so many sociological instantiations of the metaphysics of presence. Whence the ethics of dissemination begins by systematically reversing these oppositional schemes, reversing the discrimination strategically, in order finally to displace oppositional arrangements in favor of the open and nonexclusionary.

The work of dissemination is directed at constellations of power that systematically dominate, regulate, exclude. Its model is the Socratic work of delimiting the authority of all programmers, planners, managers, and experts of whatever sorts. This thinking, which situates itself on the margins of metaphysics, operates on behalf of the marginalized. It compromises the prestige of the expert, releases all the loose ends in every system, exposes the systematic violence of any tightly organized structure whatsoever (university, church, hospital, government, etc.). And it does all this not by any show of strength of its own but by letting the system itself unravel, letting the play in the system loose.

The function of an ethics of dissemination is not to try to level all institutional arrangements or to discourage the formation of new ones— Derrida, for example, is the organizer of a *College*—but to *intervene* in ongoing processes, to keep institutions in process, to keep the *forms* of life from eliminating the *life*-form they are supposed to house. It wants always to remind institutions of their genealogy and of the humble circumstances surrounding their birth and so to dispel the illusion that they have dropped from the sky. Its function is to crack hardened shells, to practice the Socratic art, to be gadfly and stingray—but always in the *polis.* It agrees that there is no human life outside the *polis,* or in a solitary, free subject— which is the sociological equivalent of Descartes's epistemological subject. The ethics of dissemination operates only in a community and in the ongoing conversation of mankind but it insists on a nonexclusionary community.

It offers no overall strategies, no total schemes or masterplans (which always proceed from master names), but only local strategies for local action—in this institution or that, in this political struggle or that. It recognizes that nothing is metaphysical or anti-metaphysical "in itself"—indeed "in itself-ness" belongs to the metaphysics of presence—but that there are only metaphysical uses or economies. (The church, for example, can be a force of liberation in one place—the sanctuary as sanctuary for the oppressed—even while it dines with the powers that be in another.) Even adopting an apocalyptic tone serves a purpose when the powers that be flood the official lines of communication with propaganda. The only system in this ethics is to try systematically to intervene on behalf of those for whom the system was *not* designed—women, students, the mad, the ill, the poor, blacks, the suffering, the marginalized of every sort. Its function is to liberate those who are trapped by systems of power, to make openings where there are none, to make room for the exceptions, the excluded, for the endless dissemination of life-styles—not by a plan for universal revolution, but by local action.

Finally, I would say that the ethics of dissemination is likewise an ethics of *Gelassenheit,* of letting be, of everything that liberates and sets free. This is an old idea, coming from the Rhineland mystics, especially Meister Eckhart.[9] *Gelassenheit* meant letting God be God, letting him be—in yourself, in others, in everything—a very nonexclusionary idea. That is why in Meister Eckhart *Gelassenheit,* letting-be, was a principle of love (*caritas*) with some teeth in it, a *caritas* put forward by a Christian which had a deconstructive kick to it. Eckhart saw the life and love of God to be ubiquitous, not confined to just a few privileged souls, not just to priests, for example, which made the churchmen of his day uneasy; or to males (he preached to women and told them that they all had the divine spark, the *Seelenfünklein*), which made these same church*men* uneasy; or even just to Christians, which made nearly all Christendom uneasy. Furthermore, he did not think that the presence of God was confined to *churches* at all, or that God necessarily prefers the Latin language, but that the German vernacular in which he preached would do just fine. And that is why the Reformation took a liking to him and why the papal inquisitors gave him a hard time. Although a high-level Dominican administrator himself, Eckhart set about disseminating power clusters in medieval Christendom, and for that he earned the wrath of the Curia and felt the blows of its institutional power.

This idea makes its way down to Heidegger, where it undergoes a wondrous repetition and retrieval—but with one thing missing, the emancipatory tone that announces the liberation of us all. Heidegger tends to be more interested in letting jugs and bridges and Greek temples be, and to let it go at that, and never quite gets around to talking about letting others be, about our being-with others as mortals. He neglects the fellowship among mortals in virtue of their common fate of not knowing the master name. I do not think there is anything in what he says that excludes his doing this. He just never gets around to it. But we can do it for him and in so doing restore to *Gelassenheit* its ethical punch (an oxymoron of which I am fond).

Although I cannot spell this out here, I think that a good deal of what Heidegger is up to is found in this notion of *Gelassenheit* as "openness to the mystery," as a deep respect for the world, for others, for the gods. *Gelassenheit* is the thoughtfulness that lets the self-withdrawing be, which understands that we are but pointers bent in the direction of what withdraws, and that the ultimate ethical posture is the humble bow of one who bends in its direction. But deconstruction warns us not to take these meditative spirits for fools. They have been trained in martial arts.

— 6 —

The Obligation to Will the Freedom of Others, According to Jean-Paul Sartre

Thomas C. Anderson

The recently published *Cahiers pour une morale (Notebooks for an ethics)* of Jean-Paul Sartre (written 1947–48)[1] leaves little doubt that most standard interpretations of his early view of human relationships are incorrect. This posthumous work makes it clear that not even the early Sartre believed that human beings are necessarily in conflict, nor that all social relationships are ultimately hellish in nature. In other words, *Being and Nothingness* was not meant to be a portrayal of the unavoidable structure of interpersonal relations; rather, as Sartre himself indicates there in a strategically placed footnote,[2] and states explicitly in *Cahiers,* it describes encounters between inauthentic human beings who have not exercised a pure reflection and undergone a conversion. "*Being and Nothingness* is an ontology before conversion," Sartre asserts on the third page of his *Cahiers.* "After conversion," he adds, "there is no longer an ontological reason for struggle" (CM 26). Later, in *Cahiers,* he again refers to *Being and Nothingness* and states that conversion can transform the "hell of passions described [there]" (CM 515).

Since in other places I have already discussed at some length the notion of conversion (also called pure reflection) which Sartre treats extensively in his *Cahiers,*[3] I will simply note here that it involves the refusal to value the impossible goal we humans naturally seek, namely to be God, and the choice instead of man, or more precisely human freedom, as its primary goal and value. And it is concrete human freedom that is chosen, freedom immersed in a world of other free human beings who inevitably objectify it and deform its projects. The converted individual chooses to *accept* this objectification by others as the inevitable price of the human condition, and by acceptance removes one of the main sources of antagonism and conflict among human beings. In *Cahiers* Sartre also explains that conversion "transforms" the narrow alternatives for human relations, as object to subject or subject to object, presented in *Being and Nothingness.* He offers an extensive discussion of comprehension, an act in which it is possible to be aware of another not just as an object but as a free subject,

63

and even primarily as the latter. He speaks also of the possibility of "reciprocal comprehension" or "reciprocal recognition" of freedoms, something
he admits was absent from the ontology presented in *Being and
Nothingness.*[4]

Not only does *Cahiers* show how human relationships of genuine intersubjectivity—each subject willing the freedom of the other—are possible, it
goes further and designate such relationships as the goal of morality. Sartre, in his notebooks, presents as his moral ideal the city of ends, a classless society, the reign of freedom, a society in which each wills the freedom
of all.[5] And in numerous other works of this early period also, it is such a
society that Sartre proposes as the moral goal human beings should strive to
realize. (In fact, I believe that this goal remained primary for him throughout his career.)[6] Thus it is not enough to say that for Sartre, even the early
Sartre, human relations *can* be basically positive in nature, and that individuals *can* recognize and will each other's freedom. For he advances the
much stronger moral claim that they *should* be so, that each of us should
take as our primary moral obligation to will the freedom of others, the
realization of the city of ends. Of course, given Sartre's rejection of all
objective or transcendent values, the basis of such obligation cannot be
some intrinsic dignity or worth naturally present in all human beings. The
purpose of this paper, then, is to analyze the major argument or arguments
Sartre does offer in his early works to support his contention that each
person should will the freedom of others. (Actually, I use the term "argument" here advisedly. It might be better to say "suggested argument,"
since nowhere does Sartre set forth a detailed, step-by-step logically tight
demonstration.)[7] Specifically, I will try to determine the degree to which
Sartre successfully establishes not only that one should not interfere with
the freedom of others, but also that one should positively assist, promote,
and enhance that freedom.

One final point before I begin my analysis. In his last years Sartre
stated that he had worked on three moralities over the course of his life.[8]
Although this paper concentrates on the first of these, this limitation is not
as severe as it might appear. Space prevents me from showing this here, but
I believe that Sartre's later moralities did not involve wholesale rejection of
his earlier, but rather, as he himself said, an "enrichment" of them. One
example of this, which I have already noted, is that the ideal of his early
morality, the city of ends, remained his primary moral goal throughout his
life, although its content was progressively enriched. Furthermore, it is in
his so-called first morality (and only here, to my knowledge) that Sartre
offered anything close to adequate reasons to demonstrate that each person
should will this ideal and choose the freedom of all. I turn, then, to his
argument.

Universalization

Almost all who have written on the topic have recognized that in *Existentialism and Humanism* Sartre offers something like an appeal to universalization to support his claim that, "I am obliged to will the freedom of others at the same time as mine." Thus, he states: "When we say that man chooses himself we mean that each one of us must choose himself; but by that we also mean that in choosing himself he chooses all men." And he explains, "In effect there is not one of our acts that in creating the man whom we wish to be, does not create at the same time an image of man such as we judge he ought to be." Although these suggestions have some resemblance to a Kantian notion of universalizability, note that Sartre's key word is "image," not rule or principle. He does not say that when I choose I implicitly propose a rule which all persons in morally similar situations are to follow. Rather he says that when I choose an ideal for myself, "I am creating a certain image of man," I am presenting an ideal of what "man . . . ought to *be*."[9]

I have argued elsewhere that as it stands Sartre's assertion here is too broad;[10] I do not believe he is correct in maintaining that every time I choose something as good or valuable for *me* (or what I ought to be), I in effect choose it as good or valuable for *everyone* (or what everyone ought to be). It seems to me arbitrary to claim that moral values and obligations always pertain to those aspects of a situation that are in principle repeatable and never to the situation's irreducibly *unique* features. In my moral experience, at least, the most morally relevant features of my concrete situation are sometimes my unique individuality or my situation's unique characteristics. In such experiences the moral value-obligation pertains to me not insofar as I am similar to other human beings, but insofar as I am a unique individual—and it would be question-begging in the extreme to claim that such experiences cannot be *moral* experiences. I submit, then, that only if the good or value I choose for myself is rooted in what I believe to be good or valuable for me insofar as I am a human being can it be claimed that when I choose, I, at least implicitly, create an image (ideal) of what "man" should be.[11]

Nevertheless, let me immediately add that Sartre is correct when he claims in *Existentialism and Humanism* that when I choose my freedom as my primary value I in effect propose that one's freedom should be one's primary value. For, he says, the reason I should choose my freedom is because it is the source of all my values.[12] But this reason, this fact, is indeed part of the universal human condition for Sartre; each person's freedom is the source of all of his or her values. Freedom is a good for me precisely in that respect in which I am the same as all other human beings, and so in choosing my freedom I do in effect propose an image of what other human beings should be—namely, they should be individuals who choose their freedom as their primary value. Still, how does it follow from this that I, or anyone else, am obliged to choose as valuable anyone's freedom other than my own; that "I am obliged to will the freedom of others at the same time as mine"? This conclusion will result only if a necessary connection can be established between my proposing that each person's freedom should be *his* or *her* supreme value, and my choosing his or her freedom as a value for *me*.

The best argument that I have found in support of such a connection is given by Linda Bell.[13] Invoking Sartre's inextricable linking of choosing and acting, she reasons that if I will that others choose their freedom as a value, this must mean I will that they act in accordance with their choice. But "if I will that others act in accordance with their choice of freedom as a value, I must at least will that they have the freedom thus to act. Must I not then will that they not be oppressed?" Moreover, she adds, since "to value is to act," this means that I myself must act against oppression of them.

This is a strong argument and may well be what Sartre has in mind but does not explicitly say. It surely does seem that if I will that others value their freedom (in other words, if I propose as a value that others value their freedom), it would be inconsistent for me to oppress or otherwise interfere to prevent them from acting according to their choice. It may also be inconsistent for me to will that others value their freedom and yet not also work against third parties who seek to interfere with others' exercise of their choice of their freedom.

But, as Bell herself recognizes, to say that I should not myself interfere, or allow third parties to interfere, with others is one thing. It is much stronger to claim, as Sartre seems to do, that I must positively act to increase or enhance my own and others' freedoms and achieve the city of ends. Part of the difficulty with Sartre's argument is that it is not altogether clear just what it means to say that one should act in accordance with the choice to value freedom, or even what precisely it means to choose to value freedom. Let me explain.

To choose to value something and to act accordingly can mean, on the one hand, to strive to realize in one's life and in society the ideals in question. In this sense, to value something like justice or peace would involve acting to make them real. On the other hand, to choose to value something or someone may simply mean to acknowledge or appraise that object or person as having worth. Obviously, when an object or person already exists, to value it and act accordingly cannot mean to strive to make it real.

(To value Caesar Chavez, or my present state of pleasure, or the status quo, cannot mean to act to make them real, for they already are.) Furthermore, I can choose to value things that can in no way be made real, such as a dog I owned when I was seven years old. My point is this: to choose to value something does not necessarily entail choosing or acting to increase or promote its reality; it may simply mean to affirm or acknowledge the worth or importance of its reality (present or past).

Thus, to follow Sartre and to will or choose to value freedom (one's own or others') can simply mean willingly to acknowledge and accept as worthwhile the fact that oneself and others are structurally free and able to make free choices; this would be to admit that oneself and others are beings-for-themselves, not things totally determined by processes and forces. Action in accord with this choice would be, I suppose, to admit to oneself and others one's responsibility for one's choices and actions and not to evade this by offering excuses. Note that the freedoms in question here are our ontological freedom and freedom of choice, both of which are part and parcel of our fundamental human structure. Obviously, to value our structural freedom as a being-for-itself cannot entail to act to make it real, for it already is. Likewise, to value our freedom of choice in this sense would not mean to strive to increase it but to declare it to have worth and importance for us (and not to deny or flee it in bad faith). On the other hand, to will or choose to value freedom (mine or others') may mean to will, and hence to act, to make freedom real or more real, where the freedom in question would, I suppose, be political or psychological freedom. Again, the point is that even if one grants, as I do, Sartre's claim that in willing or choosing to value my freedom I in effect will that others choose to value theirs, this does not in itself oblige me to do any more than to affirm as worthwhile the fact that both I and others are ontologically free and can make free choices. (And, of course, in every situation human beings are ontologically free and possess some freedom of choice.) Only if we arbitrarily identify choosing to value something with choosing to make that something real (or more real), can we claim that willing freedom entails acting in the situation to increase actually or expand that freedom. (In fact I think Sartre does tend to make such an identification!)[14]

If my analysis here is correct, it means that this first suggested argument of Sartre's (as expounded by Bell) adequately demonstrates that one who wills his freedom, and thus that of others, should not interfere with or oppress the freedom of others or allow third parties to do so; it does not prove, however, that such a one must positively strive to increase or enhance these freedoms. But we should not stop here, for Sartre has more to offer in support of his position.

Interdependency

The second reason presented by the early Sartre as to why one should will the freedom of others seems to have been overlooked by many commentators. As the following passage states, it has to do with the interdependency of human freedoms.

> In willing freedom, we discover that it depends entirely upon the freedom of others and that the freedom of others depends on our own. Obviously, freedom as the definition of man does not depend upon others, but as soon as there is engagement I am obliged to will the freedom of others at the same time as mine. (EH 51–52. I have slightly modified the translation.)

The interdependency of human freedoms that Sartre has in mind here is both social-political and psychological, for in an earlier passage in that same work he writes, "The other is indispensable to my existence, and equally so to any knowledge I can have of myself"(45). Accordingly, I will investigate both kinds of dependency in order to determine how they enable him to conclude, "I am obliged to will the freedom of others at the same time as mine."

Social-political dependency

Sartre is certainly correct in thinking that since I am concretely engaged in the practical social order, my freedom is dependent on that of others and theirs on mine. Both the range of options available to our free choice and our freedom to attain the goals we choose, are heavily dependent on the will and actions of others. However, the fact of such dependence does not in and of itself oblige any of us to cooperate or to will the other's freedom. For in some situations—for example, if one is powerful enough—it could well be that one can most effectively increase one's freedom by restricting the freedom of others and forcing them into one's service. To do so would not in any way deny interdependency; quite the contrary, it readily acknowledges it. It is only if we join Sartre's earlier argument to this notion of dependency that we can obtain the conclusion he draws. In the preceding section we saw that, for Sartre, when I choose my freedom as my primary value, I, in effect, also choose that others choose their freedom as primary, and it would be inconsistent with this choice for me to oppress or restrict the acts of the other that are in accord with the other's choice of freedom, or to allow third parties to do so. If this is so, then a "discovery" of my dependency on others, that is, of my need for them to will my freedom, can only lead me to will rather than restrict theirs. However, as we discussed at length above, "willing" another's freedom does not necessarily mean that I must act actually to increase and expand that freedom. All it need mean is that I must acknowledge it in the sense that I affirm it to be of value and so do not interfere with it or allow anyone else to.

However, if the reason for my willing the other's freedom is that I need him or her to will mine, let us ask, what kind of willing of my freedom am I myself dependent upon in the practical order? Without a doubt I need and want others to acknowledge that my freedom is of value and so not to interfere, or let third parties interfere, with it. But this is hardly enough. I am fundamentally dependent on others if I am to achieve most of the goals that I freely choose, that is, I need their positive assistance, not their benign neglect. How many of the goods of life, can I alone supply for myself? Now if it is the positive assistance of others that my dependency calls for, then for me minimally to will their freedom by merely affirming it to be of value while neglecting to assist it, will hardly prompt them actively to promote mine. It is far more likely that I will gain their aid if I on my part actively engage myself in aiding them. Thus, I suggest that Sartre's argument leads to the conclusion that I should will, in the sense of actively promote, the freedom of others so that they will do the same for me. An investigation of psychological dependency gives even more support to this conclusion.

Psychological dependency

In *Existentialism and Humanism* Sartre asserts, "I cannot attain any truth whatsoever about myself except through the mediation of another"(45), and his studies of Genet and Flaubert amply illustrate this claim. Genet, for example, did not recognize his freedom to be other than a thief precisely because the society of good people branded him a thief at an early age. Likewise, oppressed masses may be so duped by their rulers that they fail to grasp their freedom to reject their masters' values. Thus, for Sartre, I depend on others not only to be free in the practical order, but even to become explicitly aware that I am free (both ontologically and in my choices). The question is, how does this psychological dependency oblige me "to will the freedom of others at the same time as mine"?

Robert Stone has responded by claiming that if the other is not free—for example, if I enslave him—he cannot "recognize" me as a free subject, and as a result I will not come to recognize myself as a free subject. He writes, "A slave can 'recognize' me only as a being devoid of subjectivity, that is, as a master. But it is my freedom, not my domination, that I need recognition of."[15] Thomas Flynn appears to make a similar claim. My concrete freedom requires the free "recognition" of my freedom by other freedoms, he suggests, because their free recognition is necessary for me to discover truths about myself, such as my moral character and (presumably) even my freedom.[16]

I think there is merit in this suggestion, especially since Sartre himself does claim that one's "freedom can be asserted only by the *recognition* bestowed upon it by other freedoms."[17] However, the meaning of the term *recognition* is far from clear. Just as with "willing" or "valuing," freedom can have various meanings, so "recognizing" someone as free admits of a variety of meanings. To recognize someone as a free subject can minimally mean to: (1) understand, or be aware, that they are not a thing but a non-determined human being who continually projects itself beyond what is toward not yet existing possibilities and goals, and (2) understand, or be aware, that their acts are freely chosen, that is, not the necessary result of psychological and environmental forces. Now, contrary to Stone's assertion that "a slave can 'recognize' me only as a being devoid of subjectivity," it seems to me that the slave can recognize me, the master, as a free subject in both of the above senses. The slave can be aware that the master is a free human being who transcends what is, toward not yet existing possibilities, and the slave can also understand that the master's very acts of enslaving (not to mention his other acts) are the result of his free choice and not merely the products of social, economic, and other conditions over which he, the master, has no control. Indeed, it is precisely the slave's recognition that the master *freely* chooses to enslave him that makes slavery the especially heinous oppression that it is. Obviously the term *recognition* is used here in a sense roughly equivalent to "to understand, to be aware of, to acknowledge or identify." The slave can understand, be aware, acknowledge, identify the master as a free subject rather than a determined thing. I take it that such recognition, which even a slave can offer, is not what Stone and Flynn have in mind when they claim that my own recognition of my freedom requires *free* recognition by other free subjects.

I would suggest that one type of recognition by others that would be applicable would be that which Sartre calls comprehension in his *Cahiers* and elsewhere.[18] Although the recognition described above is an awareness of the other as a free subject, it grasps this freedom as one objective property among others possessed by the other. It is, one might say, the kind of recognition or knowledge that is found in a subject-object relation, a knowledge by a subject that classifies and categorizes the other person as a free object. It is recognition at a distance; it does not involve entering into an intimate intersubjective union with the other subject. Thus this recognition of another subject does not grasp the other's freedom as it is intimately lived and experienced by the other. The recognition that is comprehension, on the other hand, does attain the freedom of the other as it is lived because it involves, Sartre says, a sympathetic unity with the other subject. As he explains in his *Cahiers,* comprehension involves an "interpretation" of freedoms such that each is in the other. In comprehension I fuse with the other subject's free dynamic transcendence of her facticity toward her goals and thus grasp her freedom as she lives it, not simply as an objective property that she possesses. Clearly, then, comprehension is the kind of recognition from others that one would need to become explicitly aware of one's freedom as the dynamic transcendence that one lives and is. If others grasp my freedom as an objective property of my being, that is the way I will know it.[19] And if the other is someone I oppress, this is exactly the way the other will recognize my freedom, as a characteristic of the object I am for the other. There is little likelihood that he will sympathetically unite his subjectivity with mine and attain the intimate recognition of my free subjectivity which comprehension involves. It follows, then, that if my recognition of my own lived freedom is dependent on the other's comprehension of my freedom, I must "will" the other as a free subject rather than oppress the other.

Once again, however, we need to specify the meaning of the phrase, "will the freedom of the other." Does our need for the other's comprehension require us actively to promote her freedom or simply to acknowledge it to be of worth? It seems that strictly speaking only the latter is required, for, although Sartre states that comprehension involves "respect" for, and not rejection of, another's freedom, he also insists it is not "adoption" of this freedom or its goals.[20] Thus it does not seem inconsistent with my need for others' comprehension for me to refrain from actively promoting their freedom, since the comprehension I seek from them itself involves only their respect for, but not necessarily their adoption or promotion of, my freedom. But it would certainly be inconsistent with my need to have others comprehend my freedom were I to reject or repress theirs, for they will hardly be willing sympathetically to unite their freedom with mine if I do so. On the other hand, if I do take positive actions to assist others, they will likely be more inclined to unite with me in comprehension, than if I merely respect their freedom and refrain from interfering with it. In other words, although my need for comprehension by others may not, strictly speaking, require me to promote their freedom, it surely makes it prudent and reasonable for me to do so.

There is yet a third, and stronger, sense of recognition, one which more clearly includes a positive evaluative dimension than the above two. I suspect it is this notion of recognition that Sartre and his commentators have in mind when they assert that my recognition of my freedom depends on others' recognition of my freedom, for to recognize others in this third sense means to consider them to be of value. Thus when oppressed peoples demand recognition they are not, I take it, just stating that they want others to understand or be aware that they are free human beings and not things; they are also demanding that they be treated as having a certain value and dignity. To need this kind of recognition of one's freedom, then, is to need it to be valued, approved, by others. The claim of dependency is that I myself would not recognize the value or worth of my freedom if others did not do so. Psychological studies (such as Sartre's *St. Genet*), which show that children who receive little positive valuation from others tend to have a very negative self-image, provide testimony to the need for this kind of recognition. Furthermore, in Sartre's universe this evaluative kind of recognition is even more important, because he believes that the only sources of meaning and value that exist are free human beings. Since he also believes that one of the, if not the, most basic needs of a human being is for a valuable and meaningful life, it is essential that one receive the evaluative recognition of others. Of course each individual can freely choose to confer value on his own life and it will thereby have value. However, if other freedoms also recognize my value, this will enrich the solitary worth I give myself. It follows, then, that I should recognize (value) the freedom of others inasmuch as it is the source of their valuation of me. Failure on my part to do so will mean that any value or recognition they offer me, even if positive in nature, will be worthless in my eyes. Moreover, it is far more likely that they will recognize me to be of value if I so recognize, rather than ignore or repress, them.

Even more important in this regard is Sartre's suggestion that the recognition-value I especially want is from those who choose to offer it freely, rather than those who offer it because their situation almost forces it from them.[21] The recognition-value I receive from my vassal or slave is worth something, for even they are not mere things but free subjects, albeit in a very restricted sense. Yet the value to me of their recognition is minimal compared to that which I impute to the recognition by an equal. This is because the extreme psychological and physical dependency of the former on me almost compels them to value me. Someone who is not in such a relation of dependency is much more free to value me or not, and, therefore, if they do so, their recognition-value of me will be significantly more meaningful to me (just as freely given love is far more valuable to its recipient than love obtained under duress). For the same reason the recognition-value I receive from a child, or from an adult who is emotionally a child, is worth less in my eyes than that from a mature adult. The recognition-value I receive from those whose existence is consumed by poverty, ignorance, disease, and oppression is not as valuable to me as that which I receive from those whose freedom is not so impoverished. For, again, it is unlikely that those who suffer such deprivations will recognize me as anything more than their possible benefactor, if even that. They have little freedom or ability to recognize or value me as the free individual I am. If this reasoning is correct, if I especially desire recognition-value from those who offer it freely, not because of dire need or extreme dependency, it follows that I should strive to aid others in achieving their freedom. In other words, I should work to promote Sartre's city of ends, that society in which individuals are equals, freely able to recognize and value each other as ends.

Conclusion

Sartre's appeal to dependency, coupled with his version of the universalization argument, seems to me to demonstrate not only that I must not interfere, nor allow others to interfere, with the freedom of others, but also that I should actively promote their freedom. Since I am dependent on others if I am to *be* free in the concrete order and to *be aware* of and value my freedom, I ought to acknowledge, value, and promote their freedom since that is the most likely way of encouraging a similar response from them. Since it is especially from human beings who are free from dire need or extreme dependency that I want recognition and valuation of my life, I should endeavor to aid others in achieving that freedom.

What remains unclear to me is the extension of this notion of the other. Although Sartre occasionally speaks of willing the freedom of *all* others, this seems simply to be exaggeration. His argument from interdependency obviously implies that I have no obligation to will the freedom of those whose lives and subjectivity I can never touch nor they mine. A more serious question, however, is whether, and to what extent, I am obliged to promote, or even acknowledge, the freedom of those whose lives are only minimally linked to mine. Sartre's argument appears to be so based on self-interest (for it seems to advise me to value and promote other's freedom so that they will value and promote mine) that it would hardly require me to promote the freedom of those from whom I can expect little or nothing in return. However, we should take seriously his phrase, "the city of *ends*," for it indicates that Sartre is not advocating that we turn others into mere means for our personal justification. As I noted earlier, if others become simply my servants or slaves, they are not able to offer me the meaning and value I desire, the affirmation of my being by free and independent subjects. That is to say that only individuals whose freedoms I respect as ends in themselves can give to my existence the kind of value affirmation I crave. Still, the question persists. Just who am I obliged to treat as ends, according to Sartre's dependency argument? In particular, to what extent am I required to acknowledge and promote the freedom of those whose existence is hardly linked to mine at all? Inasmuch as my psychological dependency on many others is slight (for example, I experience little need to receive recognition-value from most of the humans on this planet), my obligation to will their freedom is correspondingly slight. Likewise, if my socio-political dependency on others is small, and I suspect there is little that many human beings can do to enhance or restrict my freedom, my obligation to will their freedom is also minimal. Thus, while Sartre's appeal to interdependency does establish an obligation for me to promote others' freedoms as ends, it appears that this obligation does not extend nearly as far as I believe he wants it to, namely, to the most wretched of the earth and to the promotion of a *worldwide* classless society and city of ends.

Yet I do not want to end on a negative note, for in a 1964 lecture on morality Sartre took a number of new and interesting positions.[22] In that lecture he rooted moral values not in human freedom but in human needs, and proposed as his moral ideal and goal integral humanity, that is, human beings with their needs fulfilled. Now if human need is the basis of moral value, and if it could be shown that this entails that human beings have a legitimate claim on, or right to, those things necessary to fulfill their needs (such as by an appeal to a moral principle that promotes maximal individual well-being for all), then perhaps it could be argued that others have some responsibility to aid them in attaining such goods. This would mean that even the peasant in some remote corner of the fourth world could rightfully claim the assistance of all who have the ability to help. It would mean, therefore, that each human being would have the obligation to will and promote the integral humanity of all, to the degree that he or she is able. Such a moral norm was, I believe, the one that Sartre himself lived by.

III

An Other Voice

— 7 —

On the Advantage and Disadvantage of Nietzsche for Women

Debra B. Bergoffen

I. Friedrich Nietzsche's critique of Western culture was never intended as a critique of patriarchy. He did not, for all his analyses of and insights into the nihilisms of Western culture, focus his attention on its patriarchal structure as a possible source of its nihilism. Nationalism yes.[1] Patriarchy no. This does not mean, however, that Nietzsche's analyses are not relevant for contemporary feminist thought; for if it is true that patriarchy is a dominant and pervasive feature of Western culture, then a critique of the culture must at some level be a negation of its patriarchal value/power structure. The task then is to find the thread of Nietzsche's thought that is pertinent to the contemporary feminist project.

That a critic as acute as Nietzsche was not aware of the patriarchal dimensions of Western culture, is a silent testimony to the power of patriarchy and to the ways in which it makes women invisible. This is all the more striking in view of the fact that the question of woman is scattered throughout Nietzsche's works. It is not that Nietzsche is silent on the question of woman—his reputation as a misogynist is not based on the absence of speech—but rather that what he has to say about woman is stereotypical of nineteenth-century male biases and irrelevant to the central issues of his philosophical project(s). Or so it appears. Jacques Derrida and more recently Ophelia Schutte and David Krell have suggested that the philosopher whose preface to *Beyond Good and Evil* asks whether truth might be a woman was more preoccupied with the woman question than has been previously recognized and that this preoccupation is more ambiguous and more central to his thought than is usually understood.[2]

It remains the case, however, that in addressing the question of woman and in indirectly challenging the symbols of patriarchal power, Nietzsche did not establish definitive links between patriarchy and nihilism. The point of this paper is to suggest that these links can be established if we pursue the lines of thought begun by Nietzsche's analyses of the prevalent mode of Western temporalization—historical consciousness.

Deciphering the relationship between Western historical consciousness, nihilism, and patriarchy entails exploring the ways in which the male
and female relationships to time have been dichotomized within Western
culture. It involves discovering the ways in which the female appropriation
of time within Western culture offers alternatives to the nihilisms of patriarchal historicism. This feminist perspective shows the eternal return in a
new light. It suggests that the eternal recurrence is somehow entangled in
the story of woman and pursues the question raised by Krell: "What binds
Calina (or any woman) to noontide and to Nietzsche's thought of
thoughts?"[3]

My first hypothesis may be formulated as follows: As an attack on
Western historical consciousness, the eternal recurrence is also a refusal of
Western patriarchy. Within this refusal is an affirmation of Western female
temporality. In rejecting the male-female split characteristic of a patriarchal
culture, the eternal return offers the possibility of a heterosexual-
androgynous transvaluation of the meaning of human historical existence.

In calling the eternal recurrence a heterosexual-androgynous structuring of time I mean to suggest that the eternal return entails a recognition of
difference which refuses to succumb to reductionist or dialectical-synthetic
suppressions of the other. Neither heterosexual nor androgynous can, by
itself, carry the full weight of this recognition and refusal. Though "heterosexual" carries the sense of difference, it also conveys oppositional and
domination meanings of otherness. Though "androgynous" calls forth the
relational structure of otherness, it also carries meanings of the fusion and
obliteration of difference. In linking heterosexual to androgynous I intend
to call attention to the eternal return's recognition of the difference
(heterosexual)-relation (androgynous) structure of otherness, and to insist
that within the context of the eternal return difference does not entail domination and relation does not mean synthesis.

Even the most cursory look at Western culture reveals that within the
West reality has been divided into a public and private sphere and that this
division is not gender neutral. The public sphere—the domain of political,
civic, and historical existence—is reserved for the male; the private sphere,
the domain of the family, is designated female. This is not to say that
within the West women have been entirely excluded from the public domain
but rather to say that the public domain has been identified as the nonfem-
inine (anti-feminine?) domain and that a woman can enter this domain only
with difficulty, that is, by renouncing, masking, or repressing the feminine
dimension of her existence. As Julia Kristeva puts it:

> We cannot gain access to the temporal scene, that is, to the political and
> historical affairs of society, except by identifying with the values considered

to be masculine (mastery, super-ego, the sanctioning communicative world that institutes stable social exchange).[4]

Kristeva's words alert us to the relationship between temporality, masculine values, and the public domain and indicate the power of the masculine perspective; for from her vantage point, there is only one temporal scene, the scene of history and politics. This is, I shall argue, the position of patriarchy. That is, in equating human time with historical time, patriarchy refuses to legitimatize or recognize the temporality it designates as feminine. The eternal recurrence, however, disturbs the formula which equates time with history.

II. Freud's *Civilization and Its Discontents* helps us understand the gender specificity of the public-private distinction. In that work Freud teaches us that the family and the state confront each other as advocates of different value systems and that these systems reflect a fundamental split whereby the principle of Eros is bifurcated into the principles of Eros and Ananke. Further, he identifies woman as the embodiment of the principle of Eros and man as the advocate of Ananke. Freud notes that the female principle of Eros is gradually excluded from the domain of civilization until it is ultimately situated in opposition to the sphere of Ananke, functioning as its antagonistic other.

In his analysis of the male-female conflict which permeates civilized life, Freud echoes the voice of Sophocles, whose *Antigone* explores the meaning of the male-female dichotomy as it portrays the consequences of a woman's attempt to challenge the male domination of public life. Though often read as a study in the conflict between the rights of the individual citizen and the authority of the state, the *Antigone* may (should?) also be read as a reflection on the male-female dimensions of the public-private disjunction of Western civilized life. Antigone is not just any citizen. Indeed she, because she is a she, is no citizen at all. As a woman, she confronts the state as the sister of a citizen. She demands his rights, not hers. Antigone as woman (*qua* woman) has no place or rights in the public arena.[5]

Where Freud and Sophocles teach us to explore the value antagonisms embodied in the gender disjunction of the public and private domains, Nietzsche alerts us to the necessary temporal distinctions embedded in this dichotomy. Nietzsche's analysis of the essential relationship between temporal meaning and human existence tells us that the diverse meanings of the public and private domains must be articulated temporally. That is, it is not simply (or even complexly) the case that within Western culture male and female came to represent distinct value systems, but also the case that they are required to live time differently. The evidence here is not difficult to find. The public domain is the domain of history. The private domain is that of nature. Men make history; women make babies. Men produce; women reproduce. Men create; women re-create.

The ways in which these diverse meanings of the male and female become disjointed and dichotomized value systems, with the male, implicitly anti-life articulation of reality dominating the female appropriation of the world, is suggested by Haunani-Kay Trask when she writes:

> Man, who does not experience physical reproduction, appears to transcend life through his cultural projects. Consequently, man comes to value invention, symbolization, and action more than the reproduction and repetition of life. This superior valuation separates the animal from the cultural, the repetitive from the creative. Because she is associated with both the animal *and* the repetitive, woman is subordinated to man as nature is subordinated to culture.[6]

Nietzsche is not in principle opposed to this division of being. There is a sense in which he recognizes it when he writes, "history . . . I take it to be the eternal masculine. . . ."[7] Neither is he opposed, in principle, to the valuing of the historical above the familial. To hope to find him assisting the feminist project by invoking the principle of equality is to look to the wrong philosopher with the wrong perspective. Equality was never one of Nietzsche's calling cards. The principle of life affirmation, however, was.

III. Though Nietzsche is unconcerned with the division of Western reality into public and private domains along gender lines, and though his discussion of the nihilism of Western culture takes little notice of the family or the female, Nietzsche's claim that historical consciousness is life-denying may be seen as an attack on Western male temporality, that is, on a patriarchal system which excludes Eros from the domain of necessity. From this perspective, the eternal recurrence—the articulation of time offered as an alternative to the nihilism of Western historical consciousness—may be understood as a structuring of human temporality that refuses the gender split as it negates the disjunction between creation and re-creation.

According to Nietzsche the essence of Western historical consciousness is to be found in its nihilistic desire to negate the value of the present. On the one hand, linear developmental time imposes the weight of the past on the present. The past is said to be the causal origin of the present. It is the authoritative source of the present insofar as it is seen as carrying the meaning of the present within it. On the other hand, linear teleological time negates the value of the present in the name of the future, which holds its meaning or fruition. The present, then, is the causal product of the past and the incomplete meaning of the future. In and for itself it is nothing.

Although from a purely logical point of view the meaning of the present cannot tolerate the contradictory demands of historical consciousness, Nietzsche sees the simultaneous pull of the meaning of the present to the past and to the future as a function of the nihilistic desire articulated by the Western sense of history. Within the context of a nihilistic culture the life affirmation inherent in the meaning of the present is drained away from itself in all directions so that it cannot under any circumstances become visible. To live historically is to reduce the present to a parenthesis between a glorious past and a glorified future. Historical living, whether it falls prey to the temptation to value the authority of the past more than the life of the present, or yields to the inclination to sacrifice the life of the present to the promise of the future, must, by virtue of invoking the value of history, abandon the value of life.

If we apply our orienting hypothesis to Nietzsche's critique, that is, if we, invoking the work of Freud and Sophocles, identify the nihilism of historical consciousness as a sign of patriarchy, then Nietzsche's call for transvaluation must include a demand that feminine temporality be explored for possible antidotes to the nihilistic poison. If historical temporality is the time of the male (i.e., patriarchal time), what is the temporality of the female? If Nietzsche's discussion of historical consciousness is not a description of Western consciousness per se but a depiction of the public-male domain of Western culture, can we articulate the features of Western female temporality in such a way as to discover whether it reflects and reinforces or deflects and refuses the nihilisms of patriarchal historical time?

Within Western culture, female temporality, the time of the family, is the time of the erotic and repetitive. The woman of Western culture is asked to repeat the role of the mother. Unlike the male, who is required to leave the home and create a place for himself "in the world," the female is allowed to leave the home of her mother in order that she may become a mother in a home of her own. Unlike the male, who is asked to embody the value of transcendence, the female is asked to be the eternally present mother.[8]

Jane Gallop points to the psychoanalytic sources of this sexual bifurcation of temporality when she describes the different positions from which the girl and boy discover that the mother is castrated (sic). Though children of both sexes experience this discovery as an irretrievable loss, the boy can refuse to recognize that the discovery of the mother's castration is actually the discovery of his lack by insisting that the moment of loss has not yet arrived. That is, as possessor of the penis, he can assure himself that castration is a threat he can escape by controlling the future. Biology offers no such assurance (or none that are credible) for the girl. She must experience herself as lack and can only experience this lack as transcendable, that is as a loss, by inferring a past without lack. Her sense of loss is "inferred on the basis of a retrospective view that sees the past as fuller than the present."[9] While the male then is oriented to the not-yet as the time of threat and transcendence, the female is nostalgically turned to the imagined has been.

Although both of these readings of the meaning of the mother are mis-readings, both in the shared experience of the mother as castrated and in the disjunctive experiences of the meaning of castration as immanent or already undergone, they represent diverse ways of coping with the real loss of the mother as MOTHER. While the boy denies the loss (he is not yet castrated), the girl cannot. Her misreading allows her to harbor the hope (always frustrated) of recovering the loss. By accepting the possibility of refinding the mother by becoming the mother again, the woman pursues and perpetuates her misreading of castration and allows the man to believe that he can both escape castration by controlling the future and refind the MOTHER by possessing a wife-mother.

These sexually distinguished misreadings of the discovery of one's sep-aratedness or alienation from the mother provide the conditions for the male's desire to be thrust into the historical time of transcendence, and the female's desire to enclose herself in the natural time of recurrence. The woman, hoping to recapture the presence of the pre-castrated mother, may be said to be oriented toward time in a transformative mode. Hers is the time of nostalgia. The man, hoping to escape becoming the castrated mother, may be said to be directed toward time in an appropriative mode. His is the time of projection. These diverse male-female misreadings of the castrated mother then generate different understandings of the meaning of and need to cultivate power. For the male, power is equated with domination;[10] if he can exercise power over the future and others he can escape the fated castration. For the female, power is understood in its trans-formative sense; by transforming the givenness of her being she can escape her castrated status.

It perhaps should not surprise us that in the confrontation between the temporality and values of transformation and domination, domination should come to dominate. Nietzsche's place in this confrontation is in part suggested by Trask's observation that the circle imagery of the eternal re-currence recalls the imagery of Adrienne Rich, for whom the womb, the pot, the urn, and the circle represent transformative power rather than dom-ination power.[11] (That the story is not this simple is seen when the power advocated by eternal recurrence is placed within the context of the will to power. But that is for another time.)

IV. In helping to clarify the sources of the patriarchal disjunction and di-verse valuation of temporal realms, the psychoanalytic perspective makes it clear that it would be a mistake to say that in being asked to be the mother again the female is being asked to allow the past to dominate the present, for this is a historical way of speaking. It carries an implicit devaluation of feminine time and appeals to the male orientation toward power. To speak of allowing the past to dominate the present suggests a struggle among temporal moments and implies that this struggle is inappropriately resolved when or if the past becomes a privileged moment.

This way of speaking, by representing the woman's present as the moment which (ought to) transcends the past, assumes that there is only one mode of the present—the historical present. But what needs to be emphasized is that the woman's original refusal of historical time, which is then reinforced by her being barred from historical activity, means that the female present cannot be the historical present, a moment in a transcendent, teleological relationship to the past. It must be a present without a historical past—that is, a psychological, biological, cosmic present.

It is here that something promising emerges. The meaning of this form of presence invites exploration. We must try to understand the difference between a present that is the present of a familial, genealogically conceived past and a present that is the present of a patriarchal, historically conceived past. If the nihilism of patriarchal historical consciousness lies in its negation of the value of the present, the way in which female ahistorical temporality embraces the present may be the key to transcending the nihilism of history.

We begin by suggesting that the repetition articulated in familial/erotic temporality and devalued as uncreative by patriarchal historical consciousness acquires a new value in the context of Nietzsche's critique. Instead of accepting historical consciousness's meaning of repetition as the time of unfreedom and the uncreative, we are led to ask why a nihilistic appropriation of time would devalue repetition. We are led to suspect that this devaluation is a part of the nihilistic strategy against life. We wonder whether the devaluation is a sign of a threat, that is, a sign that a temporality which values repetition may threaten the nihilistic project of patriarchal historicity. Under the influence of these suspicions we propose to examine the ways in which patriarchal historicism masks the threat posed by the time of erotic repetition to the devaluation of life embedded in historical temporality. Under the influence of these suspicions I propose a second hypothesis: As an affirmation of presence and of the genealogical and the erotic, a feminine transformative temporality is an anti-nihilistic but humanly incomplete affirmation of life.

Of particular interest is the way in which historical consciousness reduces the meaning of repetition to mere redundance, for with this reduction the relationship between re-creation and creation is severed. Nietzsche's critique of Western historical consciousness suggests that uncovering the sense of this reduction of the meaning of repetition may be the key to deciphering the nihilism of patriarchal historicism.

Instead of linking the meaning of repetition to variation and the meaning of variation to creativity, as in a musical repetition of or variation on a theme where the relationship between repetition and variation articulates the meaning of creativity, patriarchal historicism links creation with novelty. From this perspective repetition is seen as the antithesis of creativity. The creative is the new, the not yet, the un-present of the future. It is represented as the unique, as that which transcends or escapes the present. If Nietzsche's insights regarding the link between nihilism and historical definition are attended to, however, we will not be misled by the historical definition of creativity. Neither will we be lured to abandon familial temporality for the historical existence of the public domain; for we will have learned to see the historical devaluation of the familial/erotic as a nihilistic attack on the transformative meaning of power and creativity.

If Nietzsche's critique of historical nihilism saves us from the mistake of adopting the values of the patriarchal public domain, his doctrine of the eternal return prevents us from prescribing a simplistic cosmic temporality as antidote to the nihilism of the historical time of patriarchy. Though patriarchal historical consciousness may be nihilistic, historical consciousness itself cannot be refused. To be human is to be historical. It is to be aware of past and future and to understand oneself as living in the imperfect tense. Whereas the innocent animal and child enjoy their lack of memory by naturally living in the presence of the present, the human sense of presence cannot escape the power of memory. That is, the human present can never be a complete presence, a present enclosed on itself. It must be a present in which the fullness of presence is entangled in transcendence. Whereas the animal and child affirm life naturally, the human adult must cultivate an affirmation of life through the proper cultivation of memory and forgetfulness.[12]

If Nietzsche's critique alerts us to the improper cultivation of memory and forgetfulness perpetuated by patriarchal historicity, it also warns us that the refusal of memory and forgetfulness is impossible. Thus we see that although Western feminine temporality may escape the nihilisms of patriarchal historical consciousness, it cannot itself be the answer to Western nihilism as long as its meaning is confined to the unhistorical. That is, though the time of the feminine may be seen as refusing the devaluation of the present embedded in patriarchal historical consciousness, feminine time, insofar as it is severed from public time, cannot counteract the nihilism of the culture. The value of the feminine must be brought to the domain of history and the meaning of history must be brought to bear on the life of

Eros if the overcoming of one form of nihilism is to avoid becoming another form of nihilism, the negation of the meaning of human time.

Within the structure of the gender-distinguished public-private disjunction of time, female temporality escapes the nihilisms of historical consciousness without escaping the nihilistic project of patriarchal historicism. If the proper cultivation of memory and forgetfulness are essential to the meaning of humanity, then any temporality that avoids this cultivation is inherently nihilistic. This is precisely the situation of feminine temporality within Western culture, for it is situated as the Other of historical consciousness, and the task of valuing and cultivating memory and forgetfulness is given to historical consciousness. The complexity (and power) of Western nihilism is such that it operates in both the public and private temporal structures. As the Ananke-historical, nihilism cultivates the human affirmation of memory which devalues the life affirmation of the present; as the Erotic-familial, nihilism cultivates the life affirmation of the present which devalues the human affirmation of memory.

V. Nietzsche's eternal return, by realigning the times of Eros and Ananke according to the notion of genealogy, may, I believe, be seen as an attempt to avoid both of these forms of nihilism. The recurrence of the eternal return is neither identical with the repetition valued by the temporality of the familial, nor a negation of the public domain. It is instead a new way of temporalizing which refuses to allow public time to appropriate all value to itself and refuses to allow private time to be reduced to inertia. The eternal recurrence affirms the value of the return of the same, the life-affirming value of the present, as it embraces the historical sense of coming from and going toward.

In intertwining the male and female temporalities of creation and re-creation, the eternal return elaborates on Zarathustra's insistence, in "Upon the Blessed Isles," that conceptions be conceivable, that is, that the process of intellectual creation be modeled on the phenomenon of birth. In "Upon the Blessed Isles" Nietzsche appeals to the heterosexual multidimensionality of the term *conceive* in his demand that ideas be recalled to their rootedness in the earth. In the eternal recurrence, he conceives of an idea that, in its heterosexual-androgynous temporality, affirms human life. In both cases, the affirmations demanded by Nietzsche require an affirmation of what Western culture has traditionally recognized and devalued as the feminine.[13]

As the time of the *Ubermensch,* the eternal return declares the value of transcendence, the human-affirming values of memory and imagination, without endorsing the patriarchal teleology, which links transcendence to a future understood as a goal or purpose. For it is this linking that allows transcendence to dominate the immanence of presence; that is, once transcendence is understood as the yet-to-be-realized purpose of the present, the present becomes the mere instrument of the times which it is not. A means-end relationship is imposed on the temporal flow.

Like patriarchal historical consciousness, the eternal return recognizes the present as coming from a past and going toward a future. Instead of locating the value of the present in the otherness of either the past or the future, however, the eternal return locates the meaning of both past and future in the present. Because the present is an eternal return, it is past, present, and future simultaneously. It cannot be affirmed, as it is in historical consciousness, as the time to be transcended. As that which gives past and future life, the present is the valued temporal scene.

Because the recurrence is a return of a future as well as a past, and thus not simply a repetition of the past, the return can embrace the value of transcendence genealogically as it rejects the meanings of causality and teleology. The eternal return aligns repetition with transcendence. The cosmic sense of repetition is disjoined from the meaning of inertia (the sense that nothing new happens in nature) and rejoined to the meanings of transformation and renewal. The historical sense of transcendence is severed from the teleological causal structure so that instead of being conceived of as a demand to move away from the present toward a goal already there (that is, somewhere else, not here), it is understood as a demand to engage in transvaluation.

The nihilism of the teleological sense of creativity as novelty is now rejected. That is, the value placed on the new (the not present) is now understood as a ruse by which the value of the now is annihilated. Within the structure of the eternal return the value of creativity is temporalized according to the paradigm of re-creation. As renewal, re-creation is a transcendence that is going nowhere because it has already been. It is in this sense that the eternal return may be said to be a heterosexual-androgynous structuring of time: it links and affirms what has been traditionally designated as the distinct fields of female and male temporality. Within the structure of the eternal return, the antithesis between the creative and re-creative is negated. Rather than confronting each other as antagonistic partners in a master-slave dialectic, the meanings of the productive and reproductive are allowed to play into and enrich each other as both male and female are enticed to pursue the genealogical affirmation of the human life of memory-cultivated presence.

It is here that the precise sense of the phrase "heterosexual-androgynous" emerges. To suggest that Nietzsche's eternal recurrence is an androgynous temporality would isolate the eternal recurrence from the rest of Nietzsche's thought. For the concept of androgyny is grounded in the ideals of identity and equality. It is an attempt to transcend the inequalities of patriarchy by annihilating the otherness of sexuality. In androgyny, sexual differences are merged. The two become one. Nietzsche's philosophy, however, is the philosophy of the order of rank. In its refusal of leveling it cannot tolerate the equality embedded in the ideal of androgyny.

As the time of the *Ubermensch,* the eternal recurrence must affirm otherness. That the eternal recurrence cannot be simply heterosexual, at least cannot be spoken of as such within the context of Western culture, is, I hope, clear from the argument of this paper. For my point has been that within Western culture "heterosexual" has meant disjoined rather than distinct, and otherness has been a justification of and for domination and devaluation. With the phrase "heterosexual-androgynous" I intend to capture the senses in which the eternal recurrence refuses the meanings of sexual difference embedded in Western culture as it affirms the possibility of complicitous otherness. In this phrase the term *heterosexual* captures the sense of otherness necessary for genuine relationship, while the term androgynous negates the sense of binary opposition usually attached to the meaning of otherness. As "androgynous" and "heterosexual" intersect each other, neither term is allowed to solidify or appropriate to itself the full meaning of relationship.

As the temporality of the *Ubermensch,* the eternal recurrence offers a structuring of time that is at once infinite and plural. It is a temporal vision that embraces the polytheism of the world emerging in the wake of God's death, and delights in the entanglement of all things emerging in the beyond of good and evil. In this, my feminist-perspective interpretation of the eternal recurrence, I am suggesting that the fluidity of the eternal return offers a vision of male and female which breaks the boundaries of traditional Western categories. In his choice of the term *Ubermensch,* in his admonition to get beyond good and evil, where evil is characterized as an attack on and aversion to otherness, and in his inversion of the traditional understandings of the male as active and female as passive,[14] Nietzsche encourages us to articulate new meanings of masculine and feminine.

Sexual differentiation cannot designate the *alienation* of otherness to one who stands beyond good and evil; it cannot be an invitation to domination to one who rejects all pretensions of masterful expertise; and it cannot be the ground of a patriarchal hierarchy of values to one who allows his Zarathustra to invoke images of mothering as he dances his Yea-saying songs.[15] What sexual differentiation can be is suggested by the structuring of time Nietzsche called the eternal recurrence, where otherness and forms of differentiation are entangled and affirmed without being annihilated or devalued.

VI. Where does this leave us? With a few insights and some intriguing possibilities. A general insight is that Nietzsche's transvaluation of values is also and necessarily a decompartmentalizing of values according to the patriarchal designated spheres of male and female. Transvaluation is a genealogical project that invokes the erotic without allowing the erotic to be sexualized in accordance with dominant male significations. A more specific insight concerns the relationship between patriarchy, historical temporality, and nihilism. Within the Western system of patriarchy, time is bifurcated into male and female spheres of otherness. Though the male-female couple is recognized as a couple, it is dichotomized into a she who displays reproductive energy in giving birth and a he who displays creative energy in social, political, and historical activity. Nietzsche's eternal recurrence offers an alternative vision of the couple. Here the reproductive and productive are freed from their enclosure in the sexually designated private and public domains. Creation and re-creation, transcendence and immanence, male and female are intimately and complexly complicitous. On this feminist reading of Nietzsche's eternal recurrence, what patriarchy designates as disjoined male and female modes of temporalization is a nihilistic figuring of time intent on subverting an attentiveness to the ways in which the otherness of male and female must intercept and inhabit each other if life is to be affirmed. In this reading, the eternal recurrence's nonteleological joyful affirmation of life is aligned with the affirmation of feminine pleasure insofar as it is independent of all reproductive functions or goals. It is linked to what Spivak calls the double vision that affirms the feminine as it undoes sexism.[16]

This feminist reading does not come from nowhere. It is historically situated and reflects, I believe, the current state of feminist studies. While earlier feminist thought attempted to discard the sex-biased roles of patriarchal society by declaring the equality of women, current feminist work distinguishes between the notions of equality and equal status. Whether it argues for a rejection of male values or demands that the feminine be recognized as an other of equal standing, today's feminists insist on their otherness.[17] It is this affirmation of otherness within feminism that sets the stage for a receptivity to Nietzsche and opens the way for a heterosexual-androgynous reading of the eternal recurrence.

— 8 —

An Ironic Mimesis

Kate Mehuron

Luce Irigaray's doctoral thesis *Speculum of the Other Woman* shares many common assumptions with Maurice Merleau-Ponty's analysis of language.[1] Both view language as constitutively indispensable to self-reflexivity; both view the self as a languaged, metamorphic process within which fluid self-reflexivity falls short of a complete adequation of consciousness to its object.

In this paper, I will describe Merleau-Ponty's chiasmatic ontology in *The Visible and the Invisible* as an effective ironizing of transcendental phenomenology's presumption that the essence of language consists in a realm of idealized meanings, autonomous in principle from the carnal world of perceptual and linguistic significatory nexuses.[2] I will argue that Irigaray's writing style may be interpreted as intensifying the ironizing effects of Merleau-Ponty's chiasmatic ontology. Her writing style enacts what I will call an ironic mimesis of philosophical texts which she terms patriarchal. By this strategy, Irigaray hopes both to critically reveal and disrupt the idealist presumptions of our Western philosophical tradition in their ideological dimension. Thus, her writing ironically mimics the place of the feminine as it is directly and indirectly depicted by various philosophical texts.

My interpretation of Irigaray's writing style as an ironic mimesis intends to counter the predominant criticism of *Speculum of the Other Woman* that her writing style falls prey to the very definitional and biological essentialism that it attempts to subvert.[3] I find that the general undecidability of ironic reference, coupled with the parodic exaggerations of Irigaray's mimesis, eschews any easy appropriation of her discourse by those philosophical discourses which her style mimics. My reading does not conclusively refute the criticism that Irigaray's express commitments to a positively described feminine writing simply contradict the tacitly anti-essentialist trend of her mimetic style. Rather, I wish to caution any reading against either taking her text as a naive celebration of the epiphany of feminine writing liberated from patriarchal ideology, or as simply incoherent between its express aims and tacit style. I do applaud what I take to be a deeply provocative trend in her writing: the parodic exaggeration and

89

subsequent disclosure of the ideological dimensions of philosophical texts under scrutiny. What if the risks and undecidabilities of feminist irony were taken and exploited to the highest degree?[4]

Reading Chiasmatically

Let us follow Merleau-Ponty in imagining reading as a chiasmatic enactment, or variant of carnal being. To think of reading in this way is to situate it as a participatory moment within the spectacle, or within the intertwining of touch and visibility constitutive of being. The question of reading converges with the question of language insofar as both are among the phenomena of expression. Merleau-Ponty treats language presumptively as an expressive variant of carnal being that is indispensable to the movement of abstract thought. In doing so, he turns to a fundamental problem: how ideas, whether literary, artistic, dialogical, or musical, may be understood as aspects of an already intrinsically languaged carnal being.[5] Hence the fundamental problematic in *The Visible and the Invisible* concerns how it is that ideas can be understood simply as aspects of what he intimates is the ultimate fact of carnal reciprocity.[6] Because of the unfinished status of this manuscript, we have only descriptive clues intimating the direction whence his account might have gone. In this section, I am limited to isolating the most distinctive features of reading as chiasmatic enactment. I will sketch these features, beginning with Merleau-Ponty's understanding of language as an expressive phenomenon, situating its place in fleshly reflexivity.

The majority of Merleau-Ponty's reflections on language occur in tandem with his reflections on painting.[7] The former stands in analogous relationship to the latter; Merleau-Ponty explores the limits of this analogy to disclose the singularity of each. With regard to conceptual thinking and artistic idealities, Merleau-Ponty is attuned to how the genesis of both could be said to be grounded in visual and tactile experience. The commonality between these expressive phenomena lies in the pervasive degree to which invisibility, latency, and depth are fundamental in engendering and sustaining their sense. In articulating this relation, he rejects ontologies that envisage the elements of meaning in terms of dynamic oppositions: being/nonbeing, identity/difference, or intelligible/perceptible. Rather, he elaborates a fleshly ontology of sensible, perceptual experience that is characterized by elements fluidly related through enveloping, intertwining exchange. Aided by Ferdinand de Saussure's linguistic theory, Merleau-Ponty also characterizes the ontological nexus as fundamentally diacritical; meaning is engendered in the interstices of difference and opposition between binary terms.[8] Concepts and artistic ideas, on this model, are thought as meaning-effects that are completely contingent on and sustained by carnal praxis, rather than as eidetic insights that may be transcendentally secured. A further commonality of artistic ideas and concepts lies in the extent to which both rely on the dynamic character of this chiasmatic, diacritical nexus.

Mirroring is the crucial operation by which the static, diacritical values of language and artistic expression are converted to dynamic envelopment. In the realm of artistic ideas, Merleau-Ponty calls the latter carnal essences or echoes; such essences are awakened within the fleshly reflexivities of the sensible world. Our bodies participate in these carnal reflexivities; in his earlier work, *Phenomenology of Perception,* Merleau-Ponty outlines the nonthetic, oriented intentionalities of the body within the perceptible world.[9] This analysis is transmuted into the ontological dimension in *The Visible and the Invisible.* Whether ontologically or perceptually conceived, the nonthetic intentional nexuses of the lifeworld are dynamized by our bodily and languaged mimesis. We qualitatively experience the world because we meet the world and mirror its qualities by actively taking up its contours; our participative mirroring is self-referential because the world reciprocally meets us and reflects our gestures. It is as if there are

> two mirrors facing one another where two indefinite series of images set in one another arise which belong really to neither of the two surfaces, since each is only the rejoinder of the other, and which therefore form a couple, a couple more real than either of them. Thus since the seer is caught up in what he sees, it is still himself he sees: there is a fundamental narcissism of all vision. (VI 139)

This fleshly mimesis founds a fundamental narcissism on the reflexive levels of perception, language, and self; the self-reflexivity of each is contemporaneous with, and intertwined with, the others.

I propose that we think of this mirroring dynamic as metamorphic, rather than as a purely reproductive operation. Merleau-Ponty's description occasionally (as in the above passage) evokes the image of a dyadic mirroring situation; I urge that we also take into account his concerted effort to think the nonthetic reflexivities of the lifeworld through the chiasmatic figure. Whereas the dyadic situation offers only an inert and static mimetic encounter between two terms, the chiasma promises an interlacing of one term by the other—engendering a third at the intersection that inscribes both difference and unity. On this account, the narcissistic operation involves a reflectivity whose object remains at once proximal, yet excessive to the dyadic situation. In apprehending an artistic work there is a selective yet nonthetic reflectivity of the qualitative possibilities of the work: a virtual genesis of the visible by the participative mimesis of the artist, artistic medium, and the world. The sense of the artistic work remains allusive, excessive, and disruptive of any complete coincidence between the diverse intentionalities of artist, work, and world.

This understanding of the metamorphic character of mirroring includes speech as a transformative variant of carnality. Speech founds a more facile, fluid transitivity than the dehiscences of touch or visibility; its mimetic operations enact more acutely the imageless interplay with latency and depth than either of these other registers. Merleau-Ponty writes:

> As there is a reflexivity of the touch, of sight, and of the touch-vision system, there is a reflexivity of the movements of phonation and hearing; they have their sonorous inscription, the vociferations have in me their motor echo. This new reversibility and the emergence of the flesh as expression are the point of insertion of speaking and thinking in the world of silence. (VI 144–145)

In this passage, Merleau-Ponty continues to think analogously, turning to music in order to sketch the singularity of language. The dynamism of one spoken address to another is similar to the way in which we actively welcome the passage of a musical phrase. Both situations witness reverberations between interlaced participants: the echoing of certain melodic and intonational possibilities, a rhythmic metamorphosis of the sonorous world.

> And, in a sense, to understand a phrase is nothing else than to fully welcome it in its sonorous being, or, as we put it so well, to *hear what it says.* The meaning is not on the phrase like the butter on the bread, like a second layer of "psychic reality" spread over the sound: it is the totality of what is said, the integral of all the differentiations of the verbal chain; it is given with the words for those who have ears to hear. (VI 155)

One expressive situation elucidates the other; spoken address communicates via affective, intonational valences taken up by the other. Whether dwelling on spoken address, the active reception of the artistic work, or the experience of music—we are urged to think in terms of a chiasmatic nexus wherein the narcissism of touch, vision, and hearing founds an other term excessive to dyadic coincidence. Further, the metamorphic operation described above seems to presuppose that all terms in the situation are both active participants and active recipients of the others' gestures. Hence, Merleau-Ponty envisages a dynamic in which all terms both actively reach toward the other and selectively take up (partially mirror) the other; yet the intentional movement of each also surpasses and escapes the other's reflective grasp.

The singularity of language—particularly of philosophical language—is discussed in *The Prose of the World* (PW). Its uniqueness lies in its usages that attempt to retrieve things as they are, in a perfect adequation of referentiality to its object. This propensity distinguishes language from the ''mute forms of expression'' such as painting and expressive gesture; language is discontent with the latter's tacit ''coherent deformations'' and strives to grasp universal truths. Despite this intent, it culminates in the ''philosopher's failure [that] leaves behind him a whole furrow of expressive acts which enable us to rediscover our situation'' (PW 104).

I propose that Merleau-Ponty's chiasmatic thought has the effect of gently ironizing all the terms through which transcendental phenomenology may describe reflective exchange: narcissistic self-reflection, participation, intentionality, etc. Merleau-Ponty resolutely re-envisions intentionality on the model of a nonthetic, carnal nexus. His project thus endeavors to displace the transcendental dream of the absolute coincidence of consciousness with its object that subtends all traditional concepts of reflectivity. I suggest that the same ironizing awareness may be brought to bear on Merleau-Ponty's comments on the activity of reading.

Reading is also directly addressed in Merleau-Ponty's essay, ''Science and the Experience of Expression'' in *The Prose of the World*. On the one hand, a passionate dyadic mimesis is invoked:

> The relations between the reader and the book are like those loves in which one partner initially dominates because he was more proud or more temperamental, and then the situation changes and the other, more wise and more silent, rules. The expressive moment occurs where the relationship reverses itself, where the book takes possession of the reader. (PW 12–13)

Here we are encouraged to think of a fleshly initiation in which one participant provisionally fuses with an other, dominant term. On the other hand, reading receives comment in other passages where the impulse to imagine possession as a term of completion or fulfillment is tempered and qualified. The relation between text and reader is envisioned as an imaginary world occupied by those initiated into its possibilities. There is expressiveness through style.

> If he is a writer, that is, if he knows how to find the ellipses, elisions, and caesuras of conduct, the reader will respond to his appeal and meet him at the center of the imaginary world he animates and rules. (PW 89)

Through omission, incompletion—a pause, breath taken and exhaled . . . breaks in the rhythm of the writing . . .—cadences disclose the quality of passions recoiling between the significations of the text. The fusion imaged is a relation of enveloping or reciprocal intertwining in which the active and passive terms are not clearly distinguishable. Neither differentiates by virtue of taking turns in a series nor by subsuming one another through a complete realization of form. Although a sort of touch occurs in reading, it is certainly neither coincidence, grasping, nor possession in the transcendental sense of mind thinking itself in a pure communality with its object.

Reading itself is described as a species of sonorous reversibility, or an echoing, intertwining, sustaining both proximity and divergence in its provisional fusions. Our mirroring of the affective cadences of the text and its ellipses, caesuras, and elisions establishes the imaginary of the text and the space of our initiation. Reading enacts the mimetic reverberations of myself and other, where my mimesis of the unspoken latencies of the text is always already also a divergence from prosaic meaning. We could say that the stylistic interlacing incarnated by readers and texts fission and decenter habitual usages of language. To this extent, reading becomes the intoxicated shattering of the prosaic and the literal, and simultaneously the ecstasy of oblique, perhaps ironic reference.

Irigaray's Mimesis

In a popular periodical, Hugh Drummond writes:

> With all the computers, pile drivers, and rockets in the world, all those "conquests" of space and nature, all the pure power of patriarchy, there was one remaining area of male vulnerability. A man could push a button to destroy the world, but he could not until now make himself get an erection. It remained in the autonomic nervous system, out of conscious control, subject to mysterious forces like lust, witchcraft, and *relating to another human being.*[10]

Our reading is immediately confronted with a complex reading situation: a male writer writing of sexual difference as it manifests itself within sociopolitical reality. He writes from the paradoxical position of both identifying and differing from the very extralinguistic reality to which he refers. In this case, writing's chiasma involves the crossing of referential strands toward certain extralinguistic beliefs, attitudes, worldviews, and a stylistic strand of tacit self-reference, "A man could. . . ." Within that interlacing arises a third term, the phrase casting an ironic glance toward this crossing, "subject to *mysterious* forces like lust, witchcraft, and *relating to another human being.*" Animating this situation further, the mimesis of my own reading renders explicit the questions: from what theoretical, ideological, or subjective position do I read?; how does textual style incarnate and transmute sexual difference?

These questions emerge within the equally complex reading situation presented by Luce Irigaray's *Speculum of the Other Woman*. The multiplicity of voices within her text, coupled with the absence of a single, primary account of her own intentions and theoretical commitments, provokes criticism from theorists such as Shoshana Felman. Felman asks:

> If, as Luce Irigaray suggests, the woman's silence, or the repression of her capacity to speak, are constitutive of philosophy and of theoretical discourse as such, from what theoretical locus is Luce Irigaray herself speaking in order to develop her own theoretical discourse about the women's exclusion? . . . Is it enough to *be* a woman in order to *speak as* a woman? Is "speaking as a woman" a fact determined by some biological *condition* or by a strategic, theoretical *position*, by anatomy or by culture? What if "speaking as a woman" were not a simple "natural" fact, could not be taken for granted?[11]

Without denying the validity of these questions, I urge that, first, we read Irigaray's text as part of a philosophical tradition which includes a significant legacy of irony, parody, and other indirect writing styles;[12] secondly, that we resist the temptation to conflate experimental feminist writing styles generally with French feminist theory, thereby reducing its significance to a recent, temporary enthusiasm in France.[13]

It may be plausibly argued that ironic and/or parodic gestures—whether textual or theatrical—provoke a specific sort of self-reflexive questioning which places the onus of Felman's interrogation on the reader or spectator. The development of this argument would necessitate an account of the ways in which ironic and/or parodic style carries a unique philosophical value. Such an account would imply that the act of reading/spectating is a crucial active-receptive moment; there is a simultaneous play of reading's selective identification with textual voices and a decentering of habitual, conventional usages of language. The moment of decentering also implies the disruption of conventional attitudes, beliefs, and worldviews that are borne by the language employed between reader and text. The efficacy of indirect writing styles may be largely dependent on the degree to which the context of parodic and/or ironic utterance is plurivocal: providing the responsiveness of reading/spectating with a heritage of conflicting, contradictory semantic and attitudinal resources available to its selective activation. Rather than developing this argument, I want simply to note some of the ways in which Irigaray's mimetic writing style simultaneously discloses and disrupts the patriarchal ideological pretensions of dominant

Western philosophical languages. Presently, I wish primarily to focus on
certain stylistic elements within her text.

Many of Irigaray's express intentions and theoretical commitments are
collected in a series of interviews and essays, published as *This Sex Which
Is Not One*.[14] Neither her intentions nor her theoretical commitments are
systematically organized in that volume. Despite her lack of systematicity,
it is clearly premature to construe Irigaray's thought as either incoherent or
as politically naive in its theoretical stance. Rather than reconstructing her
writing into a set of theoretical statements, I wish to emphasize that Irigaray expressly rejects the form and style traditionally taken by philosophical
theory. She says:

> It is indeed precisely philosophical discourse that we have to challenge, and
> *disrupt,* inasmuch as this discourse sets forth the law for all others, inas-
> much as it constitutes the discourse on discourse. . . . Now, this domination
> of the philosohic logos stems in large part from its power to *reduce all oth-
> ers to the economy of the Same.* The teleologically constructive project it
> takes on is always also a project of diversion, deflection, reduction of the
> other in the Same. And, in its greatest generality perhaps, from its power to
> *eradicate the difference between the sexes* in systems that are self-
> representative of a "masculine subject." (SNO 74)

The "specularity" of classical philosophical discourse partially consists in a discursive economy whereby diversity and difference are systematically viewed within relations of resemblance; alterity in its specific
manifestations is systematically appropriated by the theoretical impetus toward self-same unity and identity. We have seen that the specular character
of the philosophic logos already undergoes criticism and displacement by
Merleau-Ponty's chiasmatic ontology, insofar as this ontology attempts to
think philosophical language as carnally imbricated in the world. Irigaray's
many descriptive analyses of the specularity of philosophical discourse are
deeply compatible with Merleau-Ponty's project. However, her description
exceeds Merleau-Ponty's account in attributing an ideological dimension to
its specular character; a phallocentric orientation pervades the discursive
economy of philosophical discourse.[15]

Irigaray transposes Merleau-Ponty's critique of transcendental phenomenology's dream of an eidetic analysis culminating in the ideal telos of pure
consciousness grasping itself, to a critique of the phallocentric orientation
of this dream and others like it:

> the *specular make-up* of discourse . . . An organization that maintains,
> among other things, the break between what is perceptible and what is intel-
> ligible, and thus maintains the submission, subordination, and exploitation
> of the "feminine." (SNO 80)

In philosophical discourse's phallocentric economy, the feminine remains transhistorically available as an element freely exchanged within the specular metaphorics of *anything* ranked inferior and viewed as subordinate to a higher epistemological unity, or ranked as secondary within a primary ontological unity: the phantasmic, materiality, phenomenality, temporality, the disparate, a/systematicity itself. In lieu of these phallocentric and specular propensities, Irigaray explicitly attempts to write and think in a way which exceeds these propensities, while acknowledging that her effort is inevitably influenced and partially determined by the specular discursive tradition.

Irigaray states that her style of writing in *Speculum of the Other Woman* is deliberately mimetic:

> To play with mimesis is thus, for a woman, to try to recover the place of her exploitation by a discourse, without allowing herself to be simply reduced to it. It means to resubmit herself—inasmuch as she is on the side of the "perceptible," of "matter"—to "ideas," in particular to ideas about herself, that are elaborated in/by a masculine logic, but so as to make "visible," by an effect of playful repetition, what was supposed to remain invisible: the cover-up of a possible operation of the feminine in language. It also means "to unveil" the fact that, if women are such good mimics, it is also because they are not simply resorbed in this function. *They also remain elsewhere.* . . . (SNO 76)

By the effects of playful repetition, Irigaray's stylistic strategy hopes to reveal a possibility of philosophical language which is concealed by the phallocentric character of that language itself: a specifically feminine operation. What sort of feminine specificity in language does this playful mimesis reveal?

I propose that we read much of the writing in *Speculum of the Other Woman* as parody. Irigaray's writing a/systematically plays the roles of both the feminine and the masculine; it grotesquely magnifies, exaggerates, distorts their overt and implicit places within phallocentric philosophical discourses. The a/systematicity of her writing is induced by the unique way in which parody is disparately interspersed among voices that assume the theoretic role, and among voices that are hyperbolic, aphoristic, and pathetic. We can read *Speculum of the Other Woman* as exemplifying a unique dialogicity wherein various voices retrieved from our Western philosophical tradition interanimate one another in an exchange which may incite reading to incredulity, laughter, or outrage, yet disallow theoretical conclusiveness.[16]

A bittersweet voice in "Volume-Fluidity" mimics the ambivalent exuberance of a certain feminine specificity latent to this tradition:

> For the sex of woman is not one. And, as jouissance bursts out in each of
> these/her ''parts,'' so all of them can mirror her in dazzling multifaceted
> difference. . . . The/a woman cannot be collected into *one* volume, for in
> that way she risks surrendering her own jouissance, which demands that she
> remain open to nothing utterable but which assures that her edges not close,
> her lips not be sewn shut. (SO 239–40)

We read of a dazzling jouissance *demanded* by phallocentric self-
representation; celebratory intonations of multifaceted difference simultaneously darken with the imperatives and inevitabilities imposed by our
Western discursive legacy. The epiphany of feminine writing is qualified by
reflective phrasing: ''And, admittedly, the history of this return upon herself has dispossessed her'' (SO 240). This passage deepens into a dyadic
exchange between a hyperbolic representation of the masculine and a mag-
nified feminine pathos:

> She remains outside the circularity of a thought that, in its telos, turns to his
> ends the cause of his desire: she is the unconscious basis of that attempt to
> find metaphor for an originary matrix in the sphere of intimacy with self, of
> nearness to self, of a ''soul'' or a mind. . . . Opaqueness of matter, fleeting
> fluid, vertiginous void between two, a mirror in which the ''subject'' sees
> himself and reproduces himself in his reflection. . . (SO 240)

In the following pages, I will quote passages from Irigaray's text in
full, inserting labels for what I take to be differing voices which exchange
address within the same passage. I wish to show how Irigaray's writing
animates differing voices within a dialogical interplay. Each embodies a
unique attitudinal perspective; the differing perspective of each is marked
by intonational inflection, rather than by grammatical indicators. The passage opens with a ruminative, hypothetical voice:

> [RUMINATIVE, HYPOTHETICAL] Subjecting herself to objectivization in
> discourse—by being ''female.'' Reobjectivizing her own self whenever she
> claims to identify herself ''as'' a masculine subject. A ''subject'' that would
> re-search itself as lost (maternal-feminine) ''object''?

> [THEORETICAL] Subjectivity denied to woman: indisputably this provides
> the financial backing for every irreducible constitution as an object: of rep-
> resentation, of discourse, of desire. [RUMINATIVE, HYPOTHETICAL]
> Once imagine that woman imagines and the object loses its fixed, obses-
> sional character. (SO 133)

One voice rejoins the other in a chiasma of address and response. Hence,
within the space of an opening paragraph, we find a dialogical interplay

between two voices, the theoretical and the hypothetical, that inaugurates an experiment in philosophical prose. Other voices are animated beyond this inaugural dyad, as if the chiasma of address and response interanimates third terms that seem to disrupt the static mimesis of the couple.

Following the opening passages of the same essay, I find an ironic voice introducing and subtly displacing the interlocked inertia of the hyperbolically depicted masculine and the pathetically silent feminine:

> [IRONIC] The Copernican revolution has yet to have its final effects in the male imaginary. . . . [HYPERBOLIC MASCULINE] As things now go, man moves away in order to preserve his stake in the value of his representation, [PATHETIC FEMININE] while woman counterbalances with the permanence of a (self)recollection which is unaware of itself as such. And which, in the recurrence of this re-turn upon the self—[THEORETIC] and its special economy will need to be located—[PREMONITORY] can continue to support the illusion that the object is inert. [HYPERBOLIC MASCULINE] "Matter" upon which he will ever and again return to plant his foot in order to spring farther, leap higher. . . (SO 133–34)

In the middle of this passage, the dyadic stalemate is interrupted by a theoretical intonation prescribing a systematic task. Then, a further inflection hints the emergence of yet another voice which is premonitory and wiser than the others. The latter discloses itself through a subtle mockery of the dyad's inertia. This premonitory, aloof voice cedes briefly to the hyperbolic masculine term. But the hyperbolic masculine term is rejoined by the aloof, wise voice of premonition that continues to mock the inertia of the inaugural couple, verging on a sort of (self) celebratory exuberance.

It is tempting to focus on this voice, to interpret it as the privileged representative of feminine specificity in writing. A seductive effect in reading may be produced by its volatile, expansive exuberance, the aloof distancing of its gentle mockery, and its premonitory hints intimating an elsewhere of discourse that is free of the stagnant specular dyad. "She" mockingly intertwines with the theoretical voice:

> [ALOOF, CELEBRATORY] . . . although he is dealing here with a nature that is already self-referential. Already fissured and open. And which, in her circumvolutions upon herself, will also carry off the things confided to her for re-presentation. Whence, no doubt, the fact that she is said to be restless and unstable. [THEORETIC] In fact it is quite rigorously true that she is never exactly the same. [ALOOF, CELEBRATORY] Always whirling closer or father from the sun whose rays she captures and sends curving to and fro in turn with her cycles. . . . Thus the "object" is not as massive, as resistant, as one might wish to believe. And her possession by a "subject," a

subject's desire to appropriate her, is yet another of his vertiginous failures.
(SO 134)

A reading which takes Irigaray's text to be equating feminine specificity
with what is unspeakable and altogether excessive to the constraints of discourse, may be partially disarmed by the rhetorical strength of this voice.
Nevertheless, I urge that reading yield to the possibilities of self-criticality
opened by the plurivocality of Irigaray's text. The self-reflexive question is
an implicit moment accompanying indirect writing styles: who am I in the
moment of my exuberant receptivity?

Finally, the dialogical profundity of voices and the density of their
chiasmatic interchange within Irigaray's text counters readings which find
the referent of Irigaray's "feminine specificity" in language to be clas-
sifiable in biologically or definitionally essentialist terms, i.e., categorically differentiated on the basis of any objectively fixed biological or
conceptual attribute. On the contrary, it is debatable whether the character
of such a referent may be completed by any one description, or whether
descriptiveness is even the mode by which to understandingly approximate
this referent.[17] I suggest that the dialogical, indirect style of Irigaray's prose
generates an affirmative discursive gesture that ironically submits itself to
its conventional role in philosophical discourse, yet always already remains
elsewhere than its specular nonidentity. The ironies of this submission of
voice within the dialogical textual space recur on the more global levels of
reading/spectating. Perhaps in the latter domain, the moment of laughter,
outrage, or exuberance may simultaneously identify with the beliefs and
attitudes borne by patriarchal ideology, yet rupture that complicity in the
singularity of its self-reflective response.

I submit that the allusive "elsewhere" of feminine specificity remains
an undecidable third term. It perpetually risks the specific determination of
its character and value through the dynamic chiasma of reading's active-
receptive engagement and the text's plurivocal weave. The collision of the
theoretical and attitudinal positionality of reading/spectating with the text
provokes responses of laughter, outrage, and perhaps a self-reflexive question. Irigaray writes in "La Mysterique":

> But if the Word was made flesh in this way, and to this extent, it can only
> have been to make me (become) God in my jouissance, which can at last be
> recognized. Now the abyss opens down into my own self, and I am no longer
> cut in two opposing directions of sheer elevation to the sky and sheer fall
> into the depths. I know, now, that both height and depth spawn—and slit—
> each other in(de)finitely. And that the one is in the other, and the other in
> me, matters little since it is in me that they are created in rapture. *Outside of*

all self-as-same. . . Mystery, me-hysteria, without determinable end or beginning. (SO 200–201)

What has my onto-theological legacy bequeathed me, so that I am fasci-
nated by and tempted to identify with the rapture of this voice? From what
extralinguistic perspective do I simultaneously shudder as I encounter what
is said to be (my own) mystery? Who speaks? Who will answer?

Defusing the Canon: Feminist Rereading and Textual Politics

Linda Singer

One thing that feminist philosophers have in common with their colleagues is that they have read many of the same books. One thing that distinguishes them from their colleagues is that they do not read, or have not always read, them in the same way. The configuration of this identity in difference is significant for two reasons: it is not coincidental or accidental, and it is not reciprocal. This nonreciprocity is evidenced by the fact that most philosophers have not read and have not had to read those texts that are central to the feminist enterprise.

The nonaccidental aspect of this asymmetry can be explained, in part, by reference to the conventional nature of philosophical training and certification. Although philosophers often attempt to define the boundaries of their discipline by reference to common processes, aims, or questions that are designated as specifically ''philosophical,'' in practice the unity or hegemony of philosophy is constituted intertextually, that is, by reference to a body of writing that collectively comprises what philosophers refer to as *the* history of philosophy. The semantic operation of the ''the'' in ''the history of philosophy'' suggests a singular, seamless history, which lends to the texts collected under this rubric a canonical status, a status which another authoritative text, the *Oxford English Dictionary,* defines as ''of the nature of a canon or rule; or admitted authority, excellence, or supremacy; authoritative; orthodox, accepted; standard.'' The term ''canon'' is also therein defined as ''a general rule, fundamental principle, aphorism, or axiom governing the systematic or scientific treatment of a subject'' and as designating ''any sacred set of books.''

Those texts collected under the rubric of ''the history of philosophy'' come to assume a privileged position as those that set the standard for what is philosophical, and in terms of which philosophy defines itself to itself and to other disciplines. Therefore, to be certified as a philosopher, one must demonstrate one's mastery of the canon, and, by extension, of the synthetic chronology of issues and positions that emerges from it.

Competence with respect to this history is in no way optional. It is rather presented as an epistemological imperative and as a moral obligation, as well as a condition for professional certification. From this canonical standpoint, however, feminist writing is given only optional status, as the sort of thing one can pursue in addition to and often only after one has demonstrated one's entitlement by a mastery of the canon. Conversely, and this is especially significant from the standpoint of feminists, those texts and only those texts that are granted canonical status in the discipline's self-definition are the work of white European or American men, a fact the referential rhetoric of "the history of philosophy" tends to conceal.

The rhetoric of "the history of philosophy" suggests a seamless chronology that effaces the mechanism of its construction, as well as the principles of inclusion, exclusion, and their justification in terms of an ultimately circular logic. It would seem that to determine what counts as part of the history of philosophy one would need to determine what philosophy was, yet philosophy is ultimately defined in terms of that which is acknowledged or presented as its history. Such language therefore tends to conceal the fact that there are or were potentially other candidates for membership. Describing the intertextual universe of philosophy in terms of a canon, by contrast, connotes a collection that has been formed and solidified legislatively and therefore which could, at least in principle, be otherwise.

Hence it should not be surprising that those most likely to speak of a philosophical "canon," rather than a seamless history, are those thinkers identified with the issues, texts, and discourses, like feminism, that have been excluded from that history and from the sphere of authority and privilege afforded it. To represent the unity of philosophy in canonical terms, as many feminists do, is already to adopt a critical posture toward the history of philosophy and the privilege it claims for itself as the master discourse with the power to legislate the conceptual foundations of other disciplines. It is also to bring to the foreground that which is probably the greatest source of philosophical anxiety—the recognition of philosophy's own contingency and hence its groundlessness. If philosophy lacks a necessary foundation, it is reduced to the status of just another idiolect or genre and hence loses its supremacy and legislative authority. The threat posed by feminism is substantial in that it calls into question the very nature of philosophy as such; as French theorist Jean Francois Lyotard argues, for philosophy to affirm its contingency is "to turn away from the task of speculation and cease philosophizing."[1]

This helps to explain why feminism has largely been excluded from the history of philosophy, and why this exclusion is neither accidental nor coincidental. It also helps explain the argumentative strategies employed to justify this exclusion. In her article subtitled "Sexism in the Philosophic Establishment,"[2] Shelia Ruth provides a summary of those arguments that operate by attempting to prove that feminism fails to satisfy the conditions necessary for "real" philosophy:

> Feminism is a specialized pursuit, not part of the "mainstream" of philosophy.
>
> Philosophy is universal in scope, dealing with all mankind (sic), but feminism applies to a segment of the population.
>
> Feminist issues are trivial compared to the ultimate questions philosophers ought to address.
>
> Feminist concerns are transient, bound to a particular time and place; philosophy transcends particular time and place.
>
> Feminism is sociological, political, or anthropological; it asks no genuinely philosophic questions.
>
> Feminists haven't yet learned to argue properly; they have not learned to give proper evidence for their claims; no general principles, just vignettes and metaphors.
>
> Philosophy is neutral in its analysis. Feminism is a bias.

That such arguments have had their effect is evidenced by the long-standing exclusion of feminist texts from journals, conference programs, and university curricula. *The Philosopher's Index* does not acknowledge feminism as a subject classification until 1973, and until 1980 less than ten articles per year are listed under that heading. Far more are listed under the more neutral heading "Woman," which gives some sense of the high-minded logic underlying philosophic classification. Since then some significant progress has been made. In 1986, for example, ninety-six articles are listed under "Feminism," and panels devoted to feminist theory appear more frequently on conference programs than they used to. But such progress is likely less a function of the abandonment of phallocentric bias by the philosophical establishment than of the concerted and sustained organized political activity of feminists, as well as of their continued commitment to produce work in this area, a substantial portion of which has been devoted to the rereading of the philosophical canon.

Given the way in which appeals to the canon have been used against feminism to marginalize or exclude it, it seems reasonable to ask why feminists have been motivated to reread the canon in the first place, especially since it would seem that any attempt to engage it, even critically, would involve contradictions and paradoxes of legitimacy, authority, entitlement, and desire. Why have we sought to return to the site of our own exile, and what do we hope to accomplish through that return? Can we hope to win or seduce legitimacy by engaging the mechanisms that have been used to exclude us, and if we can, what is that kind of legitimacy good for, especially if it is also something we seek to question and undermine? Can or should we hope to enjoy the pleasures and privileges of mastery, if that is precisely what we want to transform, not only, but at least in part, because it has been denied us? Can we hope to wear the emperor's clothes by revealing that he himself has none?

Any attempt to articulate the desires operationalized in feminist rereadings is subject to the dilemma and dynamics of overdetermination. There are so many reasons why feminists choose to engage the history of philosophy, many of them obvious, but such reasons ultimately fail to be either definitive or explanatory, at least in some deeper sense. But before we can address the strategic value of this practice, it is necessary to provide at least some skeletal account of the motivational logic underlying it, as a clue to the value it has had for its practitioners.

One reason why feminist philosophers reread the canon is precisely because we have already read it as part of our training as philosophers. Because acquaintance with the canon has been part of every feminist philosopher's initiation, it is not surprising that it will continue to function as a threshhold and context for our activity, even as we progressively come to question its authority, and to situate our work more and more independently of it or in resistance to it. But this historical explanation leads only to further questions, namely, why were we motivated to read it in the first place?, and how, or from what position, were we able to read it, given that the discourse marginalized or excluded us as women in the first place? Since philosophical training is neither obligatory nor coerced, nor is it a usual pursuit for women, any woman who has read the canon has done so as a consequence of some deliberate choice or decision, a choice that often must be continually reaffirmed in the face of resistance or hostility from teachers, peers, and, sometimes, family.

To sustain the interest and discipline that philosophical training requires, especially in light of the minimum prospects for economic or social rewards, one must believe in the intrinsic value of the enterprise as such. One must, at least in some sense, be seduced by the promises of philosophy, even if one also hopes to use those to subvert or transform it. What is most seductive about philosophy, I think, is its appearance of being or promising to become a self-rectifying discourse, a discourse capable of recognizing its limits and lacunae and of reforming itself in light of these recognitions. It is not so hard to understand why this should appear so attractive to feminists, who recognize that there is much to be reformed and rectified in ourselves and in the world. Philosophy is seductive because it seems to offer a mechanism both for isolating what needs to be changed and for changing it; rather than resigning ourselves merely to desiring or imagining a transformed world, we can also gain access to the rational means for constructing another one.

To the extent that one has studied and continues to study philosophy, one is invested, to varying degrees, in its promissory and optimistic economy, especially with respect to the prospects of power and authority it offers. This is especially seductive to women, because such power is represented in what appear to be gender-neutral terms, terms in which women are not by definition disadvantaged, because such power is said to arise not from contingently gendered bodies, but from minds and from a logic that transcend incarnation and dependence on the arbitrary. Philosophy appeals to some women because it offers access to that which we are otherwise denied because we are women, namely, the possibilities of self-transcendence and empowerment. Since philosophy is a discipline that advocates truth and knowledge as the foundation of power, it provides to women the prospect of empowerment and emancipation through knowing.

Such appeal is amplified by virtue of its affinity with the process by which most feminists are made, namely, the process of consciousness raising, which presupposes a similar positive correlation between knowledge, power, and self-transcendence. Part of what is liberating about consciousness raising is the process by which one comes to understand one's situation and the reasons for it in ways that were previously unavailable. Consciousness raising and philosophy are two enterprises where it is still assumed that the truth can set you free. It is therefore not surprising that some women become attracted to a discipline that defines itself in terms of the pursuit of truth, nor that we will pursue it by reading those texts in which it is allegedly lodged or in process.

But despite this affinity between philosophical and feminist practice, insofar as one is a feminist, one also stands in a problematic relationship to the history of philosophy, precisely because it is the history of one's own subjugation, as well as to the discourse that has provided many of the grounds and justifications for that subjugation. It is also a discourse that marks woman's difference in a way that is problematic existentially, conceptually, and professionally. In this sense, being a feminist necessarily entails a critical or ambivalent stance toward the promissory dimension of philosophy, since one is forced to recognize that philosophy also withholds that which it promises, namely, a truth that mitigates or overcomes the disadvantages accruing to women in patriarchy. Philosophy acquaints feminists with the logic of the fathers that has produced and kept us in our place, as well as with the mechanisms by which that operation and its consequences are perpetually effaced. To approach philosophy as a feminist is also to confront a place from which one has always already been exiled.

The recognition of this situation of exile also produces the desire to return, to take up or make up one's own place, a room of one's own. It is this desire that I believe lies at the motivational core of feminist rereadings. Given the quantity and quality of feminist rereadings that have already been produced, it seems clear that this desire must be taken seriously. But I think that feminist theory has also reached a degree of maturity that makes it a legitimate place from which to question the strategic value of continuing to pursue this practice. Such assessment is made in a context that is necessarily relative, that is, judged in light of competing values and priorities. Given the wealth of work to be done in areas of concern to feminists, the question I wish to pursue is whether continuing to reread the canon is the best way for feminists to direct their energies, or whether this practice has, in some sense, outlived its usefulness and thus should occupy only a relatively subsidiary place in feminist theoretical priorities.

In posing the question this way, I do not mean to devalue or dismiss the significance of the work that has already been done. For a number of reasons which will soon be made explicit, I believe that this practice has resulted in much very good work that has also had important political and theoretical consequences for professional philosophy as a whole and for feminist theory in particular. The trajectory of my question is rather aimed at a future that feminists will have a role in constructing. I will pursue this question by examining the different kinds of rereading practices currently in operation, and assessing the political implications of the interpretative strategies each employs. Without tipping my hand too much at this preliminary stage, I hope to raise questions about the dependence of feminist philosophy on the canon, and to indicate that such dependence may no longer be necessary, in part because of the successes feminism has already achieved.

The first point to be made is that feminist rereadings are no more monolithic in strategy or intent than is feminist theory in general. My discussion will focus on three different kinds of rereadings that differ in intent, interpretative logic, and conceptual consequences. Each has its practitioners and its critics. The first kind of rereadings are those that approach the history of philosophy in search of the ''conceptual forefathers'' of feminism. In this kind of reading, one returns to the history of philosophy in order to find or confirm the existence of earlier expressions of feminist sentiments or principles in philosophers whose work predates the rise of feminism as a social movement. One thus rereads Plato (who, incidentally, is the philosopher who has thus far been subjected to more feminist readings than any other) in order to recover his advocacy of education for women, or John Stuart Mill as an early advocate of equal rights for women, or Kant as a spokesman for equal treatment under law. Part of the intent of such readings is to show that some of what feminists are trying to do has already been done for us by the fathers themselves. We can be good daughters because we have had some good fathers. This kind of reading hopes to amplify the prospects for success in achieving feminist goals by finding the traces that already exist, making the path to liberation that much more navigable because it has already been marked for us. As a consequence of the success of these kinds of readings there is emerging a revisionist history of philosophy liberally populated with proto-feminists and feminist advocates.

It is not hard to understand the appeal of this strategy for its practitioners or, for that matter, for its audience. First, such readings help to restore faith in the rational benevolence and gender neutrality of philosophical discourse. Sexual difference therefore need no longer be seen as threatening to limit the scope, entitlement, or authority of philosophy to speak for all of us, because male philosophy can and in fact has spoken for women, and in many cases well in advance of explicitly feminist discourse. It also helps support an alternative mythos, namely, that, as David Krell says of Nietzsche, male philosophers can "write with the hand of a woman."[4] This allows for the emergence of the politically useful implication that there is therefore no particular need for women to speak for themselves, nor for philosophy to make explicit room for feminism as a separate discourse, because the fathers can and have already spoken for us, and perhaps better than we could speak for ourselves, since they are also the bearers of the argumentative acumen feminist theory is often said to lack. The strategic logic underlying such readings is to help to legitimate feminist sentiments by finding them articulated by voices that are already taken to be authoritative.

This strategy is understandable, particularly as a response to a time when the legitimacy of feminist scholarship was far more tenuous, and when intervention into a well-known tradition offered a way to introduce what would otherwise have likely been rejected as irrelevant issues. Before a profession is educated to a new language and a new literature, it is often necessary to speak in the terms that are already available, if one wishes to be understood. Because this crisis of legitimacy affected not only professional relationships but also had impact on feminists' own sense of entitlement, it is logical that feminists sought authorization for their concerns by writing within the frameworks which they had already been socialized to privilege. Returning to the canon as a forum for feminist expression was, and probably still is, one way for feminist theorists to assure themselves that they are still philosophers, and that philosophy can still be a viable enterprise. Discovering a sympathetic forefather is also one way to mitigate the contradictions that often arise between one's philosophical and feminist commitments. To the extent that such readings allow feminists to continue to work, they are valuable as survival strategies that ought not be easily dismissed.

But despite the value of these readings as self-authorizing practices, I am concerned about the misleading effects of the revisionist history that seems to be emerging from them, a history that I think misrepresents the development of phallocentric discourse and the development of feminism as a historically specific discourse of resistance. In this rewritten history, sexism, misogyny, and male privilege become phantasmic, untethered from historical roots. Masculine supremacy is a position held by no one, defended by no one. Plato is already a feminist, even though there were no women in the *agora* to hear and benefit by his insights. The discourses that have been used historically to justify women's subjugation emerge from nowhere because they belong to no one. Not only does this remove any possibility of accountability, but it also misleads us about the way philosophy has understood itself and the ways it has been appropriated by other authoritative discourses. If feminist readings end up erasing phallocentrism from the history of philosophy, we play into the hands of those who would encourage our uncritical complicity with it. With such acts of erasure, we have no way of understanding either the logic of male dominance or the possibilities of resisting it. We also help to undermine the significance of feminism as a historically specific discourse of women's resolve, by obscuring recognition of the social conditions that helped produce it and that will be necessary to sustain it. If feminism is severed from the historically specific activities and struggles of women and is treated as just another philosophical leitmotif, we lose access to the means of establishing the grounds for our entitlement in terms of our difference from the operative hegemony as well as diminish our will and power to resist it. A feminist theory envisioned even by its advocates as separable from the concrete political activities of courageous and committed women willing to pursue the unprecedented because it is unprecedented, is a feminist theory that has already lost its reason for being. It is a feminist theory that is already domesticated, capable of taking up residence in the structures the fathers have already built for us.

To the extent that we as feminists still rely on the *maitre-penseurs* for ground and support, we are still dependent upon, and therefore contained by, a phallocentric economy of approval. By remaining dutiful daughters, we limit our vision as well as our strategic options for resistance. This tactic is also problematic because it conveys a mixed message to those colleagues still unwilling to grant legitimacy to the feminist enterprise. By remaining on turf they already claim as their own, we reaffirm their hegemony through our practices, while largely relieving them of the pressure to learn to speak our language and to read the writing that does not find inclusion within the canon as currently constituted. If we continue to accommodate the existing levels of professional ignorance and indifference by sublating our difference from it, we diminish our potential for changing the rules of the game, as well as for changing the lineup of players. If we don't assume and expand the sphere of our own legitimacy, no one else will, either.

A second kind of rereading (which at this stage may be the dominant one, at least in quantitative terms, in part because in some sense it is the hardest to resist) are critical/combative readings that operate with a strategy exactly opposed to the first kind of readings. Rather than searching for predecessors, this sort of reading aims to challenge what the history of philosophy has had to say about women on the grounds that such discourse amounts to a self-interested effort on the part of men to construct women in their absence, as well as to try to justify an indefensible logic of male privilege by embedding it in codes that lend to these prejudices the force of philosophic legitimacy and authority. This kind of reading has served and may continue to serve the crucial function of establishing a basis for feminist grievances as well as helping to clarify just what we are up against. The collective effect of the work produced from this kind of reading is to intensify or revalidate our sense of the necessity and urgency for sustained feminist theory and practice, even though the styles and forms of rationale offered for male supremacy may vary historically. It also has some value in the context of enlisting other women not yet engaged in feminist struggle, by demonstrating the ways in which the history of philosophy persistently fails in its claim to be gender neutral. These critical readings help to make problematic what for many remains a persistent hope, that things will be all right if one can just find the right adopted father. Taken collectively, the force of these critical rereadings is to minimize the possibility that there is some place within traditional philosophical discourse to dwell or to hide.

Beyond the value these readings have for the community, they also serve a very vital function for the reader herself which ought not be ignored. Such rereadings often provide a way to articulate and validate what were once intuitions—intuitions of alienation, displacement, the sense of not really being addressed by the texts we spent our time examining and attempting to understand as students and as teachers. What began for many of us as a nagging self-doubt about the limits of these texts with respect to our own experience, a doubt that more likely than not we initially turned on ourselves in the form of fear of our limitations, now gains critical expression and becomes empowering, because doubt is now directed where it belongs, onto texts that either deliberately or uncritically reproduce the conditions of female absence as central to the structures of rationality as such. We can, as a consequence of engagement in this critical enterprise, come to understand better why, if rationality is predicated on women's absence, we so often thought or feared that we were crazy. We can also understand why our distress so often went unrecognized or misidentified.

But as crucial as such strategies may be in the course of a feminist's development, I do not think we ought to conceive of this strategy as a place to dwell or take root, conceptually or professionally. For one thing, such a strategy, too long pursued, tends to bog one down in the eternal return of the same—the same motifs, the same logic, the same absence. Continuing to reiterate narratives of exile does not really address the problem of where we as feminists can dwell. Continuing the discourse of absence cannot by itself produce a way to intervene and make a place for ourselves, nor can it help us to determine where we want to be. As long as one remains tied to a position of challenging the history of philosophy on more or less its own turf, we may get recognition for our grievances, but we also risk succumbing to the numbness that accrues from repetition, and thereby end up lending our energies to intensifying the force of the dominant hegemony, while diminishing our capacity to envision, demand, and produce significant alternatives. We may move from being grateful good daughters to the position of rebellious ones, but our identity and our logic still remain dependent on the discourse of the fathers.

The last and most recent strategy for rereading the canon are those that endeavor to read texts "against the grain."[5] Tactics employed in this kind of reading differ significantly from those discussed previously and are in some sense more radical, because they aim to intervene and subvert the textual mechanisms operative in phallocentric texts. Rather than addressing texts at the propositional level and extracting an explicit discourse of origins or of refusals, this kind of reading speaks against this thematic grain in order to reveal gaps and lacunae, which leave room for an interventionist activity of rewriting that introduces a feminist voice which the logic of the text is powerless to control. Philosophy is an especially important target for such tactics because, as one exemplary reader-against-the-grain Luce Irigaray puts it, "It is indeed philosophical discourse one must question and disturb because it lays down the law for all the others, because it constitutes the discourse of discourses."[6]

Reading against the grain constitutes an intervention into the phallocentric dynamic of authoritative textual closure. By reading texts in terms other than those it explicitly poses, by using one's position of difference to disclose the text's conflicts and contradictions, such readings work to disrupt the self-suturing operations used to marginalize or displace feminine voices. Often linked to the larger practice of deconstructive reading, this interpretative strategy works to call into question the self-authorizing discourse of rationality in which it is assumed that texts can and do say only what they claim to say, and with that the presumptions of traditional logocentricism to legislate the forms of interpretation and circulation to which it is subject. I have characterized these readings as radical, because they challenge the foundations of traditional reading practices, while making operational an alternative model of interpretative authority. Such readings undermine the prospect of significatory univocity by demonstrating its limits, most specifically the failure of these texts to contain and thereby dominate all that falls within their frame of reference. One consequence of this kind of textual subversion is to demonstrate that the logic that has been used to contain and domesticate women cannot in fact deliver what it promises. If the obstacles are rendered inoperative, then we need no longer think of ourselves as bound to or by them. If "phallogocentrism" can be ruptured in the process of reading, and if the text can be recognized to be complicitous with the process of its dismemberments, then these readings also open the possibility that phallocentric domination can be ruptured in other ways as well.

Feminist readings against the grain have resulted in some very insightful and, to many, unsettling scholarship. Those who are unsettled by this practice recognize its challenge to the terms upon which philosophic hegemony has been constructed and circulated as an authoritative discourse. Those readers are therefore right to be unsettled because it challenges the foundations of the privileges enjoyed by systematic rationality. The capacity of such readings to produce unease about that which philosophy has historically taken most for granted is one of its major strengths as a tactic. The question I wish to pose with respect to these readings is a strategic one, that centers around their utility as ongoing practices. Is this a strategy that feminists should expect to normalize as a competing hegemony, or should this rather be conceived as a specific tactic of accommodation to circumstances that feminists must work harder, in other ways and through other means, to change, so as to render obsolete the conditions that necessitate such reading?

My concerns about institutionalizing reading against the grain as a strategy of feminist hegemony are twofold. The first recapitulates the questions I raised in response to rereadings that aim to retrieve conceptual forefathers of feminism. Even though the logic and intentions of these two kinds of readings differ fundamentally, readings against the grain that locate or retrieve suppressed feminine voices also run the risk of severing feminism from its historically specific roots in women's deliberate and self-initiated political struggles. If a text can be read as giving voice to essentially feminist sentiments, even against its will or better judgments, the efforts of women to discover or produce the difference in their own voices is somehow devalued or effaced. If a text can be feminist in spite of itself, what happens to feminist commitment and the courage it takes to sustain it? Has the myth of authorial intentionalism been displaced only to recover the myth of the good father under another guise?

My second concern lies with the extent to which reading against the grain is still dependent, conceptually and epistemologically, on that which it operates against, specifically, the canon and its traditions of interpretation. Perhaps such readings, despite their intention to do otherwise, end up revalidating the force of the canon, by attributing to it more power and authority than it has or deserves. Reading against the grain, however, also makes room for another far more empowering and politically viable alternative that distinguishes it positively from readings of the first two types. The interventionist strategies at work in such readings authorize the recognition that the sympathetic voices emerging through this process can be affirmed not because they belong to the good father but rather to the good reader. They are thus attributable not to the canon, but rather to the gestures that work to defuse it. It is, therefore, the act of reading and not the self-sealed text that produces these voices, allows them to speak and to speak with authority. Those voices can, therefore, also rightfully be described as feminist without risk of anachronistic misdescription because they are very much our own, a product of our labor. This gesture of reappropriation not only extends and affirms the sphere of feminist discourse, it also provides a space and a way of raising what may be the most subversive and fundamental question about the relationship between feminism and canonical philosophy, namely, the question of who exactly has given birth to whom.[7]

Reading against the grain is no easy feat, not only because one must overcome deeply engrained habits of thought and protocols of readings, but also because one chooses to operate on conspicuously unstable turf, without appeal to pre-established codes of validation and verification. What is the strength of such rereadings may also turn out to be a strategic limit, namely, the decision to chart some radically new courses through old and apparently established territory. Given the political urgencies and conceptual lacunae facing contemporary feminist theory, might not the effort, ingenuity, and insight entailed in rereading be better spent trying to map some new spaces, rather than doing battle with issues and conundrums that in many respects are not of our own making? Reading against the grain may very well be the best way for feminists to reread philosophy. But at this stage of our development, there may also be other more important things to do.

This call for a new agenda that moves feminism into some new territories carries with it the desire and expectation of some specification of just what or where those new terrains are. Although I recognize the legitimacy of that desire and feel in some sense obligated to respond to it, I also recognize the problems entailed in attempting to address it in too substantive or determinate a way. Given all I have said about the limits of the discourse of prescriptive mastery, I cannot and will not try to assume the position of the legislator, authoritatively determining the direction feminist theory ought to take. To refuse to respond at all, however, would place me in the unhappy position of uncritically reproducing the dynamic of withholding the promises for which I have criticized traditional philosophy. So, like so many of my feminist foresisters, I find myself in a potentially explosive situation. The cannon I am attempting to help defuse may very well blow up in my face.

My reservations about continuing to focus on the canon lie not only with the potentially infantalizing father-daughter dynamics produced thereby, but also, pursuing this familial metaphor, with the sibling rivalries that also emerge between the sisters in such discussions, rivalries over just whose father is the best father. This does not mean that feminists ought not to engage in struggle with one another. But the struggles in which we engage ought to occur around the issues arising from the feminist theory and practice that drew us together in the first place. Rather than casting our differences in terms of a canonical logic that will always be inadequate to our needs because it systematically excludes them, we ought be articulating and working through our differences with respect to the conceptual, epistemological, and ethical questions that emerge and have already emerged in the context of our theoretical and political activities as feminists. We need to address the questions we have produced ourselves, rather than those we have inherited.

Suppose, for example, we divest ourselves of the traditional trappings and codes of authority: how is our own discourse to be authorized and legitimated? What, if anything, entitles us to speak for or on behalf of other women? Is feminist politics possible without some form of legislative and articulatory authority? If we succeed in undermining, at least for ourselves, the hegemonic relation between knowledge and power, how ought this relationship to be reconstituted? What model of truth ought to underlie liberatory discourse? How is such truth to be produced, validated, criticized? What kind of model is appropriate for feminists to advocate or exercise? In what relationship does or should this model stand to truth and knowledge? Should feminism aim to consolidate its force as another local hegemony? If so, on what basis? Does any discourse of foundationalism reproduce the dynamics of exclusion we ourselves have criticized? If feminists cannot constitute some common ground, how is political activity in its name possible? What would feminism be if separated from the possibilities of mobilizing women's energies and commitments?

In suggesting a move into new territories I do not mean to imply that feminists are free to ignore or dissociate themselves from their own intellectual histories, or from the larger forms of thought that have produced them as well as the possibility of feminist theory as a historically specific response. Insofar as feminist theory emerges within patriarchy as a form of resistance, it is to that extent also dependent, conceptually and genetically, upon it. One can no more simply declare oneself free of one's conceptual heritage than one can choose to think of oneself as free of the influence of parental and familial heritage (much as we would sometimes like to). We are all the daughters of fathers, many of whom were in close enough proximity to us as we were growing up to have been influential factors in determining directly and indirectly the kind of people we have since become. But though these influences persist, happily and unhappily, we have grown up and moved out of our fathers' houses to homes and offices of our own. Though we may sometimes feel haunted by their presence, sensing dimly or clearly how they continue to work in us, we have also managed to get on with it, in part by struggling to take from that inheritance what we can use, and leaving as much as possible of the rest behind. We have developed the power and resources to separate our agendas from theirs and get on with them.

Feminist theory is growing up as well. The volume and quality of the work we have produced and continue to produce serves as testimony to the nonnegotiable legitimacy of our enterprise. We are becoming less dependent on canonical codes of recognition and validation as a consequence of the progress we have made in developing a forum for the kind of work we want to do. As feminists we may be at a place where the dependency we once felt, and which was perhaps appropriate, is no longer necessary or desirable for our own survival—existentially, conceptually, or professionally. We may already be in a better position than we realize, a position from which we are empowered to ask our own questions, rather than continuing to try to respond to those we have been left with. Such questions are vital not because they liberate us from the effects of this past, but because the answers we produce together will help determine our future.

IV

Attending to the Cultural Other

— 10 —

Alma Gonzalez: Otherness as Attending to the Other

Michael D. Barber

I

Several years ago, a woman, recently arrived from Mexico, asked me to take her two children, Oscar and Alma, ages nine and eleven, to a city clinic to receive vaccinations required for entering school in the fall. It was a blistering hot, humid day in the middle of summer, and our car lacked air conditioning. I maneuvered furiously through the afternoon traffic, honking, changing lanes rapidly, cursing impatiently at those cars that slowly accelerated as though there were not the slightest hurry in the world. Alma, from the back seat, interrupted my raging war with the sluggish mass of automobiles. "Look at that poor little old man (*viejito*) in that car next to us," she said. "He is so old and so tired and so hot that he doesn't even have the energy to roll down the windows of his car." After a pause, I informed her that the little old man was considerably better off than we were, with our windows wide open, gasping for whatever stifling air was available.

In later reflection, my bemusement over the naiveté of this stranger to advanced technological culture gave way to questions about my own possibly condescending attitude toward her. Howard Schwartz and Jerry Jacobs argue that researchers must disengage themselves from paternalistic responsibilities to train or teach or deliver social services, if they are to learn from "cultural troublemakers" such as Alma.[1] Could she, by disruptively saying things that are never said or breaking rules that are never broken, teach me to observe better the familiar in which I was naively immersed?

After all, however mistaken she may have been about air conditioning, she was at least worried about the old man next to us, in contrast to my nearly absolute disregard of those around us. But, in my defense, surely one cannot drive an automobile and remain attentive to others in the way nondrivers can, unless one is uncaringly willing to endanger the lives of all around oneself. A brief digressive phenomenology of driving is called for.

Driving an automobile demands inevitable technical concentration that prohibits us from easily noticing horizonal occurrences unless, by chance, someone calls them to our attention. Even if we were driving on a deserted road, our involvement in instrumental action would constrict observational possibilities. Things become even more complicated when we drive on a crowded street because there we enter into a network of gestures, signals, and actions in which we can, in addition to carefully controlling our automobile, orient our actions toward other drivers strategically or communicatively, to borrow descriptive terminology from Jürgen Habermas.[2] In strategic driving we exert pressure on another rational agent in order to achieve our rational-purposive goal, in contrast to seeking to negotiate a common definition of the situation. Anyone who has ever been tailgated by a massive semi at seventy miles an hour on the Jersey Turnpike has experienced another's strategic driving. But one can also drive communicatively, oriented toward reaching understanding with other drivers, not primarily aiming at one's own success, but trying to negotiate, through gesture, action, and the manner of driving, a common definition of the situation at hand such that mutual plans of action can be harmonized.

In the example of our traffic jam above, insofar as I impatiently attempted to dominate the other drivers around me, honking, pressing them from behind, cutting them off, or denying them access wherever possible, I oriented myself strategically. I was thereby diminishing the possibility of paying attention to these drivers even further than the technical demands of driving made necessary.

Of course, even the strategic trucker is not completely oblivious to the tailgated driver's perceptions; the truck driver expects that the driver of the car will experience terror and get out of the way. Similarly, my strategic driving included anticipating the reactions of my competitors. Even the most ruthless self-interested agent—for instance, some of those described in modern game theory—must engage in some truncated form of *Verstehen* in order to play successfully. And, besides, I was not so absorbed in driving that Alma's comment was lost upon me. On the continuum between purely instrumental and purely communicative action, I may have leaned toward the instrumental pole, but communicative elements were present.

Likewise, Alma was not as technically naive as I had supposed. Much later, when I inquired whether she had ever seen air conditioning before that incident, she informed me that, although it was uncommon in that part of Mexico from which she had come, she had experienced it before. Hence, in the incident with the old man, although acquaintance with air conditioning pertained to her stock of knowledge, her relevance system led her to focus on the imputed suffering of the old man and to bypass completely the technological dimensions of the situation. Had she alluded to those technical characteristics first of all, her wonder about the old man's pain may never have developed at all.

These striking differences in our relevance systems at work in this incident point to our fundamentally different stocks of knowledge with their differently ordered typifications and relevances. These stocks of knowledge, in turn, manifest the radically divergent socio-cultural settings and histories from which we emerged. In a trip to Alma's small town in Mexico years later, I discovered some of these socio-historical factors—what Alfred Schutz called "because motives"—that might explain her reaction to the *viejito* in his air-conditioned automobile.

II

The because-motive analysis in this section will begin with a completed act, Alma's comment, and seek out those prior historical-environmental conditions that shaped her act and her stock of knowledge from which the act proceeded. Since it is impossible to give an account of *all* those historical-environmental factors, we must select interpretively those past experiences and environmental conditions relevant to the completed act. In effect, we will be using Alma's alertness to the old man's plight as a hermeneutic clue guiding us to those elements in her past and present and in her social affiliations that might have prompted her to be so attentive. I will argue that her attunement to the old man and her liberty of self-expression reveal the influences of her family; her status as a child, a female, and a Mexican; and mythic currents in her background. No mechanical, cause-effect relationship is being imputed to these factors prior to the completed act.[3]

Alma's mother had been abandoned by her first husband, who migrated to the United States, leaving her alone with seven children, ages one to seven. After years of lonely struggle raising these children, she developed a relationship with a man in a nearby town and gave birth to Alma and her brother. When the children were still very young, their father was shot to death while accompanying a friend who had been involved in a feud with another group, who ambushed the both of them. Years later, because of the mother's growing difficulties in raising Alma and her brother alone, the other seven children, who had since migrated one by one to the United States, arranged to bring their mother and the two children to the United States the very summer when I was taking them to the clinic.

Alma's stepbrothers and sisters became adults before their time, sharing responsibilities in their fatherless family with their mother. Hence, children in the family, down to and including Alma and her brother, were permitted and encouraged to express themselves freely like adults. The family still laughs about the time when Alma, at age eight, refused to baby-sit for her older sister's three little children and remarked to the others, "They aren't my kids. If she [her older sister] doesn't want to take the responsibility for raising them, then why did she bring them into the world in the first place?" A day later, she showed up at the sister's doorstep asking the sister if she could "borrow" (*prestamelos*) the three little children to play with them. Nowadays, following this pattern, the family delights in the uninhibited cursing that the two-year-old daughter of one of the sons regularly administers to her mother and father. Alma's ability to express herself freely, not to worry about whether others might think her unsophisticated because she did not know about air-conditioned cars, could be traced to her family, in which children are welcomed into adult discourse, in which incongruous comments provide amusement instead of meriting disapprobation, and thus in which cultural troublemaking is fostered more than usual.

Furthermore, a child, free of adult responsibilities, can wonder about those around her with the leisure Aristotle considered necessary for philosophizing. If driving a car involves an adult in repeated choices between problematic possibilities, a child in the back seat faces a world of open possibilities in which anything can become questionable. Her interests are not fixed by relevances intrinsic to a project at hand, and so she can adopt new, unexpected thematic relevances.

Alma's Mexican heritage also played a role in her attentiveness to the elderly man beside us. During my visit to her town in Mexico with a stepbrother and sister, we simply did not have the time to visit all the elderly aunts and uncles and grandparents to whom the returning family member is obliged to pay his respects. In such a family structure, typically Mexican, respect for the elderly occupies a high position in systems of relevance. Because of that same respect, for example, Alma's older brothers and sisters did not hesitate to arrange for their mother and her two children to come to live with them in the United States, in spite of the expense and overcrowding that resulted. It is no wonder that the diminutive *viejito,* laden with affectionate connotations, is almost never replaced by the more neutral *viejo* in Mexican usage.

Sex roles in Alma's hometown are rather clearly defined. Men drive trucks, labor in sugarcane fields, brave the dangers of the sugarcane factory (one man perished in an acid vat in the factory during my visit), and succumb to violence between feuding factions. Women manage the home, cook, wash clothes, raise the children (even when husbands abandon them to seek work in the United States), and mourn the victims of masculine violence. They tend the sick, as I discovered when, during a sickness I experienced there, women of the *pueblo* administered injections and brought me soft foods daily. Such sex roles, insofar as they are rigidly defined, of course, merit no endorsement or justification by a secularized theodicy that points to the "greater" good to which they give rise. Nevertheless, women formed under such norms often emerge with an acumen for attending to (in the perhaps related senses of both *taking cognizance of* and *treating medically*) those who are fragile, ill, or helpless. Did Alma's empathetic response to the old man next to us echo the age-old lament of Mexican women in the face of suffering or violence, such as the violence that deprived her of her own father? Such a lament would be as old as Antigone's defiance or the Trojan women's protest.

Finally, Alma's relevance system reflected a mythic world view. On numerous occasions I have spent hours listening to her and her older brothers and sisters, in their twenties, narrating stories about ghosts, enchanters and enchantresses, spirits of the dead taking vengeance on their living enemies, etc. Repeatedly I have found them much more willing than I was to place credence in such occurrences. An often-recurring story, for example, is that of the three enchantresses from the Falls of Varral near their home in Mexico. These three irresistibly beautiful women attract the attention of men wandering alone in the hills above the falls. These men, who cannot divert their gaze once it has been drawn to the enchantresses, follow them and are never heard from again. Perhaps through the paradoxical vehicle of sexist myth, women do recover a little compensation for the daily tedium of cooking, cleaning, and child-rearing culturally imposed upon them. If, according to Jürgen Habermas, the mythic world view constructs narrative explanations of the world under the influence of mythical powers and fails to differentiate the objective, subjective, and social worlds,[4] then these stories qualify as mythic. Contrary to objective, empirical evidence, the mythic world view, from out of its own subjective resources, peoples the world with spirits and agents who take up their own perspectives on this world. Similarly, Alma's placing in total abeyance her own familiarity with air conditioning in order to engage in a compassionate reading of motives and attitudes onto the driver contiguous to us resembles this mythic refusal to submit to empirical-technical constraints.

III

The incident described and the reflection it provoked show interesting parallels with the concepts and processes of technical phenomenology, as articulated by Edmund Husserl and Alfred Schutz. By expanding on these parallels, I hope to pinpoint more clearly Alma's otherness from myself.

The natural attitude, as Schutz describes it, tends to suppress reflection and divergent viewpoints. Since the pressing pragmatic purposes of the natural attitude leave little time for questioning, the member of the cultural ingroup resorts to "the ready-made standardized scheme of the cultural pattern handed down to him by ancestors, teachers, and authorities as an unquestioned and unquestionable guide in all the situations which normally occur within the social world." The ingroup member applies these ready-made recipes for action out of "habituality, automatism, and half-consciousness." Due to this dominant pragmatic motivation, the denizen of the natural attitude may even look upon persons as things to be handled, as Schutz's own language suggests: "The world of our working, of bodily movements, of manipulating objects and *handling things and men* constitutes the specific reality of everyday life." While this reifying tendency easily leads to overlooking the conscious, interpreting activity of the Other, it is also reinforced by the social style of the natural attitude, in which it is generally assumed that everyone obviously sees things the same way. This style becomes evident in the astonishment, usually followed by a reproach of doubtful loyalty, when ingroup members discover a stranger who does not accept their cultural patterns as the natural and best possible solutions to any problem.[5]

My behavior in the incident recounted exhibited these characteristics of the natural attitude. Driven by practical aims and, beyond that, by a highly instrumental, noncommunicative orientation, I was all too willing, at first, simply to dismiss Alma's offhand remark as showing nothing but cultural naiveté in the face of what was obviously air conditioning. This automatic response, of course, maintained a domain for me in which I was at ease, manipulating the practical situation at hand, and protected me from uncomfortable questions, for example, about my instrumental-strategic attitude and relevance system. The grip of the natural attitude upon me was so tenacious that even in reflection I could, at the start, justify my inattentiveness as "normal" and demanded by the requisites of safe driving. Finally, only subsequent reflection would lead me beyond my initial simplistic conceptualizations of myself as entirely instrumental and Alma as entirely instrumentally naive.

The sluggishness of this passage of reflection to a more reflective stance within the natural attitude, coupled with the self-protective social style of that attitude, illustrates how very difficult it is even to come to the awareness that there is another way of looking at a situation in common—for instance, that a person of another culture approaches that same situation with a relevance system quite distinct from my own. This natural-attitude resistance to recognizing the Otherness of the Other no doubt underlies the claim of Schwartz and Jacobs that for the sociologist the mere adoption of the scientific attitude is not enough. They urge, in addition, association with those already in possession of "unnatural natural attitudes"—strangers, novices, cultural troublemakers, and misfits—who deprive the researcher of social and technical competences, especially if he gives up the socially fixed role of dispenser of social services, which confines him and his client within regularized, natural-attitude typifications.[6]

Of course, even to be aware of the hold of the natural attitude indicates that we have somewhat escaped its spell, however much we may fall short of that reflective disengagement which Husserl believed a fully implemented formal phenomenological reduction could achieve. The encounter with the Other and the reflection initiated by such an encounter can achieve effects resembling those of formal phenomenological reduction. Just as the Stranger, according to Schutz, becomes conscious of their own *thinking as usual* and learns, through bitter experience, that the "normal way of life is always far less guaranteed than it seems," a similar self-discovery and de-absolutization takes place in those who directly relate with the Stranger and so insert themselves into a situation analogous to the Stranger's.[7] When the natural attitude's blinders to Otherness fall from our eyes, we can recognize some of our own intentionalities, including relevances, through which the world is given to us, as never before, as well as recognizing that other intentionalities are possible and that our own are not absolute.

Paying attention to the unique attitude through which the world is given to the Other, an attention wrested from the natural-attitude tendency to attend to the attending of the Other in a truncated fashion, only insofar as pragmatic purposes require, opens up a rich field of conscious experience, as does reduction. Alma's Otherness, the Otherness of a child, a female, a rural Mexican with proclivities toward the mythic, were manifested precisely in her ability to attend to the ways in which the Other, the old man beside us, was attending to our common situation. Her remark stimulated me to become attentive to her attentiveness to his way of attending to the world. This consciousness of another's consciousness of another's consciousness replicates on a social plane what Edmund Husserl described as intentional implication, in which there can be memories of perceptions or memories of memories of perceptions and so forth.[8] Through Husserlian reduction and the breaking in of the Other upon us, meanings, interpersonal otherwise, burst into bloom; and the practical citizen of the dreary, unidimensional natural attitude gets a glimpse of how richly meaningful the world of our animistic, mythic predecessors must have been.

IV

Jürgen Habermas's account of communicative rationality informs this paper beyond the explicit borrowing of the descriptive concepts of

communicative and instrumental orientation for my phenomenology of driving. The interchange between Alma and myself, between her culture and
my own, has included, I hope, a symmetry and mutuality of critique. My
critical questions surface in my moral alarm over the suppression of communication through violent feud or sexist reification and my cognitive-
instrumental rejection of mythic ontology.[9]

On the other hand, my pragmatic, even strategic de-personalizing and
de-intentionalizing of the situation at hand stands out as restrictive, in sharp
contrast to Alma's more bountiful ascriptive personalizing and intentional-
izing of it. Paradoxically, someone whose relevances have been shaped in a
culture in which sexism, violence, or mythic dogmatism threaten to abolish
communicative rationality has shown herself at times further along on the
road toward communicative rationality than one formed in a cognitive-
instrumentally advanced society. It is not surprising that the potential for
communicative rationality should be found even in a context hostile to such
rationality. After all, technologically advanced Western societies have not
snuffed out the potential for communicative rationality even though those
societies have jeopardized communicative rationality through their one-
sided emphasis on cognitive-instrumental rationality.[10] In the search for
communicative rationality, mythic cultures may have much more to teach
their more cognitive-instrumentally developed dialogue partners than Habermas's condensed critical treatment of the mythic world view suggests.

While ascriptive personalization and intentionalization may humanize
a culture impoverished by de-personalizing and de-intentionalizing disen-
chantment, such ascriptive intentionalization is finally only en route toward
communicative rationality. The reading in of meanings and intentions,
while an improvement over the neglect of rich meanings at hand, can also
involve an imposition of interpretive schemes on another to which he or she
might not assent, especially if that self-critical reflexivity, which in Habermas's view is a condition sine qua non of all rationality,[11] is lacking. The
next step in Alma's interpretation of the old man would have been to inquire whether he would find her interpretation of his interpretations of his
situation acceptable, as Schutz's postulate of adequacy would require of the
sociologist.[12] Such self-criticism would serve to safeguard the Otherness of
the Other and bring to fulfillment a telos toward which mythic wonder
about the Other is already headed and which the instrumentally-strategically
disenchanted are in danger of forgetting completely.

The very framework of communicative rationality itself depends on
that shattering of presuppositions which phenomenology and the breaking
in of the Other upon us effect—in order that the Otherness of the Other
might be glimpsed in all its distinctiveness.

— 11 —

Decentering the Self: Two Perspectives from Philosophical Anthropology

Kenneth Liberman

Egocentrism in European Culture

Martin Heidegger has identified an egocentrism which operates at the origin of Western philosophical thinking. With the Cartesian "I think," an egoity appeared and became the essential definition of humanity.[1] The I provided an origin from which a certain but egocentric and dualistic universe was secured for Western experience.

> The motive of this primary orientation toward the subject in modern philosophy is the opinion that this being which we ourselves are is given to the knower first and as the only certain thing, that the subject is accessible immediately and with absolute certainty.[2]

> This egoity already appears in the form of the *certum*, the certainty which is nothing other than the guaranteeing of what is represented for representational thinking.[3]

The I is the original ground of unity and has also provided the model, since Leibniz, of the unity which was then attributed to every being. The independent origin of the self provided the possibility for worldly entities to be likewise independent and self-originating. The dualism that lies at the basis of representational thinking was thus instituted. As the origin of Western humankind's certainty about the reinterpretation of experience as objectivity and representedness, this I was accentuated[4] and Western humankind became intoxicated with it: "In this fundamental certainty man is sure that, as the representer of all representing, and therewith as the realm of all representations, and hence of all certainty and truth, he is made safe and secure; i.e. *is.*"[5]

The origins of this origin are at once Jewish and Greek, "the historic coupling of Judaism and Hellenism."[6] Judaism fostered the idea of an individual soul, at once divine and eternal, as well as an ethical imperative that accompanies it. The word that was with God instituted a logocentric rationality that totalized human experience and permitted self-righteousness to proliferate. A proclivity toward absolutism, not inconsistent with Judaic thought (even in its ethical domains), ironically prepared the way for a totalitarianism that consumed Jews. It was the Greek democracy which introduced both civil liberties and civil authority. The "citizen," free and self-certain, engaged himself in the free pursuit of ideas and selected democratically the optimal solutions for humankind. Yet that very freely established civil authority killed Socrates, the thinker who was most committed to free inquiry—too much free inquiry threatened to undermine the unity that established the certainty of civil authority. Already, at the dawn of democracy, a reified rationality installs an imperialism of *theoria*.[7]

The marriage of the idea of self and of civil authority propelled the political imagination of the Enlightenment and still characterizes the West today. Self-certain, rational individuals, protected by the Declaration of the Rights of Man and its progeny, freely select in a Hobbesian fashion a civil authority that in reality tolerates little diversion from the accepted corpus of reified truths (*theoria*). It is pertinent to note that Descartes's first moral rule in his epochal *Discourse on Method* was "to obey the law and customs of my country" and church.[8] Civil society reproduces these autonomous and autochthonous individuals whose confident self-righteousness is so pervasive in Western democracies, including Reagan's America. This self-certain egoism leads to a self-certain logocentrism. Michael Ryan describes the political tradition in the West which such a possessive individualism and logocentric rationalism have produced:

> Hobbes demonstrates the relationship between the metaphysical concept of the logos as a point of absolute cognitive authority, from which laws issue in an unequivocal language that excludes all possibility of ambiguity of intention or interpretation, and the absolutist political concept of a sovereign who represents the whole state and who is the unique source of laws whose authority is incontestable.[9]

Are we Greeks? Are we Jews?[10] Ostensibly acting as our own foundation and orienting ourselves to a final judgment in which we stand in "spiritual isolation,"[11] we are free and we are alone. Morality is personal, itself predicated upon the egological "I think," and ethics is egocentric. Such an ethics does not propel us toward our fellow humans but isolates us from them. Describing Protestant America, Weber writes:

> This consciousness of divine grace of the elect and holy was accomplished by an attitude toward the sin of one's neighbor, not of sympathetic understanding based on consciousness of one's own weaknesses, but of hatred and contempt for him as an enemy of God bearing the signs of eternal damnation.[12]

It is the Jew-Greek Husserl who bears philosophy's rationality into the modern era. Because Husserl's truth is founded upon the self and its original experience, "egocentrism operates at the heart of pure phenomenology."[13] Western metaphysics retains its grounding, and its totalization goes unchallenged. Derrida equates this "transcendental oppression" with "the origin or alibi of all the oppression in the world."[14] Logocentric rationality is established as the white mythology:

> Metaphysics—the white mythology which reassembles and reflects the culture of the West: the white man takes his own mythology, Indo-European mythology, his own *logos,* that is, the *mythos* of his idiom, for the universal form of that he must still wish to call Reason.[15]

It was Heidegger who called this rationalism and egocentrism into question. Departing from Husserl's transcendental phenomenology, Heidegger pursues an origin that is founded not so much in the self as in Being and society. For Heidegger, "the egoity of the individual does not become the center of the entire problematic."[16] But Heidegger's break with egocentrism is equivocal. Our philosophical systems are generated by egocentrism, and yet they are called upon to evaluate this egocentrism; the West is able to stumble away from its egoism only haltingly. The early Heidegger writes, "The proofstone of philosophical truth consists solely in the loyalty the philosophizing individual has to himself,"[17] but he cautions that this is not a narrow egoism but an ontologically 'authentic' self, an ego subordinated to being: "It is equally necessary not to start simply from the subject alone but to ask whether and how the *being* of the subject must be determined as an entrance into the problems of philosophy, and in fact in such a way that orientation toward it is *not one-sidedly subjectivistic.*"[18]

Levinas calls this ontological imperialism, wherein ethics is subordinated to ontology, and he considers it dangerous. Certainly, the morality is logocentric. And despite Heidegger's critique of Husserl's *cogito,* he does not abandon that autonomy that characterizes the *cogito*'s freedom. The integrity of the self is preserved, and "Heidegger remains tributary to the Western tradition by declaring that comprehension is the fundamental Existential."[19] Freedom precedes responsibility.

Levinas declares that we live in a tragic form of liberty. The tragedy rests in a liberty of self-reliance, of rugged individualism, in which we are isolated from our fellows. Instead of this competitive liberty and its egological morality, Levinas commends to us submission to a social responsibility in which the other is the natural basis of morality, a basis that transcends our individual foundation. Taking his lead from Heidegger's critique of Western philosophy as an egology, Levinas asserts that we must not begin with the self's relation to itself. As citizens or as philosophers we are addressed first and most immediately to the self's relation with others; in Steven Gans's words, "The ultimacy of the other is prior to and the condition of our own life-world experience."[20] This responsibility precedes freedom, and the self is decentered toward the other. Levinas's thought summons us to a dislocation of our identity.[21]

Decentering the Self

In post-phenomenology no longer is the *cogito* the origin of epistemological inquiry; likewise, in sociology and anthropology the *cogito* as a model is more neglected than ever. Possibly the postmodern disillusionment with rationalism is infecting social inquiry generally, but it would seem that the turn away from the *cogito* is motivated in a more positive fashion by the discovery of more fruitful origins of social being. These "origins" are less unitary and expose us to a less deterministic universe, but they offer more fecund insights into human affairs. In a word, social scientists are directing themselves more toward processes than toward foundations, more toward praxis than toward grand theory, and in this turn the self is being decentered: the self is inscribed in a world it does not found. In Derrida's words:

> There is no subject who is agent, author, and master of *differance*, who eventually and empirically would be overtaken by *differance*. Subjectivity—like objectivity—is an effect of *differance*, an effect inscribed in a system of *differance*.[22]

Differance is not a concept; it is an activity. It does not settle into a stasis or permit itself to be reified but is a shifting system of adjusting relationships. According to this view, the self is a transitory product of these shifting relationships, not the foundation of society but the transitory result of a system of activity.

Neither is the self the point for inaugurating sociological analysis. A thoroughly radical philosophical sociology cannot rely upon Western metaphysics alone but must disclose the shifting system of relationships that is productive of an egological space of one sort or another; it is a "system of *differance*" that provides openings for actors. This 'deconstructive turn' is one that is poorly accommodated by a philosophical rationalism that is committed to the tyranny of *theoria*, and so philosophical inquiry is seeking new directions. "Even for a philosopher, the theoretical ideal and the realm of representation are not the most radical and not a universal perspective.''[23] What can be more radical than philosophy is sociology, because the world is more imaginative than theory. The self does not precede social interaction; it is embedded in the practices of an interactional system. For Simmel, a selfhood was always a function of consociality. According to Clifford Geertz, thinking itself is a public activity. And this view is shared by Harold Garfinkel, who has claimed that thinking needs to be discovered in the world, where it is always located, as the ordinary and naturally organized activities which it is. In a parallel vein, Foucault's inquiries are not addressed to the ideas subjects have in their minds, but to that which unifies their practices. And even the social psychologists (still immersed, molasses-like, in the model of the *cogito*) admit that the self is a social process, not independent but contingent.

As philosophical inquirers into the self, we do not want to restrict ourselves to the ideas, theories, or philosophies of the self which dominate our society or other societies. It is more productive to address ourselves to that system of naturally organized social practices that constitutes the ordinary life of a community. We need to locate, as a discovery, a network of relationships that is pre-conceptual (yet which, in fact, is the very locus of conceptual life). We must relocate self and personal identity within a system of interaction that provides the places and orientations for self-presentation and self-assertion. Such processes are the origins of the person. The self is contingent and decentered; it is not an internal essence, nor necessarily an eternal one. There is no "inside" apart from the world. We are caught up in processes that we do not control, although it is the operative notion of Western rationality that we do control them.

Levinas asks, "How does philosophy emerge from life? What and how are the relations between existence and philosophizing?"[24] This is not a question to be overlooked. Sociology cannot be ignorant of philosophy, first, because no society is without its theoretical life, which in turn motivates (and even constrains) social activity and, second, because a philosophically unsophisticated sociology inclines toward a naive empiricism. However, compared with philosophy, a philosophically sophisticated sociology has more direct access to the world, which is capable of generating more possibilities than even philosophical imagination. Like phenomenological philosophers, phenomenological sociologists revere reflection and immerse themselves in the texts of phenomenologists, but they differ in that they seek their discoveries in the world of social activities. They do so merely because of a principled dedication to empirical research; they do so because of their wonder in the face of how the world copiously demonstrates phenomenological notions at work. Such worldly demonstrations exceed the abilities of the imagination; hence, the wonderment.

Western civilization may be facing a crisis at the limits of rationality, and the limits of self-certainty may have been reached; however, it is unlikely that transcending these limits will be the achievement of philosophy. Any transcendence will only be the accomplishment of social practices themselves. Derrida did not invent the decentering of the self, the self is already in the process of being decentered. Derrida, Levinas, Heidegger, and others are only chroniclers; their power rests only in a capacity to focus public attention. Philosophy follows history.

One method of gaining a clearer view of the possibilities of this self-decentering is to examine the selfhood that is operative in some non-Western traditions. As we seek to comprehend the limits of the self, perhaps the experience of other societies can offer us some clues. We do not want to concentrate such a philosophical anthropological investigation upon the formal or theoretical formulations of selfhood that such societies have developed as their own reifications, however vital such reifications are to the social order. Our first task—sociology's first task—is to locate the practical environment of social activities within which a self can function; the description of any indigenous philosophy of self would be only corollary to this social environment. Indigenous philosophies of self, while providing important perspectives and hence a component of this analysis, must be assessed in light of the actual systems of social interaction to which the mode of selfhood is contingent. An examination of the self in two non-Western societies, Australian Aboriginal and Tibetan Buddhist, yields some significant contributions capable of informing current thinking regarding the decentering of the self. These observations are the fruit of two years each with Aboriginal people and Tibetan people and rely upon investigations carried out within the Aboriginal and Tibetan languages.

The Self in Central Australian Aboriginal Society

Aboriginal people are the antithesis of Europeans: they are not egoistic. Individuality is neither sought after nor missed. An Aboriginal person does not wish to be a unique human being; on the contrary, he or she wants only to be the same as everyone else. This is reflected in their paintings, which do not bear any personal authorship nor are the products of any artistic license. Such a lack of egoity is considered by European Australians to be a sign of backwardness, primitive and uncreative; the Aboriginals, however, find solace in their solidarity with others. Similarly, they do not litter their landscapes with their personal names, and even the latter are changeable. Their identity is not a self-possession but is the identity of the totem, an essence that fundamentally belongs to others.

Their social life is characterized by an obsession for consensus, a preoccupation with a network of others that founds its own certainty. This certainty is never theoretical; it is not divorceable from a social solidarity whose principal features are congeniality and harmony. Although not always achieved, such an immediate congeniality is the abiding preoccupation of Aboriginal social life. They are rarely competitive and defer to the wishes of any occasional assembly of fellows. Above all, they avoid "personal" exposure and avoid exposing others. They do not look directly into the eyes of the persons they are addressing; in fact, they generally do not address individuals but address an occasional gathering as a whole, and their own participation is anonymous, the participation of Anyman.

Decision making is corporate and out-loud, and proceeds by consensus without the direction of formal leaders (though there are elders and men of eloquence). This consensus is not the result of a negotiation of individual wills—the consensus is all that appears and builds upon itself; it is consensus each step of the way. Participants do not voice "personal" views so much as they produce summaries of their image of the consensus at any given moment. Turn-taking dyads are not the routine; individuals are not addressed, and individuals do not have the right of reply. Individuals do not possess turns, and they do not take turns. Rather, discussion proceeds all at once or by way of a round-the-rally process of accretion that I have termed the serial production of summary accounts.[25] This serial production of summary accounts is a sophisticated and competent interactional system that sounds something like an auction without the auctioneer.

As a matter develops in discussion, the utterances of the participants are summaries of what the collectivity has concluded so far. These summary accounts are a process of verbally formulating, and thereby making publicly available, the developing account of a state of affairs that is emerging as a collaborative production. One's participation is not on one's own behalf but on behalf of all, or at the worst on behalf of an associate. There is little attachment to one's "own" views, for this system of interaction provides little space for egoistic participation. Failing any provision for such participation, there is little egocentrism. Aboriginal people are 'inscribed' into the 'text' of their social interaction. They are not selves in the sense of Western metaphysics; they are not autonomous centers.

My own response to the Aboriginal system of interaction is noteworthy. I was incapable of sustaining my usual egoistic self-presence. From time to time my self-centered orientation would intrude, to be met with the kind embarassment of my Aboriginal fellows, who did not pay it any mind. But for the most part the interactional practices themselves left me with few openings for exercising my egocentric rationality. I have my Aboriginal self, and I have my European self; but in both instances they seem to be provided for me by the competent system of interaction at work in Aboriginal and European societies. Deflecting my self-orientation toward the collaborative purposes of the Aboriginal group did not require deliberate action or restraint on my part; rather, once I had mastered the Aboriginal language and discourse practices it was almost impossible for me to sustain anything other than the decentered self available to Aboriginal social actors. What was more astonishing to me was that I also developed more awareness of and concern for the feelings of others. The delight I experienced regarding this was matched by my disappointment at how rapidly such concern dissipated when I reentered European systems of social interaction. These latter interactional practices were originary to a similar degree, and they obliged me to exercise European selfhood.

Another ethnographer of the Aboriginal people of Australia's central desert has commented in a recent study that Aboriginal people "speak with amazement that whites are able to refuse a person 'to his eyes'. This is to recognize no relation to the other, to assert one's total autonomy."[26] Such antagonistically structured behavior is scandalous and is a major reason why Aboriginal people have chosen not to assimilate into Anglo-Australian society. For their own part, Anglo-Australians view the Aboriginals' preference for their own primitive society as evidence of their backwardness. Their lack of attachment to their "own" views has been taken as evidence of unreliability by some political leaders. Aboriginal school children, unversed in egoistic self-presentation, are considered intellectually retarded. Nevertheless, their system of interaction is essentially egalitarian[27] and serves as an effective bulwark against tyranny. As another anthropologist has commented, "In some ways they were more skillful than we are at limiting the free play of men's combative propensity."[28] Especially, their system of interaction removes the possibility that rational goals or a codified morality would turn and make instruments of people themselves, the possibility that ethics would be separated from responsibility. On occasions, I found myself at cross-purposes with Aboriginal people: at their request I would organize a meeting to discuss land rights with governmental representatives or put together a trip to a sacred site several hundred miles distant, and I would become so absorbed with the accomplishment of such plans that I would overlook that locally produced congenial interaction that was the more important and abiding concern of Aboriginal people. To speak in Levinas's terms, within the Aboriginals' serial production of summary accounts, the face of the other is never absent.

Finally, if their ethics is spontaneous and rarely occluded by a logocentric rationality, they do not have anything like a "higher" morality that is recognizable. Aboriginal people do not have the notion of an individual soul; rather, their soul is possessed by another—not by persons or demons but by that life-force that takes the form of a natural species and which dwells in that sacred location (e.g., hill or waterhole) from which an Aboriginal's soul emanated and to which it will one day return. Even at this more theoretical level the Aboriginal's identity is corporate and not individual. The result of this cosmology is that Aboriginals do not have a self for which they are responsible—hence they do not have a morality akin to European morality. There is the face but no Judaic-Hellenic law. This is the fascination of their folklore and mythology. Incredible epics ensue, heroes and heroines prevail and are subdued in turn, but there are no moral lessons. My inquiry is not complete, but I believe that the reason for this absence is that there is no self-certain selfhood which could provide the origin for such a moral dimension. Without an egoity at the center of their social universe, a logocentric morality has no object to which it can direct itself. There is always, however, the face of the other. But it is an other different from Levinas's other, who demands recognition as autonomous. The Aboriginals' other is not autonomous; it too is decentered.

The Self in Tibetan Society

In his introduction to a 1968 volume of papers from an international conference on the self at the University of Hawaii, entitled *The Status of the Individual in East and West,* Charles A. Moore discounts the cliche that opposes Western individualism and "the ethical autonomy of the individual" to "oriental despotism" and the downgrading of the individual.[29] Colloquial thinking in the West has presumed that in the East there is little respect or dignity for the individual, a situation from which the West recoils or at most responds by sending missionaries. Today, twenty years later, the smugness of such comparisons has almost disappeared. Not only have Japan, Korea, Singapore, and other Oriental societies outperformed the West by the latter's own economic standards, but the West itself has been faced with the post-rational disillusionment with individualism. Western societies are faced with a breakdown of ethics; in American cities individuals shoot people not for money or out of jealousy but for no reason at all. Now at the limits of a self-certain logocentric morality, the Western view of Oriental society is less confident.

The ground of such a moral comparison was misplaced in any event. It was tautological in that the basis of ethics was presumed to be that self which is the origin of philosophy and morality in Western civilization; with such a basis the West was bound to prevail. If we accept that ethics rests in the priority of the other, then the outcome of such a cross-cultural comparison is not so certain.

The origin of the ethical perspective of Tibetans, inherited from Mahayana Buddhism, is a refusal to become absorbed with one's own personal liberation. Instead, one dedicates all of one's energies to helping to bring about the enlightenment of others. This dedication is sustained until the very last being is led to enlightenment; only then does one enter one's own liberation. While there is an obvious selflessness to such a religious practice, it is worth noting that the "one" who dedicates "oneself" is an ego-ity. In spite of theoretical elaboration regarding how the egoless person is one who is prepared for liberation, the Tibetans retain a stronger egoity than do the Aboriginal people. Possibly this is because the Tibetans dwell in a more philosophical realm, and their ordinary social practices betray their theorizing. The Tibetan "selflessness" (*bdag-me-pa*) is much more abstract and less immediate than the Aboriginal person's.

There is an abiding individuality among Tibetans, although it is an individuality without individual-ism. Even when they are debating the issue of selflessness, their debates proceed according to a dialectical philosophical structure sustained by a system of interaction that is antagonistic. These antagonistic social practices, such as their forensic debates, produce egoistic individuals. As one commentator has remarked, "The academic training in formal debate, inherited from the great Indian monastic universities and refined in Tibet over centuries, is an extraordinary technique in ego-broadening."[30]

Nevertheless, the force of Tibetan philosophy and religious practice is directed to the overcoming of egoistic orientations, and such practices have their effect. Most Tibetans engage in Buddhist thought training, by which one's attachment to one's ego is diminished and one's generosity is increased. Such thought training takes the form both of regular meditation and everyday practices designed to break the self-habit. One such thought training is illustrative:

> When accompanying anyone
> I shall view myself as the lowest
> of all and in the depth of my heart
> shall hold dearly others as supreme.
>
> When others, out of jealousy,
> treat me badly with abuse, insults and the like,
> I shall accept their hard words
> and offer the other the victory.[31]

For many persons in the West the notion of "thought training" implies a possibly dangerous abandonment of personal responsibility for one's actions. The idea that one's mind may be "trained," or made to conform to an external system of beliefs or ethics, undermines the precept that morality depends upon the sovereignty of the individual will. Westerners who prize their creative individuality and independence of judgment would be reluctant to submit to such a comprehensive and effective system of thought training. In response, Tibetans attribute such objections to the egoism they view to be characteristic of Western life. They view the self-habit as so embedded in a person's behavioral patterning that only an unremitting attack upon such habitual behavior will result in any lasting transformation. Thought training is not the tyranny of external belief but liberation from self-deception.

The Tibetan mode of selfhood might be described as standing midway between the egoistic self of the West and the decentered self of Aboriginal people from Australia's central desert. As with the case of the Aboriginal people, humility is the rule, and self-praise is poor form. The personal names of Tibetans may change two or three times during a lifetime and often reflect a religious affiliation. In the folk religion, persons engage in a meditative practice in which one visualizes oneself as a particular deity, and the aim is to practice such visualization so thoroughly that the identity and characteristics of the deity (e.g., compassion, wisdom, fearlessness, etc.) overcome one's personal identity. While the practice is mystical, the exaggerated selves of ordinary persons are also mystical, and probably less congenial. The many mountains and peaks of the Himalayan range do not bear personal names. Tibetan painters do not sign their work and do not innovate. They do not worry that this is a lack of respect for the autonomous individual, for they view such autonomy as an intellectual distortion. Several young Tibetan men who were selling religious paintings at a gathering of several hundred thousand Tibetans at Bodh Gaya, the site of Buddha's enlightenment in India, explained to me with some satisfaction that all of the paintings for sale were unsigned. Their tone was critical of the egoism of European society which exhalts all achievements as individual.

In Tibetan society there are two forms of discourse. One includes a mundane vocabulary, to be employed when referring to oneself; the other contains an honorific vocabulary, which is applied to others. In this way the priority of the other is declared in all public settings. When I was first learning to speak Tibetan, I would confuse these vocabularies and occasionally apply honorific terms to myself and the mundane terminolgy to others, until one day a middle-aged Tibetan lady accused me, with a note of disgust, of having too high an opinion of myself. But such a formal humility is a peculiar double-edged sword: the more humble one can be, the more status one accrues. It is a sword that in cutting down one's self can cut others at the same time.

It is worth remarking also that in Tibetan society personal relationships are highly formalized. The relative absence of social status in American society leads to seemingly continuous negotiation of status in interactional settings; since status is in part undetermined, it is up for bid, and a competitiveness ensues. Such competitiveness is enhanced by the socialization of children in sporting competitions and by antagonistic legal and civil interactional formats. In traditional Tibetan society, aristocratic forms dictate clearly one's position, and so aggressive presentations of self become pointless.

The fundamental task of Tibetan social praxis is to overcome the self-habit, a central aspect of which is the notion that one as an egoity is one's own foundation.[32] With Tibetan Buddhists there are two sides to this praxis—one called Wisdom, which refers to philosophical reasoning and understanding, and one called Method, which refers to engaging in everyday social practices which enhance one's natural sense of compassion and increase one's generosity to the point that generosity will arise spontaneously even in the face of one's enemies. The Tibetans, like the Aboriginal people, base their ethics upon the face of the other, though they also have a meta-discourse on ethics that is theoretical. Wisdom and Method, philosophy and compassion, are always conjoined, and the seminal Prasangika Madhyamika commentator, the philosopher Chandrakirti (in Tibetan, Dawa Dragpa) commences his fundamental treatise with a prostration to compassion. Tibetan philosophy itself, though formal and syllogistic, is not founded upon a self-originating ego. Madhyamika philosophy, the system of philosophical tenets that predominates among Tibetans, does not treat a theoretical consciousness as primary; rather, philosophy is a means by which obscurations to the understanding that one's self is not inherently existent can be removed. Philosophy leads to the recognition that one is fundamentally, 'originally', self-less. As the fifteenth-century founder of the Gelugpa sect of Tibetan Buddhism, Tsong Khapa, has written, "Especially for an egocentric person the sole door for determining the exact reality of things is the text on valid reasoning."[33]

The mainstream Buddhist philosophers were typically non-egocentrist and critical. They were opposed, philosophically and religiously, to egocentric philosophies and were not at all mystical in their approach. They generally accepted that the mind itself does not exist on its own basis but is a pragmatic and conventional attribution to the activities of thinking. Apart from thoughts, nothing substantial exists. Further, the origin of philosophical views is not personal; although logic and reason are the proper grounds of knowledge, individualistic departures are considered egoistic, especially when they are propelled by a relentless syntax of logocentric conceptual manipulation invested with considerable conceit.

The sense of self as an origin, which is the object of the Tibetans' philosophical criticism, may be a concept but it is not predominantly a philosophical phenomenon: "Self-sufficient existence is not just a philosophical phenomenon; it is innate, born with us due to the conditions of former actions and afflictive emotions."[34] The self-habit arises naturally: "Without any reasoning and through the force of habituation, the mind conceives of an I that is self-sufficient, able to establish itself naturally or inherently existent from the start and fused with the appearance of mind and body."[35] This concept I is a way of viewing the world, or rather a way of being in the world, but it is not an entity that really exists. Just how it operates in the world is a practical concern, for Tibetans and sociologists alike.

The I is imputed upon the mind and body. It exists not ultimately or by itself but only in dependence upon mental and physical aggregates. As cited by the eighteenth-century Tibetan scholar Jang-gya, the Buddha compared the designation "self" to that of a "chariot":

> Just as a chariot is designated
> In dependence upon collections of parts,
> So conventionally a sentient being
> [Is designated] in dependence upon the aggregates.[36]

A chariot is nothing separate from wheels, reins, a driver's seat, etc., yet it is not simultaneous with them. There is no essence "chariot"—remove one of the wheels and where in the wheel is "chariot"? It is simply a conventional designation, with no independent status.

Similarly, the self is a conventional designation without independent status. What is the relationship between the person and the mind and body? The Tibetans approach the matter logically. Is the self that is the basis of the conceptualization "I" the same as one's mind and body or different from them? If the self exists independently, then it must exist either as the same or as different. If it is the same, it would be redundant; also, it would have to exist in the hands, legs, etc. If one cut off a leg, would the self be at all diminished? Further, if long, beautiful and flowing hair or an attractive musculature were the self, would the self disappear or change when baldness or obesity set in? So the self is not the same as the mind and body; it cannot be found there. Can it be found elsewhere? If it were different from the mind and body, it would not have characteristics in common with them, and this would be absurd. Further, it would have to be observable separate from a knower, doer, thinker, feeler, etc.[37] It would be impossible to apprehend the self without the mind and body; therefore, neither does it exist as different from them. The conclusion to be drawn is that the self does not exist, except as a convention.

Following Buddhist epistemology, the Tibetans are thorough in investigating the play of relations by which an egocentrism is maintained:

> When I say or think, "My mind," "My body," "My book," and so on, I seem to be first, and then the thing owned appears to depend upon me. The I is the owner, controller. It seems that this I does not depend upon the mind or body; rather, the mental and physical aggregates seem to depend on the I. Due to the great force with which we conceive this, the I and the mental and physical aggregates appear to be, respectively, the controller and the controlled.[38]

The I arises as a system of differences, but it is dependent upon this system; its independence is only an illusion. Robert Magliola has made a similar observation when comparing the thought of Derrida with that of the founder of Madhyamika philosophy, Nagarjuna: "Derrida's own different activity can be compared with the differential frequenting identified with Nagarjunism. . . . the Nagarjunist is aware . . . of a kind of off/self that moves freely between the objectivism of ego and pure devoidness."[39]

The self, then, is an illusion, but whose illusion is it? Even in formulating the question there is a hidden egoity, a double illusion which the Tibetan Buddhists are concerned to root out. Although there is nothing like a Judeo-Christian soul in Mayahana Buddhism, the Tibetans do find something that they call emptiness and which is not nothingness. It is neither presence nor absence:

> Not empty, not nonempty.
> In this way everything is explained.
> Existence, nonexistence, and existence.
> That is the middle path.
>
> The existence of nondual phenomena's nonexistence
> Is the Characteristic of emptiness.
> It is not existent, yet not nonexistent.
> It has the characteristic of not being the same or
> different.[40]

Not having the certainty of the 'I think', the Tibetans are less prey to a logocentric rationality, and the world they turn toward is not reinterpreted as objectivity and representedness. In the citation above of Derrida's assessment of Levinas,[41] I provided only part of the pertinent clause; here is a fuller citation: "The thought of Emmanuel Levinas can make us tremble. . . . this thought summons us to a dislocation of the Greek logos, to a dislocation of our identity, and perhaps of identity in general."[42] The decentering of the self leads naturally to the decentering of everything, for without one pole of the dualism, duality collapses. Yet the Tibetans do not adhere to a nihilism, and this is in the same way that deconstructive thinking is not a nihilism:

> The non-egocentrist outlook is essentially critical of all givens, not by taking as ''given'' the essential unreliability of everything, as does the absolutist skeptic, but by never being satisfied with any supposedly analysis-proof element, and by sustaining the critical process itself as a valid mode of thought, cultivating a high tolerance of less than absolute security.[43]

This critical process is extended to the world. Conventional distinctions are retraced back to their origin in a relation of differences. A substance bearing attributes does not exist apart from these attributes; hence, it does not exist substantially. No distinction between substance and attributes can be sustained. This echoes the deconstructive argument of Jonathan Culler: ''What is said to 'ground' a proposition proves to be itself part of a general text.''[44] In the words of the ethnomethodologists, topic and resource are confused. It would not be a false comparison to suggest that Nagarjuna's argumentation in his *Treatise on the Middle Way* is deconstructive. Nagarjuna considers that a condition or cause cannot be such by its own nature. It becomes so in dependence upon the arising of the effect. Why, for example, conceive of a mover who exists independently of movement?; for without the latter there surely is no mover: ''Indeed, how appropriate will be the view that a mover moves? For, a mover without movement is certainly not appropriate.''[45] Similarly, it is foolish to conceive of a seer who sees, for if such a seer were established on its own, one would suppose that it might exist without any seeing: ''As a seeing activity which is presently not seeing is non-existent, how is it justifiable to speak of a seeing activity which sees. . . . The seeing agent does not exist whether it is with or without the seeing activity.''[46] There is only the seeing activity, without origins.

This line of thinking extends to persons, who are falsely conceived as containers for their activities and characteristics; in reality there is no underlying ''essence.'' The self is inscribed in the social text; it does not exist apart from the text. The self is deconstructed only because it already is deconstructed. The analysis only repairs the confusions introduced by an egocentric rationalism.

Conclusion

Aboriginal people and Tibetans decenter the self largely through spiritual practices. Although this is effective for them, such spiritual practices will not serve for contemporary Western civilization. In the West we need to provide reason as a basis—reason is our own spirituality, our own metaphysics, the metaphysics of that which glorifies the 'I think'. To ask us to abandon our tradition of rationality would be more than could be accepted or that would be tolerated. But the question that remains for us is, can we decenter the self enough to establish a new ethical fabric, less self-indulgent and with a more corporate orientation, and at the same time overcome the autocratic rationality that has plagued us through the centuries? This is the ultimate challenge.

From the Greek democracy to our own, rationality has been the foundation of society. It has provided civil authority with its confidence: "And as the man of action binds his life to reason and its ideas, in order to avoid being swept away and losing himself, so the seeker of truth builds his hut close to the towering edifice of science in order to collaborate with it and to find protection."[47] There is no path for us but reason, but already social movements in Europe and America are rejecting logocentric rationalism, not in an irrational or messianic fashion but with a sober post-rationalist orientation. The Earth First! environmental activists, for example, subscribe to a "deep ecology" in which the egoity that founds nature is abandoned. Further, in their statement of twelve principles they soberly include the limits of rationalism in their social program:

> 4) a refusal to accept "rationality" as the only way of thinking; . . .
> 11) a willingness to let our actions set the finer points of our philosophy, and recognition that indeed we must act.[48]

And this group acted the same month these nonprinciples were published: with a kind of postmodern humility, they proceeded to climb centuries-old conifers that were slated for logging, living in them for many days to prevent the saws and bulldozers from removing them. All of the activists were jailed.

Other cultures can only give us insights into the decentering of self; they cannot tell us how to proceed. It should be clear, however, that if there are societies in which the self is decentered to varying degrees, then egocentrism is not inevitable. Such knowledge itself serves to decenter our social imagination. It remains for our own sociology or philosophical anthropology to inspect the path that lies ahead for the West. Perhaps we will be able to locate a new mode of self, one with no other ontological grounds than that we are alive. At any rate, at this stage it is an inquiry to be pursued.

V

The Destabilized Subject

— 12 —

The Subjectivity of the Speaker

Eleanor H. Kuykendall

In recent French feminist philosophies of language there are two conflicting tendencies. The first is to consider uses of language as creating or constituting gender, and the second is to consider biological sex as somehow creating or constituting language. Advocates of the first view, including the existentialist Simone de Beauvoir[1] and the materialist Christine Delphy,[2] have been critical of advocates of the second view, such as the feminist theorists Julia Kristeva,[3] Luce Irigaray,[4] and Annie Leclerc.[5] But Kristeva, Irigaray, and Leclerc, as well as other French feminist theorists who advocate versions of the second view, differ sharply among themselves in their conceptions of the sex of the speaker's subjectivity.

It is my contention that all further attempts of these French feminist theorists to show that the speaker's 'I' is gender-specific—male—or ought to be gender-specific—female—fail at some point. Their alternative interpretations of the speaking subject's 'I' are bewildering: Beauvoir's rational, self-reflective, Cartesian 'I' or 'je'; Kristeva's pre-rational, pre-Oedipal— pre-linguistic—mother-infant bond; or Irigaray's newly feminine 'I' speaking in her own voice. In succeeding sections of this paper I argue that each of these alternatives imposes a systematic ambivalence on the speaker, who must vacillate among these uses of 'I'. First, I compare conflicting analyses of uses of 'I' given by Beauvoir, Kristeva, Irigaray, and Monique Wittig; and second, I examine uses of 'I' in examples of acts of promising given by Beauvoir, Shoshana Felman, and Leclerc. In the third and final part of the paper I conclude that this inquiry into its linguistic origins pushes subjectivity to its limit in an ontology experienced through language, but not through language alone. Speakers both revoke and restore the ontological foundations of its use in each new utterance of 'I', whenever the inevitable inconsistency of that use comes to consciousness.

The Engenderment of the Divided 'I'

There is no question among contemporary French feminist theorists whether the 'I' is divided: everyone agrees that it is. But otherwise their

145

arguments differ, sometimes with reference to the same example. Thus Beauvoir, Kristeva, Irigaray, and Wittig have all given explicit linguistic analyses of uses of the first-person singular pronoun in arguing for the claim that, in speaking, the utterer of the 'I' is fundamentally ambivalent. Yet Beauvoir locates that ambivalence in the gender-neutral vacillation of a self-reflective consciousness searching outward, while Kristeva finds it rather in the subject's eternal return—or retreat—to pre-Oedipal feminine preconsciousness, predecessor of the cognitive 'I'. Irigaray finds in impersonal and passive substitutes for 'I' and 'you', which evoke separation and distance, an ambivalent self-reference—officially gender-neutral but covertly masculine—which catches female speakers between those two alternatives. Wittig, through her rewritten 'j/e', attempts, as she explained recently, to disclose this imposition of masculine consciousness upon the female writer—herself—in order to overcome it. These examples from French feminist theorists outline a complex conflict among their conceptions of subjectivity primarily based on written French, a divergence on the question whether the ambivalence of the speaking subject is a genderless or a gendered condition, and whether or how the speaker must transcend that ambivalence in becoming subjective.

Beauvoir offers us a classic Cartesian introduction to the split subject: individual in its origin, searching outward toward others like it, separate nonetheless from those others:

> The ambiguity of our condition is that we are bound precisely by what separates us. I mean that I am I for myself alone. But each of you is I for yourself alone. It is a common condition to which we are subject in a radically separate way, one from the other. . . .[6]

This conception of subjectivity, in which consciousness is originally separate, makes no distinction of gender, nor does it implicate language in that isolation. But in a passage from *A Very Easy Death,* which Beauvoir wrote at about the same time as the lecture just cited, she describes her mother's anguish in response to a lack of access to language: "At the time when her emotional life was at its most tormented she possessed no doctrine, no concepts, no words with which to rationalize her situation. . . . she *lived* against herself."[7] And in a novel written at about the same time, Beauvoir describes a mother's inability to communicate with her daughter as a failure of language created by her own ambivalence—as the lack of "a common language."[8] Beauvoir's Cartesian, divided subject, separated from itself as well as from language, thereby is transformed into a feminine subject whose ambivalence is created by her lack of access to language. But Beauvoir goes no further in characterizing that mother-daughter ambivalence as specifically feminine; and it is in the uses of language, or *langage,* rather than in the structures of language, or *langue,* that she locates the mother's search for a common language. The ambivalence of Beauvoir's "speaking subject" is not original to it as feminine. The alienation of mother from daughter is simply an aspect of a more profound ambivalence.

By contrast, Julia Kristeva presents an account of a divided subject far removed from Beauvoir's; it is Freudian in its ontology and its ethics. Kristeva's argument transforms Saussure's transparent conception of the linguistic sign in rational discourse into an irrational intervention of the semiotic through written or spoken prosodic structures, or sound. Subjectivity is divided between a feminine, pre-Oedipal, pre-ethical preconsciousness and a masculine, post-Oedipal, separate ego. But it follows from Kristeva's account that the speaker of 'I', who thereby employs a cognitive use of language made possible only by separating from the mother, speaks in the masculine. Feminine communication, which precedes the 'I', precedes rationality and morality as well.

Kristeva's primary concern has been the literary analysis of the subjectivity of *avant-garde* male writers, in whose texts she locates a gap between the communication of the author as individual writer and the communication imposed by the social institution which is language use. In that gap, in certain literary texts, she locates the dissolution of the subject. The dissolution of the subject proceeds, for Kristeva, as a "logic of dialogism" in which, first, there appears a "logic of distance and of relation between different terms of a sentence or narrative structure" and, second, a "logic of analogy and of nonexclusive opposition, in opposition to the level of causality and of identifying determination."[9] The Freudian anti-logic of the first term of this "logic of dialogism," which opposes an analysis of sound—prosody—to that of symbolic meaning, turns that opposition again against the Cartesian/Chomskyan identification of syntax with logic in the second term.[10] The process is continual, dynamic, diachronic, so that the writer of the literary text, through the disintegrated perception of his own subjectivity wrought by that text, thereby transforms himself and the reader together as subjects in process, continually recreating the origins of unconscious knowledge of language.[11]

Although in later writings Kristeva has announced a "heretical" or maternal ethic which she conceives as specifically feminine, she offers no feminine alternative to the ontology of her early "logic of dialogism." It follows, and in several places she argues this point explicitly, that the feminine, which she identifies as semiotic, is the mother-infant bond ruptured in the child's acquisition of the cognitive knowledge of syntax and word meaning taken by Chomskyan linguists to count as language. Kristeva also characterizes feminine consciousness, in Freudian terms, as an outlaw consciousness—irrational, and so outside the rational ethics inaugurated through the child's acquisition of the superego.[12] An "ethics of linguistics," Kristeva argues, ought to make available as linguistic knowledge the communication through sound and gesture of the early mother-infant bond, recreated in *avant-garde* writing.[13] What is communicated is not cognitive information but rather a reaffirmation, through sound and bodily gesture, of the boundariless continuum between mother and infant which it is a necessary condition of Freudian ethics to break. But this conception of the subject in process, which dissolves female subjectivity entirely, fails to answer—indeed it does not attempt to answer—the question of the engenderment of subjectivity as feminine. Rather, it leaves no place for it.

Luce Irigaray, who began her career as a psycholinguist rather than a literary theorist and who has been sharply critical of the Freudian-Lacanian arguments on the unconscious origins of subjectivity embraced by Kristeva, critically examines the dislocation of the 'I' in the impersonal or passive constructions of scientific writing, which pretend to an objectivity which conceals the masculine:

> If I suppress the 'one', 'it', the high-toned impersonals in scientific language, I am often obliged to transform into the passive voice, to acknowledge my affections, to say that I am not an absolute subject, not a pure act. I do not simply order, I am ordered.[14]

For Irigaray my explicit avowal of my own authorship in speaking and writing becomes my moral imperative—and a specifically feminine imperative. For, as she elaborates, in impersonal and passive constructions I cannot presuppose my own agency, for I cannot speak it.

Monique Wittig develops this argument in contrasting her experiment involving a split 'j/e' of *The Lesbian Body* with the English translator's rendition of the split 'j/e' as passive,[15] which she finds inadequate:

> The j/e with a bar in *The Lesbian Body* is not an I destroyed. It is an I become so powerful that it can attack the order of heterosexuality in texts and assault so-called love. . . . This I can be destroyed in the attempt and be resuscitated. Nothing resists this I (or this tu which is its same, its love), which spreads itself in the whole world of the book. . . .[16]

In this argument Wittig is seeking a linguistic revolution available only in the written language, for the 'j/e' with a bar in French can no more be pronounced than can the English 'I' with a bar which is a literal translation of her experiment. But the presuppositions of gender in the speaker's use of the first-person pronoun are more subtle in French, as Wittig remarks in the same article, in that in French past participles and adjectives agree in gender with the sex of the person referred to by the first-person pronoun. In English gendered reference must be made sociologically, since it cannot be done grammatically.[17]

But Anne Zribi-Hertz, who is not a feminist theorist but a linguist, has distinguished between ordinary passives, in which the subject is mentioned, and no fewer than five kinds of impersonal passive constructions in French. In ordinary passives, past participles and adjectives must agree in gender with the subject "acted upon," as in "J'ai été frappée," "l'étudiant a été frappé par le flic," "l'étudiante a été frappée"; or "I was struck," "The student was struck by the cop," "The student was struck." Even impersonal passives can be distinguished among themselves by the oblique mention of a subject in some of the forms, as in "Il a été frappé une étudiante," or "There was a student struck."[18] Irigaray's and Wittig's arguments for the first-person pronoun do not take account of these nuances of the passive, in which my identity as a subject acted upon, or "subject in process,"[19] can be only partially concealed from you. Irigaray and Wittig have not yet shown how in my explicit avowal, in the first person, I can constitute or create myself as gendered, transcending the passive.

The Engendered 'I Promise'

Yet only in direct avowal can I as female subject deconstruct the ambivalent 'I' of traditional discourse, which is masculine, and reconstruct it in my own voice. But my ambivalence—as genderless or as gendered—goes beyond the syntax to my own conflicting moral attitudes toward my use of that syntax—between my sincere intention, and my power to complete the contract with you that, in uttering the words, I undertake.

Traditional speech-act theory is founded, however, on the presupposition of unambivalent discourse, in which, as Austin wrote, "Believing in other persons, in authority and testimony, is an essential part of the act of communicating, an act which we all constantly perform. It is as much an irreducible part of our experience as, say, giving promises. . . ."[20] But promising depends, for Austin, upon the cooperation of the participants; successful promising, he did not say, further depends upon allegiance not only to a linguistic community but also to an ethical community formed by members with compatible goals and powers to act. This community is traditionally presumed to be gender neutral. Yet a recent example of promising given by Beauvoir, as well as specific discussions of the speech-act of promising given by Felman and Leclerc, begin to suggest that my sincerity intersects with my power to carry out the act in subtle ways when your power to act, and mine, are asymmetrical. In certain cases, though not in Beauvoir's, this asymmetry varies by gender.

It appears that Beauvoir is evoking a gender-neutral community when she records, in a poignant passage, an exchange between Sartre's physician and herself once she learned that Sartre's death was imminent:

> "Promise me that he won't know he's dying, that he won't go through any mental anguish, that he won't have any pain!" "I promise you that, Madame," he said gravely. A little later, when I had gone back to Sartre's room, he called me. In the corridor he said "I want you to know that my promise was not mere words. I shall keep it."
>
> [Sartre] did not suffer during the few days that followed.[21]

This exchange has all the appearances of a linguistic as well as an ethical community in which the speakers all have confidence in one another's authority and testimony. The grammatical requirements for promising, according to Austin, are fulfilled: the words were uttered in the first person, present tense, indicative mood. The nonlinguistic appropriate circumstances for promising, according to Austin, are also fulfilled: the physician had the power to ease Sartre's pain, he perceived that his action was in Sartre's interest as well as Beauvoir's, and he uttered the words sincerely. The physician, moreover, expressly assured Beauvoir of his sincerity; it is clear that she had confidence in him; and he did keep his promise.

Upon closer examination, however, the situation manifests a power imbalance. Beauvoir, in her role as nurturer, was at the same time powerless to assure Sartre that he would not suffer. She could only defer to and beseech the physician; the choice and the power to act remained with him. Whether the power imbalance was a matter of gender or simply of the physician's dominance of the patient, the conflict between the physician's intention and his power to cancel or withhold the promised act, as well as between Beauvoir's trust and her powerlessness in the face of both Sartre's illness and the physician's skill, constitutes an ambivalence unacknowledged in analyses of promising that neglect the power relationships between speakers and attend only to their individual and perhaps momentary sincerity.

The critic of such a linkage of gender with power will argue that despite the fact that Western medicine reserves dominance to the male physician, there is nothing essential about either Beauvoir's gender or the physician's in the interaction; and in any case the physician was acting morally. But the morality of Beauvoir's attempt to control Sartre's dying is another question; for however powerless she felt herself to be in the presence of the male physician, Sartre, for once, was more powerless still. By what right did she intervene in his dying by demanding the physician's promise?

The skeptic will counter that it is the institution of promising, and more generally of discourse, that is at stake; for the confidence in "authority and testimony" that Austin assumes as a necessary condition for all sorts of communication, including promising, is not always gender neutral. Beauvoir intervened in Sartre's dying to take a control of their relationship she did not have with him in life. For example, Sartre's collaboration with Pierre Victor, or Benny Lévy, was a source of distance between them at the end of his life, as Beauvoir herself acknowledges in *Adieux*. And Sartre did not always conduct his relationships with other women in the total transparency Beauvoir had portrayed in her own autobiography; for example, he had two volumes of *La Critique de la Raison Dialectique*, I, especially printed with dedications to other women, though all the other copies of that work bore the inscription, "To Castor [Beauvoir]."[22]

Beauvoir had to act indirectly to define Sartre's dying as a relationship with her; and although such indirection is typically feminine, there is still nothing essentially gendered about the physician's promise making, or Beauvoir's promise seeking, or her confidence that he would keep his promise. Confidence in the authority and testimony of promise givers does become gendered, however, in the literary example of the Don Juan legend rendered by Molière, Mozart, and Kierkegaard; and recently reexamined by Felman and Leclerc.

In Molière's version of Don Juan, romantic promises are made to be repeated, and repeatedly broken—so Shoshana Felman has argued. Here the power to break the Austinian presumption of sincerity in communication is masculine; the feminine recipient of the ambivalent promise cannot but be doubly bound, between the ideal of promising incarnate in her confidence in her lover, and its execution in his abandonment of her. By what power does anyone promise or otherwise speak? Is this power a matter of control of access to promising or more generally to discourse? Felman answers that this power is indeed a matter of access to discourse, through the undermining of what its participants presume discourse to create, and themselves to be.

Addressing the last question, Felman writes:

> Every promise promises the completion of incompleteness; every promise is above all the *promise of consciousness,* insofar as it postulates a non-interruption, continuity between intention and act. To the extent that Don Juan embodies the performance of promising as a performance of rupture, he becomes the symptom of the self-subverting power of the performative. Indeed, the Don Juan myth is the myth of the performative only in that the performative, pushed to its own logical consequences, enacts its own subversion.[23]

As Felman's Don Juan undermines the ethical conception of the unambivalently sincere speaker presupposed by Austinian promising, repeating his promises to marry to different women, he recreates himself in his ambivalence as an impure subject, who cannot, as in Kierkegaard's *Purity of Heart,* will one thing. He creates himself as divided, Felman argues, among many women, for "the multiplication of promises brings out the division inherent in the first person. The first person is thus itself subject to the cardinal law of number, that is, to the repetition of breaches. . . ."[24] For Felman, then, the speaker's 'I' or 'I promise' is split both syntactically and morally, reserving ambivalent betrayal for the masculine gender, fidelity for the feminine.

But perhaps speakers of both sexes alternate between the genders. That alternation would constitute a different sort of ambivalence, evocative of Kristeva's conception of the split subject, discussed in the previous section, in that both Felman and Kristeva portray the speaker's consciousness as divided in its lawful and outlaw performances in speaking. But there the resemblance between their positions ends, for it is the feminine, who has not even access to promising, who is outlaw for Kristeva; the masculine, who breaches the order of ethical and symbolic normality, becomes instead outlaw for Felman. In either case, insincerity, as in the inability to resolve ambivalence in promising, is gendered as the power to redefine the institutions of romantic commitment.

Yet Leclerc argues that the masculinity of Don Juan's abuse of his power to promise, and by extension the masculinity of his abuse of discourse, are nothing but literary conventions. The Don Juan of Mozart and of Kierkegaard's "Diary of a Seducer" from *Either/Or* is a stylized figure of love said to be masculine, and certainly a man, but scarcely virile in that he never separates himself from women—never does anything but seduce.[25] There is a "pact of love" between real men and women, Annie Leclerc continues, and this pact is more than the promise of a certain conduct, or the accomplishment of a certain work:

> They promise to renew their promise indefinitely. They promise to keep their promise, but independently of all promises. For their promise does not have to be kept unless it could no longer be offered, to be respected unless desire is there no longer. . . . They swear to each other to be faithful not by faithfulness to a specific pledge but through the unlimited duration of the gesture engaging the pledge.[26]

Leclerc also writes that if the day comes when a lover says, "I don't love you any more," the rejected lover justly may "cry treason," for a love which speaks itself is "the very gesture of the promise."[27]

Both Felman's and Leclerc's opposing interpretations transform the example of a specific speech act, promising, into a description of a continuing commitment, a perpetual dialogue, in which speakers of either sex have to control the terms of communication—to transform or to subvert their acts—so as either to continue the communication or to bring it to an end. My subjectivity is gendered, not in my uttering an isolated 'I', but in my continuing to speak with you when the power relations between us depend on gender. The engenderment of my power to speak cannot be discerned alone in the structure of my words or yours; yet anything other than my first-person 'I', or yours, evades the terms in and by which we communicate.

Engendered Subjectivity Subjectified

I cannot continue this dialogue, then, on its previous terms. I must write in the first person, must avow, unambivalently, my own autobiography, if I take seriously the challenge to become subjective—the moral imperative—that is implied by the positions I have introduced above. But if I take seriously the ontology which supports that imperative, then I must also recognize that as speaker or writer I change over time, as do you. Since we are all subjects in process, I must respect in you as in myself the possibility of mutual transformation as, alone, I speak or write. But if I regard you as separate and distant from myself—especially, if indeed you are very far from me—how can our words transform us? And what has this regard to do with my sex, my gender, or yours?

Beauvoir is inconsistent, urging a practice of reciprocity and mutuality that does not follow from the Sartrian conception of the alientated self she presents elsewhere; in later years she characterizes that mutuality as feminist.[28] Irigaray, however, is emphatic, in writing that in good faith I cannot use 'it', 'one supposes', 'it may be inferred that . . .' to communicate with you when I mean 'I'. My own 'I', Irigaray adds, is necessarily feminine when I speak to you, as Irigaray urges women to do, as "meme" or "same."[29] But how is this possible?

I find it extremely difficult, if not impossible, always to write 'I' to you, when I do not know you: to address you in the first person I must continually go back and revise my own sentences; I fall back into the passivity wrought upon me by the passive and indirect structures I have learned from academic writing. But if I speak to you in English in the feminine, how do you and can you hear me as feminine? Or rather, how can you not so hear me? If my speaking voice, my sex, is my birthright, I speak in the feminine as a matter of course. If I must learn to speak in the feminine as I learned French, the ethical implications of my speaking or writing to you in either language complicate our communication far beyond sound or syntax. And writing is another question.

Si, par example, je t'écris en français, je me te rends étrange, et dès que je t'écris en français, je me récrée dédoublée devant toi. Je suis tombée dans le trou qui m'écarte de ma langue maternelle, pendant que je me ref-ère. If, for example, I write to you in French, I make myself a foreigner to you; and as soon as I write to you in French, I recreate myself as split. I have fallen into the gap which separates me from my native language, while I refer to myself, in written French at least, in the feminine. But most of these gender-specific references to myself in written French disappear when I speak.

Have I not fallen into English, in the same way? If first you spoke French, in what gender do you now read me? If first you spoke English, in what gender do you read me in French? By the participial endings in French I write myself as feminine, and can do no other. By the lack of gendered endings in English I rewrite myself as genderless. Which is more distancing: my transformation from English to French, if first you spoke English, or from my gendered to my genderless affirmation, since you who are my "same" are women? If you speak French, I write French to you in solidarity but as a foreigner; if I write French to you when you cannot understand me, then I write to you also as a foreigner, distancing myself from you. If we both speak both French and English, we comprehend to-gether the abyss between the two languages. In that comprehension we cre-ate another kind of solidarity. Ought I, can I write English in the feminine, in the same way? And in any case ought I, can I write to you that way? And can this writing take the place of speaking?

I feel myself incarnate in the words I write in English, but not engen-dered. In writing 'I' and 'you', I write neither your sex or my own; yet my words are the material of our bond. I type 'I' and 'you' into my computer: as I transform the images on the screen, do I so manifest my subjectivity as feminine? Not in English, though the material of all of my speech or writ-ing informs my communication with you.

Yet I cannot but speak in the feminine, as soon as I pronounce the words in my own voice. Here I reach the limits of my own subjectivity. You or I speak; we come into a contact that our utterances create and sustain. But when we speak—in English or in French—what we say to each other, with each other, depends not alone on English or French; not alone on the pitch and timbre of our speaking voices. What I can say to you, with you, depends on how we recognize one another, through language and beyond. Recognizing one another, we transcend the linguistic structures through which we communicate, sometimes ambivalently, alternating genders; sometimes transparently.

Then I cannot, finally, depend on the syntax of an elusive 'I' or 'je', or of elusively constructed promises, to discern in what gender or genders I speak or write. My 'I' persists as the trace of my own reflection, gendered as it may be. In each new act of speaking or writing to you, with you, I transcend that engenderment and recreate it.

— 13 —

Lacan's Other and the Factions of Plato's Soul

Joseph Grange

The work of Jacques Lacan has transformed the theory and practice of French psychoanalysis.[1] Even more radical is the way in which his thought restores to psychology its philosophical foundations. My purpose is to demonstrate the extraordinary philosophical resonance of Lacan's *"Other"* (his term for the Freudian unconscious).[2] This will be done by employing Heidegger's concept of retrieval (*Wiederholung*) whereby a central moment in the history of philosophy will be deconstructed to show the philosophical ground of the human psyche and its relation to the Lacanian *Other.*

The text selected is Plato's analysis of the factions of the soul in the *Republic* (Book IV, 434–455). This moment in Plato's development contains a vivid and at the same time richly ambiguous statement about the relation between *logos* and the human psyche. Its ambiguity is necessary, for Plato could *not* think through to the end the full import of his teaching. His "unsaid" will be expressed by Lacan. The upshot of this investigation should be the refounding of this question: What is philosophical about psychology? Lacan's *Other,* understood through this retrieval of Plato's thought, provides a stunning answer—everything genuinely psychological must be philosophical.

Why do we select Plato? In a sense our selection is arbitrary, and, if Lacan is correct, every significant thinker must have touched on this *Other,* albeit without full comprehension. Still our concentration on Plato to the exclusion of others is justified in two ways. Plato foretells in an almost eerie fashion the conclusions Lacan will reach some hundreds of years later. More important, Plato sets forth for the classical world and the modern epoch the basic parameters of the structure and function of the human psyche. He, therefore, provides a measure by which the reach and depth of Lacan's teachings can be judged.

In *Being and Time* Heidegger demonstrates the radical temporality of human being (*Dasein*). One consequence of this is the realization that the human self can authentically comprehend itself in its past, its present, and its future. This act of authenticity is accomplished when "It 'fetches' (*-holt*) its self all over again (*wieder-*), and this re-fetching, or 're-trieve' (*Wiederholung*), is the achieving of There-being's [*Dasein*] authentic past, [that is to say,] of the self which already is-as-having-been."[3] Retrieval is therefore the act whereby we own our past and are owned by its meaning. This assumption of temporal responsibility establishes the grounds of our finite transcendence, the very Being of being human. For Heidegger human being is finite inasmuch as it is thrown into a world not of its choosing and immersed in the beings of experience. As such the human self is through and through historical. Transcendence is the other dimension of human being whereby the meaning of this historical deposit is appropriated by the human self and owned up to.

The ultimate meaning of this process of finite transcendence is time, and, therefore, alongside this personal act of authenticity resides the history of philosophy, in particular those moments of self-understanding achieved by the great philosophers. Who are the "great philosophers"? Those who have thought the Being Question through to the limits of their time and self-understanding. Thus: a human self not only has at its disposal its personal history to be retrieved for the sake of authenticity. It can also encounter those moments in the history of philosophy when thinkers have come upon the essential insofar as it relates to the question of Being and being human. Both dimensions—the personal and the historical—are necessary for the achievement of authentic self-understanding. One way the personal level can be encountered is in the psychoanalytic act—listening to the *Other*. The historical is retrieved when a thinker who has touched the Being Question is retrieved in all the original power of his questioning:

> By the re-trieving of a fundamental problem we understand the disclosure of its original potentialities that long have lain hidden. By the elaboration of the potentialities, the problem is transformed and thus for the first time in its intrinsic content is conserved. To conserve a problem, however, means to retain free and awake all those interior forces that render this problem in its fundamental essence possible.[4]

As used in this study retrieval focuses on a moment in philosophy when a thinker most nearly came upon the relation of the self to an other.

An Overview of Lacan's Thought

The Newest Saying:

The unconscious is structured in the most radical way like a language.

Jacques Lacan[5]

Who is Jacques Lacan? Variously regarded as charlatan or genius, psychoanalytic hero or self-interested quack, we leave to others the task of estimating his personal worth, and focus on the central tenets of his work.[6] For the present we restrict ourselves to three aspects: the mirror stage; the relation between language and the psyche; and "The Name of the Father." Once these themes and their interlocking relations are grasped, we can turn to the philosopher we seek to retrieve.

The Mirror Stage

Lacan's thesis is fairly straightforward and can be formulated in this manner:[7] sometime between the ages of six and eighteen months, the infant gains an initial and foundational experience of its own unity by catching sight of its reflection; hence the phrase, "mirror stage." This formative moment serves a dual purpose: it supplies the previously inchoate mass of energy with a form—the image of which will ground the infant's sense of "I." This image, in its turn, will "establish a relation between the organism and its reality—or, as they say, between the *Innenwelt* and *Umwelt*" (E 4). The consequence of this primordial and unavoidable act for the psyche is disastrous, for the infant sees the world askew, and the resultant miscognitions (*mèconnaisance*) will beset the human ego for the rest of its days. Although this "I" is imaginary at the outset, the infant senses its "I" as real and is convinced of its beauty, power, and central position. Thus emerges "the imaginary," one of the triad of worlds that Lacan sees encircling the human psyche. (The other two—the symbolic and the real—will be encountered later.)

Based in the imaginary, this "I" takes on the characteristics of the paranoid: it is "the assumption of the armour of an alienating identity, which will mark with its rigid structure the subject's entire mental development" (E 4). And so we meet for the first time a Lacanian "other," a term that will go through many changes before our study concludes. Its present significance lies in the fact that the "I" sees itself as other but thereby initiates a process of self-identification by falling in love with what it is not. So begins its futile quest for satisfaction in and through the other. This other that it desires is usually the mother who stands in for the intervening environment and its objects. The shift is subtle, various, and little noticed but of excruciating importance. The infant sees all the objects of its world as infested with itself and so desires them as itself. Given this primal scene of miscognition, we can understand better Lacan's sympathetic rendering of the madness of our adult world:

> We can thus understand the inertia characteristic of the *I*, and find there
> the most extensive definition of neurosis—just as the captation of the subject

by the situation gives us the most general formula for madness, not only the madness that lies behind the walls of asylums, but also the madness that deafens the world with its sound and fury. (E 7)

Captation indeed! But soon to become a captation that is really a capitation.

Logos and Psyche

The Oldest Saying:

You would not find out the limits of the psyche, even though you should travel every road: so deep a *logos* does it have.

Heraclitus[8]

Heraclitus tells us that the boundlessness of the psyche is due to the depths of its *logos*. Lacan could not agree more, and in "The Function and Field of Speech and Language in Psychoanalysis"[9] he lays open in the most direct way the reason this is always so: "the unconscious of the subject is the discourse of the other . . ." (E 54). Now what does this mean? It says that the ego—outcome of the mirror stage—does not exhaust the boundaries of the subject. It affirms that there is a realm of speech not at the disposal of the subject which addresses the subjectivity from out of its own origins. It, therefore, tells us the shape, function, and structure of the unconscious: "For interpretation is based . . . on the fact that the unconscious is structured in the most radical way like a language" (E 234). The Lacanian formula—"structured in the most radical way like a language"—is the heart of his contribution to psychology. All the implications, consequences, and elaborations of Lacan's thought arise from this discovery. The true other—or, as Lacan would put it, *the Great Other,* as distinct from the imagistic other of the mirror stage—reveals its essence. It is a *logos* that bears in its being all the lineaments of the laws of language as discovered by modern linguistics.[10] We find the linguistic being of this *Other* etched in the two transformative powers of the dream-work. It will be recalled that Freud discerned two primary ways in which the dream worked to distort its meaning and thereby hide its significance (the latent content) inside its apparent meaning (the manifest content). One way was "condensation," whereby a single image or idea or event acts to collect an entire chain of meanings whose associations can eventually be unraveled. The other was "displacement," where the felt intensity of one idea or image was torn from it and handed on to another idea or an entire chain of associations where the original strength was used up and dissipated. The work of Jakobson supplied Lacan with a way of understanding the linguistic roots of these psychological processes. For according to the *Fundamentals of Language* all meanings relate along one of two fundamental axes—that of combination or that of selection.[11] Combination is represented by the linguistic act of metonymy, where the meaning resides in a contiguity spanning the constituent elements, as in parts and wholes or effects and causes. Selection operates by way of metaphor, where one term is used to replace another. Now it does not take much to see that metonymy and metaphor are the linguistic counterparts of displacement and condensation. Thus on a structural level we have an equivalence between the dream-work and the laws of language.

The evidence for the linguistic base of the unconscious does not, however, stop there. Lacan turns to the work of Saussure to develop further the consequence of this languagelike other.[12] The essence of Saussurean linguistics lies in the relation between the signifier and the object signified, and this relation is entirely arbitrary inasmuch as the word employed for the idea can be different in different languages (window, *fenêtre*, *ventana*). The object signified is dominated by the signifier. Lacan uses the following formula:

$$\frac{S}{s}$$

where S is the signifier, s the object signified, and the bar represents the splitting of the relationship. It is the split that interests us, for it demonstrates graphically how the so-called real things of the world are subject to language for their existence. The conclusion to be reached is that language constitutes a world in which we live and move and have our being. It is *not* ours but we anchor our being in its regions. The extent to which this is true for the human subject will be discussed in the next section, "The Name of the Father." But we should note that not even the material things of this world in all their brute neutrality are immune to the invading power of language. Lacan sketches the following and then provides an amusing but revealing commentary:

LADIES   GENTLEMEN

> A surprise is produced by an unexpected precipitation of an unexpected
> meaning: the image of twin doors symbolizing, through the solitary confine-
> ment offered Western Man for the satisfaction of his natural needs away
> from home, the imperative that he seems to share with the great majority of
> primitive communities by which his public life is subjected to the laws of
> urinary segregation. (E 151)

The point is that not even a wooden object (door) can escape the domination of language. What is signified is barred from direct entrance into our
consciousness. Mediated by language, the signified retreats before language, which through its power lets that which is signified be. To quote
Lacan: "From which we can say that it is in the chain of the signifier that
the meaning 'insists' but that none of its elements 'consists' in the signification of which it is at the moment capable" (E 153). The result of this
combination of psychoanalytic doctrine and linguistic science is a radical
turn for psychology. It is a turning away as well as a turning toward. What
is to be turned away from is any understanding of the human psyche as a set
of instinctual responses to environmental stimuli. Such mechanism or biol-
ogism fails to capture the essence of psyche—its *logos*. The future of psychology—that toward which the Lacanian turn is directed—is the field of
speech, language, and discourse. Hence, the words of the introduction to
the Discourse at Rome: "It is our task to demonstrate that these concepts
take on their full meaning only when orientated in a field of language, only
when ordered in relation to the function of speech" (E 39).

One last dimension of the relation between *logos* and psyche. Because
of the barred relation between the signifier and the signified we are
"forced, then, to accept the notion of an incessant sliding of the signified
under the signifier . . ." (E 154). In the discussion of the mirror stage we
saw the captation of the Ego by its image and foretold it as a "capitation."
This beheading results from the sliding of the signified under the signifier.
How and in what ways this act is carried out is about to be seen. For now,
let us note that the "I" of discourse receives its meaning from what it
signifies. Thus the "I" is an indexical sign of a signifying process whose
meaning does not rest entirely upon the wishes and intent of its author.
There is an *Other* who speaks to me and through me. What happens to the
subject when its discourse originates from another place?; when "The
Other is . . . the locus in which is constituted the I who speaks to him who
hears . . ." (E 141)? The sliding of the signified becomes "the fading of
the subject."[13] This radical ex-centricity of the psyche from its own subjectivity comprises the whole domain of the decentered self. Such heteronymy
is necessary for human growth and development. Its initial stirrings are felt
when the child first discovers language and thereby pronounces the name of
the father.

The Name of the Father

If the unconscious is structured like a language, then it cannot be known until it speaks. This *Other* is spoken by the human subject, and, therefore, the moment of first speech is the crucial moment when the speechless one (*in-fans*) meets the *Other* and capitulates to the *Other's* demand that it be human through speech rather than through the satisfaction of its instinctual desires. The paradigm of this achievement and its significance is Freud's famous story of "the good little boy," where the hiding and retrieval of objects is accompanied by an "o-o-o-o" and an "a-a-a-a," which for Freud were attempts at expressing the German *fort!* and *da!* (disappearance and return).[14] Freud sees in it the great achievement of instinctual renunciation whose cultural significance lies in the child's ability to let his mother go away. But on Lacan's reading much more is at stake. This act of primal speech represents "the games of occultation which Freud, in a flash of genius revealed to us so that we might recognize in them that the moment in which desire becomes human is also that in which the child is born into language" (E 103). What occultation? the magic of language, which allows for presence in absence and absence in presence by constituting a realm of significance within which the human subject can play. Inducted into this realm by owning its speech, the child submits to the demands of culture, renounces its instinctual gratification, and seeks satisfaction through the expression of its desires rather than the actual winning of its wants.

Thus it happens that an entire symbolic domain is superimposed on the natural, and this field of experience is through and through linguistic. Following Levi-Strauss, Lacan writes, "The law of man has been the law of language since the first words of recognition presided over the first gifts . . ." (E 61). Now, we have already seen that language is an arbitrary set of symbols that demands that we play by its rules. In learning to speak, then, we learn to submit to the laws of language and thereby to the laws of culture together with its kinship rules, marriage ties, and hierarchical structures. Thus: "The primordial law is therefore that which in regulating marriage ties superimposes the kingdom of culture on that of a nature abandoned to the law of mating. The prohibition of incest is merely its subjective pivot . . ." (E 66). The entrance into language represents our willingness to bend natural desires in the direction of human culture. And we know that this human achievement has occurred because we can speak about it and acknowledge its success or failure through approval or prohibition. Language, with its fundamental subordination of the signified to the signifier, achieves for humans what they cannot do for themselves: the regulation of desire through the creation of the word.

Why call this law "the Name of the Father"? In the first place, the Oedipal stage, which stands as the entrance to culture, has within its triangle of relations an absent partner, the Father, who like the signifier dominates the instinctual *ménage* by his absence and through that absence makes his (the law's) presence felt. But, more important, it is history that warrants this phrase: "It is in the *name of the father* that we must recognize the support of the symbolic function which, from the dawn of history, has identified his person with the figure of law" (E 67). But why "name of" rather than simply real "father"? Because we are now in the realm of language, which is the equivalent of the realm of law (E 66), and, therefore, the whole scene shifts to an "other" place—the place of the Other which is structured like a language. This brings us back to a previous moment when we mentioned that for Lacan three levels of experience must be acknowledged. The *symbolic* is the level of language, the genuinely human with which we are now engaged. The *imaginary,* which was the subject matter of the mirror stage and whose *relicta* constitute the domain of neurotic symptoms, is a form of inadequate language, a futile style of speech. And *the real* is the not yet symbolized or imaged; that which is impossible as such since it has not yet been articulated.[15] But as this analysis has shown, it is the realm of the symbolic with its linguistic structure and concomitant universal laws that provides the human with its worth. Therefore the human realm (which, after all, it was Freud's self-chosen task to address) is the realm of language. Therefore, also, Lacan can say: "It is certainly this that demonstrates that the attribution of procreation to the father can only be the effect of a pure signifier, or a recognition, not of a real father, but of what religion has taught us to refer to as the Name-of-the-Father" (E 199). This paternal function, now deprived of its genital significance, constitutes the world to be inhabited by the child, who must now channel his wants through the labyrinth of language—a task that will consume its days:

> Symbols in fact envelop the life of man in a network so total they join together, before he comes into the world, those who are going to engender him by 'by flesh and blood'; so total that they bring to his birth . . . the shape of his destiny; so total that they give the words that will make him faithful or renegade, the law of the acts that will follow him right to the very place where he *is* not yet and even beyond his death; and so total that through them his end finds its meaning in the last judgment, where the Word absolves his being or condemns it. . . . (E 68)

By learning to speak, the subject lets the law of culture into its being and, thereby, acknowledges the presence of the *Other.* Henceforth, that

Other will speak through the subject, and the quality of that speech—full, empty, banal, repetitive, strained, serene, delusional, or evocative—will express the level of satisfaction attained by the subject's collaboration with the world of culture.

Now from all this—the mirror stage, *logos* and psyche, and the name of the father—there emerges the most persuasive evidence for the validity of "the talking cure," Freud's first patient's description of psychoanalytic treatment. When we speak, we express our desires. If we refuse to express them—that is to say, repress—then the *Other* will still have its say. It will speak in the form of symptoms, in neurotic styles, or even in delusional madness.[16] Dream analysis, free association, and slips of the tongue are those ways in which, in the analytic setting, the *Other* speaks. Listening to the *Other* is what analysand and analyst do. When the subject can recognize the *Other's* discourse as one's own—in either a forgotten (repressed) or a failed (inadequately felt) or a new (originally felt) way—then this assumption, carried out in speech, of the subject's humanity constitutes the core of one's recovery as a person. To quote Lacan: "The unconscious is that chapter of my history that is marked by a blank or occupied by a falsehood: it is the censored chapter. But the truth can be rediscovered [by psychoanalysis]" (E 50).

There is much more to be said, and a thorough presentation of Lacan's thought would demand that we demonstrate:

> how the basic dynamic of the human subject for Lacan is not libido, as it is for Freud, but desire, as it is for Hegel; how the desire e-rupts in the infant in the rupture of the dyadic, quasi-symbiotic relation with the mother by which the infant experiences in its separation from her the negation of itself, hence, its *manque à être*—its own lack of (or, better, want of) being, out of which its wanting (its desire) is born; how this desire is essentially a desire to be desired, i.e., to be recognized as an object of desire by another; and, finally how the child's desire—its endless quest for a lost paradise—must be tunnelled like an underground river through the subterranean passageways of the symbolic order. . . .[17]

But we have done well to glimpse the major stopping places of Lacan's odyssey, and our task is not to explicate its totality or even justify its claims. We are after its philosophical resonance. We ask: Is there anything in the history of philosophy that, properly retrieved, would lend credence to his views? Does the work of other great thinkers shed light on Lacan's revolutionary rereading of Freud? A fresh reading of Plato strongly suggests that Lacan's *Other* has had a central place in Western thought, albeit a dimly understood one.

Plato and the Factions of the Soul

In the previous sketch of Lacan's thought, the place of the subject as center of conscious thought and action was radically questioned. Its centrality was undermined by its relation to an other that in the mirror stage stood in its place—a place of miscognition. This shift was but a prelude to a more profound relocation—that brought on by recognition of the *Other* when language is acquired. The subject, finally, was seen as a linguistic event that is itself through its self-expression. But this moment of self-manifestation lacks the cheer often associated with autonomy, for, in language, what is signified "slides under the signifier." Thus the I that speaks is not the irreducible source of its verbal manifestation but rather submits to the law of language, thereby showing others more of what it is not (its desires) than what it is (an indexical sign tied to the movement of speech).

This decentered self has its center elsewhere: in the locus of the *Other.* And this *Other,* in its turn, is structured like a language. A fading subject and a speaking *Other,* therefore, constitute the major findings of Lacan that we wish to bring to bear upon Plato's thought.

Of all the strange moments in the history of philosophy none seems so strange as Plato's description of the soul (psyche) in the fourth book of the *Republic*. There we meet a human soul that in its division against itself resembles an inchoate case of schizophrenia. Now, as every undergraduate in philosophy knows, the received tradition takes no notice of this bizarre natal condition. Quickly—much too quickly—Plato's analysis is hacked up into a tripartite soul whose harmonizing is to be brought about by the power of reason.[18] Enthroned as arbiter of the warring factions, reason sets the destiny of Western psychology up to the advent of Freud, who then is regarded as the one who dethrones reason or at least establishes a rival, the unconscious.

But such a conventional view of Plato's thought is unconvincing when read in the light of Lacan's theory and retrieved in the Heideggerian sense of setting free the possibilities of the text. We begin by listening afresh to the tale of Leontius:

> "Leontius . . . was going up from the Piraeus under the outside of the North Wall when he noticed corpses lying by the public executioner. He desired to look, but at the same time he was disgusted and made himself turn away; and for a while he struggled and covered his face. But finally, overpowered by the desire, he opened his eyes wide, ran toward the corpses, and said: 'Look, you damned wretches, take your fill of the fair sight.' "[19]

The traditional interpretation of this story is quite straightforward. A man overcome by desire rebukes his offending organ and at the same time gives it satisfaction. The tale, thus understood, shows both the failure to restrain our desires and the possibility of improvement. This improvement, of course, depends upon increasing the control of reason over the appetite. So goes the received tradition.

But let us look more closely, for the point of the story is to establish that the human spirit is not the same as its desires and that, furthermore, this same aspect of the human person seeks to ally itself with the commanding aspect of the psyche, *logos*. Without this tripartite division, the human being would be reduced to a binary opposition: instinct *versus* reason. Such a condition is the basis of schizophrenia. Double messages destroy the possibility of an integrated personality. Socrates himself provides the interpretation: "Don't we notice that, when desires force someone contrary to the calculating part, he reproaches himself and his spirit is roused against that in him which is doing the forcing; and, just as though there were two parties at faction, such a man's spirit becomes the ally of *speech*."[20]

These two citations require the closest scrutiny, for in them resides the skeletal outline of Lacan's *Other*. We begin by examining the Greek words used by Plato to make his point. First there is *epithumia*, translated as "desires"; then, there is *thumos*, translated as "spirit"; finally, there are in the text variants of *logos* which are translated differently as "the calculating part" and then as "speech" itself. We see at a glance that two parts of the soul are related in the very terms used, *thumos* and *epithumia*, but that the third part has no precise term, and, more wondrous, *thumos* gives itself to *logos* rather than to its cognate, *epithumia*. Now what are we to make of this strange situation? Spirit bends away from that which springs from it (*epithumia*) and aligns itself to a part (*logos*) with which it seemingly has no connection. Why would the human spirit reject its offspring and make common cause with that which is foreign to its being?

Lacan might respond this way:

1. *Epithumia* is an erratic trajectory that signals an emptiness. Thus desire announces a want-to-be and suggests that something is lacking.

2. *Thumos*, often used for psyche itself,[21] is the human drive toward being itself and suggests the inclination toward wholeness and integration that slumbers in the heart of the human.

3. *Logismos* (the word in the text) is that component of the psyche that arrives to lay out the bounds of action. As such it measures out (calculates) the norms whereby the person can achieve a sense of being.

I said that speech "arrives" because both in the story of Leontius as well as in its gloss the happening of speech is never explained. It suddenly takes up the situation and resolves it, either by way of recrimination, as in the case of Leontius, or through direct appeal to *thumos*. The issue can be clearly stated: why does Plato assign to *speech* the task of reconciling the differences between *thumos* and *epithumia*? Spirit (*thumos*) by itself cannot separate itself from its desires (*epithumia*). Its closeness to its own being—desires are an eccentric of spirit—requires an other to arbitrate between these factions. *Logos* lays down the law, and from that standard justice can emerge. Plato emphatically declares that spirit is on the side of speech: "In the faction of the soul it sets its arms on the side of the calculating part."[22]

What are we to make of this *thumos* that is its own being, that sides with what it is not (*logos*), and that struggles against its own effects? Plato provides the answer when he likens *thumos* to a child that, spirited though it be, requires the leavening of that part which calculates in order to be human: "For, even in little children, one could see that they are full of spirit straight from birth, while, as for calculating, some seem to me never to get a phase of it, and many do so quite late."[23] Spirit stands ready to accept the advice of speech and, further, to lend its strength to the voice of this other so that desires do not run away with the soul. Or, in terms already used, Plato is describing that moment when desire becomes human through articulation in speech. The stern tones of the father are to be heard in this last selection: "Doesn't his spirit . . . form an alliance for battle with what seems just; . . . and not cease from its noble efforts before it has succeeded, or death intervenes, or before it becomes gentle, *having been called in by the speech within him like a dog by a herdsman?*"[24]

The speech within him is the law laid down by the name of the father. The clamoring of desires caught in the orbit of their own self-negating drive is stilled by the norms announced by the Other and accepted by the human spirit throughout the ages. From the perspective of retrieval, Plato could not be fully aware of his discovery, and the vacillation between "calculation" and "speech" in his text serves to underscore the unsaid of his doctrine. What remains thoroughly remarkable in Plato's account of the factions of the soul is his steady reliance on speech as the decisive intervener on the side of the human. It is our bias toward reason in its modern forms that leads to the mistaken conclusion that Plato is offering a rational psychology as the solution to human happiness and well-being. But the reason of the *Republic* bears in its being the hallmarks of a speech that is heard by the human spirit as coming from a place not its own. Further, this speech breaks up the homology between spirit and desires, sending the latter packing and calling spirit to its destiny. Justice, the Good, and human happiness depend upon this speech for their being. Finally, whatever hope there is for human integration depends entirely upon this discourse of the other. Its ascendant place in the Platonic soul is clearly marked and its power equally well defined. When heard, the human spirit hearkens to its call. Its deep appeal to the human spirit and its capacity to dispel, at least for a time, thralldom to desire are the signs of its otherness. Without this other that for Plato is a discourse to be heard by the human spirit, there would be no beauty, no harmony, and no drive toward that which separates the human from the animal.

In sum, Plato offers us a psyche split between its desires and its drive toward wholeness and justice—a psyche that must be called back to its own being by a speech that is within it but not at its disposal. Now, even the most casual reader of Plato's text must be struck by the tenuousness of the relations between the factions of the soul. It seems as though this soul could be exploded by the slightest breeze of desire; in fact, its own being (*thumos*) seems to be radically threatened by its own effects (*epithumia*). But the term, explosion, does not adequately describe the perils of the psyche. If we look once more at the Greek words, we can identify clearly wherein lies the most dire threat to psyche's well-being. The trajectory announced by desire is of a distinct kind: its movement is caught by the preposition, *epi,* which in its most radical sense means "upon."[25] Thus the trajectory of desire always comes to rest upon a place. Desire in its want-to-be fixates itself and settles into a place that satisfies. This downward fluttering of *thumos* lets spirit fall down, rigidify, and in effect petrify its being. The armoring of spirit cancels its ability to move, change, and participate in the world. It is not an explosion of itself that threatens psyche but rather an implosion whose congealed energy restricts spirit's drive toward being-in-a-world. The neurotic style is characterized by being "stuck"—an impassive solidity that is the soul's only defense against the presumed hostility of the world. Spirit has come to rest (*epi/thumia*) upon an object that freezes all sense of interaction.

Logos, on the other hand, never lets spirit (*thumos*) fixate itself; never—so to speak—lets it down. Lacan tells us why: "We can say that it is in the chain of the signifier that the meaning 'insists' but that none of its elements 'consists' in the signification of which it is at the moment capable" (E 153). In other words, the peculiar property of language is that meaning rolls through it. There is never a place upon which meaning permanently settles. Contrary to desire, which drives *thumos* downward into a place (*epi/thumia*), *logos* (language) drives *thumos* beyond itself, stretching the meaning of its being. Language, therefore, breathes life into spirit and turns it upwards from the corpse of desire whose bloated visage Leontius's speech rightly condemns.

Finally, we must ask about the tension between *thumos* and *logos.* Why is it that spirit, though it naturally aligns itself with *logos,* does not always heed its call? The answer would seem to be in the mirror stage, where the ego, assuming its alienating identity, also takes up fear as its basic posture.

To defend its own being, however misunderstood, the ego focuses upon its desires and with all the insistent clamor of the child seeks a fixed point as the fulfillment of its own emptiness. The conclusion should be obvious: the ego can never be the center of meaning nor can its incessant cries ever be satisfied. When does genuine meaning arise? When cries are converted into language and the process of education begun. Thus the Socratic project of a unique paideia for the citizens of a healthy city-state takes on new meaning. The harmony to be wrought from the war between the factions of the soul is not to be won by the triumph of reason. That harmony, hallmark of the Good, is experienced through language, which, when acquired, speaks the boundaries of desire and delivers over spirit to its destiny: to move into the world through incessant spirals of meaning. These orbits of significance do not end but expand and contract with the rhythms of our cultural milieu. Thus consciousness awaits its expansion from the treasure of language—a dispensation that is not always forthcoming.[26]

The human self is a linguistic event that Lacan characterizes as ''rings of a necklace that is a ring in another necklace made of rings'' (E 153). Serpentine, annular, coiling into interlocked patterns of meanings: such is the fabric of psyche when Plato is retrieved in the light of Lacan's work.

The *Logos* of Psyche

We conclude by bringing together into their original unity the oldest and the newest sayings concerning the soul and language. In so doing a glimpse of the meaning of the self and its potential for being will be had— little more than that can be accomplished at this time. Two sayings, separated by some 2500 years, address the psyche in similar ways.

Heraclitus says: ''You would not find out the limits of the psyche, even though you should travel every road: so deep a *logos* does it have.'' The soul is boundless because of the depths of its possession by *logos*. Why do boundaries vanish when the *logos* of psyche is understood? *Logos* is not a thing or entity that can be defined and limited. Rather it is that clearing within which beings come to meaning. Lacking any boundaries, its depth is an unfathomable abyss.[27] Such is Heidegger's understanding of *logos,* and it is worthy of consideration that even in his earlier period Heidegger maintained that speech, *rede, logos* is a unique existential structure of the human being.[28] The relation between *logos* and the human being is, therefore, an essential and binding one.

Heidegger lays down what is at stake when human beings speak:

> To say is *legien*. This sentence, if well thought, now sloughs off every-
> thing facile, trite, and vacuous. It names the inexhaustible mystery that the

speaking of language comes to pass from the unconcealment of what is present, and is determined according to the lying-before of what is present as the letting-lie-together-before. . . . The *logos* by itself brings that which appears and comes forward in its lying before us to appearance—to its luminous self-showing.[29]

When, therefore, human beings speak, they announce themselves as that moment of mortal disclosure that lets beings, including themselves, be present in their self-showing. And human beings do this by yielding to *logos* which "by itself" lets this domain of meaning declare itself. So the saying of Heraclitus declares that the psyche can never be defined because it belongs not to itself but to *logos,* that other region where Being shows itself. The destiny of psyche—its health and its very being—becomes transparent. To be human is to be "the shepherd of Being" and thereby safeguard language as Being's house.[30] The oldest saying tells us that psyche is not its own but belongs to an other: to logos, the act of "collecting which brings under shelter."[31]

But in terms of the human person: what is brought under this shelter? The newest saying tells us that "the unconscious is structured like a language." Keeping in mind the main tenets of Lacan's teaching, we see how this newest saying bears upon the sheltering of the person. The unconscious is not a surdlike cesspool of repressed drives. Nor is it the bastion of the irrational, unknowable, and removed from the realm of human discourse. Rather, it, too, "rules unnoticed" and its call to our being invites us to assume the full speech that defines our ownmost potential for being. This is "the speech within" that calls us back to our selves—a self, paradoxically enough, that requires an other for its well-being. Without language we would never experience *human* desire. Our life, like the animals, would be given over to the gratification of instinct. Through language we can *express* our desires and, thereby, gain a foothold into the human. Furthermore, language as the bearer of human limits lets lie before us the proper way to be. It sets the conditions of desire but at the same time lets that desire be expressed. Language, therefore, is also the shelter of the human—through it we live and have our being. Without language, we are dumb in the root sense of absurd—without meaning and therefore nonsensical.

I said at the outset that the most radical consequence of Lacan's thought was that he once more made psychology philosophical. Heidegger sums up most dramatically the result of Lacan's work for psychology. Writing before Lacan, he states:

> That saying as laying ruled unnoticed and from early on, and—as if nothing at all had occurred there—that speaking accordingly appeared as *legein,* produced a curious state of affairs. Human thought was never astonished by this event, nor did it discern in it a mystery which concealed an

essential dispensation of Being to men, a dispensation reserved for that historical moment which would not only devastate man from top to bottom but send his very essence reeling.[32]

And that is precisely Lacan's point! The human essence is through and through linguistic. Such an understanding of psyche "devastates man" from top (the realm of reason) to bottom (the realm of drive, instinct, and the somatic functions). Indeed, we are sent reeling but the careening of this decentered self has a road map, protean though it be. It is into the loops of language that we reel and the spool of our being is wound into those rings of a necklace that is itself a ring in another necklace. Reels on reels that make up our humanity.

What, therefore, is philosophical about psychology? We have retrieved Plato's analysis of the soul by way of the work of Jacques Lacan, seeking to establish a free space within which the possibilities of Plato's text could play. The most direct answer to our question is: everything about psychology is philosophical, for the very word itself asserts that the *logos* of psyche is its subject matter. This *logos* is spoken in various tones and registers throughout the twistings and turnings of the history of Being. We have set free only one instance of its unfolding, albeit a crucial one heard at the inception of the classical Greek period. In so doing we glimpsed the staying power of Heraclitus's oldest saying. The *logos* of psyche is the subject matter proper to psychology. All attempts at reductionism are laid low by these ancient words. To set a governing principle from whence human behavior ensues is to let the spirit of psyche fall down to the level of instinctual response. The *epi* of *thumos* cannot be the goal of psychology: its *logos* can never be pinned down, found out, and exhausted.

What lies ahead for psychology if it regains its origins and once more becomes philosophical? Certainly, the validity of Freud's "talking cure" is restored. What passes between analyst and analysand is a privileged hearing of the *logos* of psyche. To speak the *Other* as one's own is to be healed of the curse of egoism. The suggestive force of Lacan's insights reaches still further. Today, attempts at "mind design,"[33] the construction of artificial intelligence through the use of computer analogs, dominate academic psychology. As that science inches toward a successful pass of the Turing test, it would do well to remember the deep ambivalence of Plato's "speech within." As our translator's cautious hesitancy between "calculating part" and "speech" reveals, patterns of information might very well have more to do with the disclosive power of *logos* than with the binary power of cybernetic operations. If so, efforts to duplicate human consciousness will amuse and even dazzle but will fall down exactly where thought begins:

''Speech, in the speaker, does not translate ready-made thought, but accomplishes it.''[34]

Merleau-Ponty's words call us back to the purpose of this essay. We set out to demonstrate the deep philosophical resonance of the work of Jacques Lacan. As a case in point we sought to retrieve in a Heideggerian way Plato's understanding of psyche. Surely, Lacan has been able to say something which Plato could only murmur. What now stands before philosophy is the work of restoring to psychology its concealed origin in *logos*. The development of that origin is the task of those thinkers who would shy from the bewitchment of the new in order to stir once again the roots of philosophy's ancient love affair with Psyche. Unlike Cupid, whose desire engendered fateful consequences for Psyche, philosophy can let lie forth without the cupidity of presuppositions the open region wherein the *Other* speaks to the human being's essence. Psyche is far better loved by such a *logos*, and, like any authentic love affair, such a science would indeed be one of ''perpetual beginnings.'' Among such beginnings I would list three questions. They are unanswerable here but serve to sum up the results of this attempt to raise again the question of psychology's relation to philosophy:

First, is the inevitable recursiveness of language, based on its antithetical, binary structure, the reason why desire can continue to thread its way through the underground caverns of the *Other*?

Second, would a conception of the self along the lines of a linguistic event, driven by desire yet endowed with memory, grant a more authentic access to the question of the meaning of a person?

A response to both questions would go a long way toward explaining the overwhelming sense of evocation experienced by those who hear the opening words of the great epic of our age:

> April is the cruellest month, breeding
> Lilacs out of the dead land, mixing
> Memory and desire, stirring
> Dull roots with spring rain.[35]

Memory, desire, and language—a reprise of the great themes of Lacan's work. *The Waste Land,* signature of our time, epic without heroic person, bears us along the dry bed of its language until we hear *What the Thunder Said: ''shantih, shantih, shantih.''*[36] Is it then a mere literary conceit that Lacan concludes his ''Magna Charta of the new movement in psychoanalysis''[37] with the same words? This, our third and final question freezes in a single frame the poetizing thought of Heidegger, the divided soul of Plato listening to the speech within, and the Name of the Father. For what the thunder said was ''da, da, da.''

Psychology would do well to think this word image through to the end. That end would enlighten it by demanding a return to its beginnings in the oldest saying of Heraclitus, "the dark one."

14

Space, Time, and the Sublime

Dorothea Olkowski-Laetz

Let me begin by establishing a contrast. On the one hand, there is philosophy with its words, concepts, and categories for rigorous thought. On the other hand, there is the chaos of life and culture, the dispersion and fragmentation of life and thought that seem to define the twentieth century. Since technology and politics have so little time to spare, art and philosophy, typically the most gratuitous sectors of modern culture, are left with the task of cleaning up the cultural dispersion. As philosopher and art historian Donald Kuspit notes: "It's a case of bringing together a pair of weak planks in an attempt to make a strong one."[1]

Yet both philosophy and art have been grateful for the "legitimization." Attending to this problem raises them above the fragmentation and commercialization of culture. Art can turn its back on streetcar graffiti, Picasso prints, designer sheets, gallery openings. Philosophy can ignore or condemn religious cults, EST training, and the autobiographies of movie stars. Together art and philosophy retire to the library to wrestle one another.

Typically, philosophy has emerged as the victor in this match. The power of logical formulations, of categorical thinking, the sheer presence of language have all worked in philosophy's favor. At the very least, philosophical utterances place the world in spatial and temporal orders that pretend to clarity and simplicity. Philosophy participates in the culture that rejects it by policing all other aberrant forms. Curiosity becomes a criminal act.

The struggle between philosophy and art already surfaces in the aesthetical writings of Immanuel Kant. As such, they reveal a dichotomy, a division in which each side operates according to its own rules, its own logic. There is the philosophical judgment of beauty which is without cognitive or moral interest, yet which, like those interests, must have universal agreement based on an educated taste. What is important about the judgment of the beautiful is that it requires only a slight change of perspective for such a judgment to become a judgment of an object, that is, an act of cognition. But there is also the other side of this division. There is the sublime. No object of nature is sublime. No sensible form can contain the sublime.[2] This means that the sublime, unlike the beautiful, is unable to be presented and cannot even be thought in terms of the sensible intuitions of space and time, insofar as it exceeds all intellectual presentation, space and time.

The point here is that philosophy, even while pointing them out, tends to ignore dichotomy and division, sublime tangents, for the sake of clarity, simplicity, and beauty. Realizing this loss of control over its own meaning, contemporary art has worked precisely in the opposite direction. It has worked to exploit the difference between what is legitimate in philosophy and its own materials, that is, between logical discourse and paint, dialectic and earth, deconstruction and junk. It has called for a thought that orients itself according to the demands of the work of art and not according to those of logical analysis.

Contemporary visual arts are not matters of rationally determined knowing but of visual intelligibility. This intelligibility may not be separable from talk about it but does not depend upon discourse. The work of art presents its case in its own terms: the concreteness of the individual art work, its differentiated nature, its essential untranslatability into a discursive system that would seek to make sense of it while deforming or policing it.

Take, for example, Franz Hals (1580/85–1666), the Flemish artist who, André Malraux claims, inaugurated the conflict between painter and public that continues into modern art. Hals is not concerned with painting representations, faithful likenesses of individuals. He is not concerned to reflect the values of the ruling class by exalting the individual. Hals transforms his models into paint.[3] He uses pure, individual brush strokes which become the subject of his paintings. He divides the surface into definite areas of light and dark. He offers a merciless vision of reality with the immediacy of a sketch. And in these paintings nothing happens, there is no story to tell, no time, no scene.

We see this again in the work of Jan Vermeer (1632–75) where single figures pause in their daily tasks. We notice not the story that has been interrupted but rather the detachment of the painted image from anything with which the viewer may try to identify. Instead of a story, there are pure blocks of colored surfaces. They glisten across the canvas in patterns that draw us into the two-dimensional surface in a manner that is physically impossible.

In Vermeer's painting "The Letter" (1666), rectangles predominate in the floor and also in the mantle, in the paintings set behind the figures, in the solid shapes of bodies, and in the negative space of the open doorway. Thus there are no undefined or empty spaces. All the shapes on the canvas interlock, and sight weaves across them following the textures of the paint into a place of great beauty and order, created purely on canvas. Clearly the supreme value here is painting. Art is not a story with space and color added. It stands on its own, a thing apart.

By contrast, let us look at another artist of the era, Jean-Baptiste Greuze (1725–1805). His contrived genre paintings serve primarily to glorify contemporary culture.[4] They represent the idealized "natural" virtues and honest sentiments of the ordinary people, glorifying their alleged simplicity. This is accomplished by treating the canvas in a radically different manner. The space of the paintings is relatively flat. The Renaissance illusion of depth has been replaced by the small scene, defined by walls like a stage. The contrived lighting is predictable in its imitation of natural light coming in through the window. The figures are caricatures or types. Greuze borrows from Hogarth's morality plays, but lacks his wit and intelligence in depicting scenes of lower and middle-class family life that are full of "natural" virtues, in contrast to the immoral aristocracy.

The question we might ask is, what had taken place to produce this change? Michel Foucault refers us to a change in the order of *knowing*. Renaissance discourse presupposed a similitude between words and things such that language was taken to be a thing in nature,[5] that is, each thing signifies to the extent that it resembles something else and so makes possible knowledge of the unseen through the seen. So for Renaissance painting, the body is the simulacrum of the soul, the visible of the invisible, the seen reflection of the spiritual reality that guides the body's movement and change.[6] Knowledge is a matter of deciphering the signs, interpreting the meaning of each resemblance, affinity, similitude.[7]

Painting in the Renaissance made ample use of foreshortening, that is, some parts of the image are diminished because perceivers do not actually see everything with perfect distinction. Since what is farthest from the perceiver is smallest, it had to be painted or sculpted proportionately larger in order to appear to be the same size as the rest of what is seen. But by the sixteenth century, painting was called upon to be planar, symmetrical, conceptual, to convey more intelligible and less optical images.[8] Similitude was replaced by rationalism, the intuition of simple natures successively combined in terms of order (simple to complex) and measurement (identity and difference).[9] Language was no longer taken to be a thing in the world but became the means of re-presenting things and what could not be represented rationally, in terms of order and identity, could not be known.

When a representation of a sensory impression appeared more like a previous one than like any other, that original representation could be recovered only in another representation. This is the very creation of Western temporality. Time is nothing but the recapture of the now, the forever-lost original in another representation. To name is to represent these representations by means of a sign that has no content or function other than to represent.[10]

Thus, Foucault points out, drawing is the first example of a sign offered by the French grammarians of the "Logique de Port-Royal." In a drawing the surface of the paper as material is effaced. The two-dimensional qualities of paint or pen as materials are ignored for the sake of what is pictured according to an ordered calculus of representation.

It is in this context that we encounter the staged narration of Greuze as well as the historical representations of Jacques Louis David: the representation of noble and serious human actions laid out in advance—relying on myth or Roman history for their models—in a homogeneous pictorial space like that of the stage. David's figures are solid and immobile, but enhanced by realistic details (hands, feet, textures of material). In David's painting "The Death of Socrates" (1787), Socrates is shown about to drink the hemlock. He serves as an example of ancient virtue and as the founder of the cult of reason; he is a model for the era of rationalism. Similarly, the painting "Marat" serves as a public memorial to the murdered hero of the French Revolution, combining a devotional image with an historical account.

In this context signs selected from out-of-doors, from "nature," were thought to be limited and inconvenient, impossible to master, rudimentary sketches at best. Artist Claude Lorraine's (1600–1682) idealized landscapes won him great favor, for in these depictions the rationalized order is disguised with nostalgia, sweetness, the impossible serenity of idealized landscapes occupied by happy herders, grazing animals, leafy vegetation. The reality of the surface as something painted is lost. Reality is confined to the limits of the frame, the general, the typical, the rational.

Lorraine's fresh and compelling wash drawings serve only as the raw material for the contrived studio landscapes. In the drawings, there is no attempt to render the scene according to accepted codes of clarity, balance, or restraint. There is only the vibrancy of the ink wash, detached from the expectations of representation. It is a site in which every image blends into the next, unifying the surface without differentiations or hierarchies of order, without representation.

Like these drawings, Kant's *Critique of Judgment* offers an alternative site detached from the categories of representation. It is not the intuition of the beautiful that provides an alternative to representation, because "in the case of a given intuition [or the beautiful], this faculty of the imagination is considered as in agreement with the faculty of concepts of understanding or reason."[11] This means that there is agreement of imagination and concepts, the condition of objectivity, the condition of logical judgments and discursive reason, even though there is no concept.

Kant makes it clear that only the sublime is unsuited to our presentative faculty, thus not conditioned by the logic of concepts. No object of nature as mechanism in accordance with laws is sublime. The sublime is "nature in its chaos or in its wildest and most irregular disorder and desolation."[12] It is nature outside of discourse, nature regarded not as mechanism (nature thought in accordance with laws) but as art, that is, art when it appears to be free from all constraints of rules, from all agreement of rules.[13]

The ultimate inability of imagination to reach the absolutely great in a progressive temporal apprehension results in a feeling of pain. But for reason the sublime is the feeling of pleasure that arises when imagination proves to be nothing in comparison with the ideas of reason. Because the sublime is painful with regard to the inadequacy of imagination, it is also violent with regard to internal sense. The time series, the flow of elements as successively apprehended, is the condition of internal sense. But the effort to receive, in a single intuition, the measure of magnitude requiring "unimaginable" time to apprehend, *annihilates* the condition of time, doing violence to internal sense. What should be given in the temporal series is given all at once as coexistent, and time is eliminated.[14] An intuition of the absolutely great, the sublime, would mean the end of time and of space (insofar as, for Kant, space is derived from time), the end of representation as the play of the time series, the end of the object and the impossibility of bringing anything to presentation by means of representation.

But this sense of the sublime results in a mode of thought that is highly problematical. Jean Francois Lyotard notes that the sublime, as the failure of imagination to present an object that might correspond to a concept, results in a pleasure *mixed* with pain, insofar as understanding and imagination are never reconciled, and pain *mixed* with pleasure, insofar as we hope to reconcile them someday into a *true unity*.[15]

The failure of knowledge to represent an object that is sublime is also a failure of judgment, for it makes the formation of taste and the appreciation of beauty an impossibility. We are left confused, celebrating the powerlessness of representation, glorifying the power to conceive,[16] but immersed in a world without reality. Is it the function of the sublime to invent conceptions that are unpresentable, to conceive of utopia, or can this concept be reinterpreted in the light of some modern and much contemporary art?

Art historian Robert Rosenblum notes that within the northern Baroque tradition of sea-painting, Caspar David Friedrich's (1774–1840)

"Monk by the Sea" (1809) strikes an alien and melancholic note, strange both for the presence of "so dense, so haunting and so uninterrupted an expanse of somber blue-grey light above a low horizon" and for the disturbing absence of any conventional components of marine painting.[17]

The painting is empty of representation, startling in that there is nothing to look at, only a single small figure facing an undifferentiated, homogeneous horizon and a bare, grey-green sky; a monk standing "on the brink of an abyss unprecedented in the history of painting."[18] The territory under observation here exceeds and counters the seventeenth and eighteenth-century commitment to order, rationality, discourse. It corresponds to what Kant calls the sublime: the formless, groundless realm of the absolutely great unable to be presented by consciousness because it is too large for either imagination or concepts.

Such a scene may be encountered in paintings of indeterminately huge expanses such as Friedrich's "Monk . . . ," J. M. W. Turner's "Sunrise with Sea Monster" (c. 1840–45), James Ward's "Gordale Scar" (1811–15), or Frederic Church's "Niagra Falls" (1857). But other artists participate in this countermovement by other means, equally sublime.

Phillip Otto Runge's "Hulsenbeck Children" (1805–06) is a closely observed image of three monstrously sized children.[19] The three fill up the entire canvas with their seemingly overgrown bodies, huge faces, and abundant energies. The space of their activity is a rejection of the ideal and measured world. The children are nearly as tall as the huge sunflowers. They loom above the white picket fence that surrounds the fields but leaves them free. Following representational principles, the town and house recede toward the horizon. Yet counter to those same principles, the girl's hand reaches out toward the house and town, and she appears ready to pluck up one of the buildings like a toy. Similarly energized children and flowers appear in other of Runge's paintings and later, in the work of Vincent Van Gogh (1853–1890). Van Gogh explodes the scale of rational hierarchies of size, painting against logic, indifferent to prettified and sentimentalized images, concentrating instead on flowers, children, and fields as images imbued with a tough energy that frightens,[20] given its vitality and the gigantic proportions these images assume in relation to the picture plane.

For both artists, these paintings have figures, but they are not representations, that is, they are not narratives set in the idealized space and time of imagination and reason. No concepts or categories enframe these images; they do not imitate nature as we "know" it. Rather, they may be called sublime images of energy and power, additional phenomena in the world, the creation of worlds, objects without categorically logical discourse but not without sense. They are art as the site of the dissolution of discourse, dissolving its spatial and temporal categories.

Perhaps the extreme of this dissolution was formulated in 1918 when Kazimir Malevich painted a work titled "White on White," a pure white square posed upon a pure white painted canvas. It is the final and perhaps most definitive disengagement of painting from the space-time continuum. Nothing painted on nothing, an event on a surface that does not signify yet responds to painting, to its insistent questioning of space, time, and discourse. The space-time continuum is eliminated in favor of a white ground that suggests an infinite surface, without any sense of scale, time, or other reference points.[21]

Other of Malevich's paintings show brightly colored geometric forms floating. Their diagonal placement suggests continual motion without representing motion. These simple colors and shapes change and create new forms subject to different kinds of classifications in relation to the artistic, personal, social, and historical factors involved in their creation. This dissolution of the spatial and temporal framework is the collapse of the logical, discursive sequence imposed upon the pictorial.

In paintings such as "Foxes," the artist Franz Marc (1880–1916) collapses time and space by bursting the animal form apart so that different parts of the animals' bodies appear scattered all over the surface of the canvas as though on a kaleidoscope in facets of form-shaping color.[22] The red pointed shape of the fox's head functions as the fundamental pictorial element. It is repeated, fades away, then is taken up in other colors and other places, sweeping across the painting, dissolving narrative sequence, the story, idealization, representation, and offering instead a surface unified by the vibrant motion of repetition of form that is color. "Matter," said Marc, "is something that man still puts up with but disavows."[23]

None of Marc's paintings seek to be representations of rationally organized reality. The world is instead inhabited by colors, forms, recognizable things refracted, juxtaposed, broken up, competing with one another but also mutually influencing one another, eternally repeated though never identical. Thus "Tyrol" includes at least three suns and three moons, unlimited refractions that may be color or form, or that may be mountains, sky, or fields, and the pictorial elements arise unsteadily from the values of the colors that form interpenetrating spatial strata.

At first glance, it seems that the Kantian notion of the sublime (inherited from Longinus, Boileau-Despreaux, Burke) acknowledges the "agitation" present in these paintings, the tension between imagination's weakness and the tremendous power of concepts. In the *Critique of Judgment,* section 28, "Of Nature Regarded as Might," Kant says that it is in the immensity of nature and in the insufficiency of our faculties to take in a standard proportionate to the aesthetic estimation of the magnitude of its realm, that we encounter a feeling of pleasure arising from pain. The gap between what can be conceived and what can be imagined kindles this pain, while it engenders pleasure in the immense power of ideas.[24] In feeling the sublime, we encounter our limitation, our *finitude*. Visual pleasure reduced to zero permits an orientation for thought no longer limited by the demands of discursive reason.

But, unfortunately, this is not all Kant anticipates with the notion of the sublime. Insofar as the aesthetic of the beautiful guarantees the development of moral ideas and produces a rational superiority with regard to the sublime, leading us to picture nature (as art) as without power over us, for Kant, the recognition of radical finitude is delayed. Even while no concept of an object can be applied to aesthetic judgments of the sublime, and we necessarily encounter detachment from the representation of the empirical contents of perception, from the rational categories and the discourse of reason, art remains subverted to moral ends. As such, art and the sublime only have value ''as a useful instrument in the realization of an end having substantive importance outside the sphere of art.''[25]

Indeed, we can see this operating in the work of Futurist painters like Picabia, Marinetti, Severini, and Balla, who saw themselves as the founders of a new series; they were the utopian phase, an arena of agitation, and the preparation for revolution in the arts. Enraptured by the machine age, the Futurists declared a new era of violence, energy, and boldness, a harsh demand for modernism.

The surfaces of their canvases are filled with overlapping planes, dramatic contrasts in shapes and colors, openly structured compositions where mass and space dissolve into lines of speed and force, diagonal thrusting lines carrying rapid physical and psychological movement. They saw the future as a universally dynamic continuum of all elements of life and culture, eliminating alienation, isolation, elitism. No doubt, the Futurists wanted their art to contribute to a large degree to the development of individual sensibilities to the point where every member of society would feel part of this unified whole.

Piet Mondrian (1872–1944) took this reorientation of perceptions one step further. He severely limited his colors to black, white, red, yellow, and blue; he restricted his forms to straight lines, squares, and rectangles, producing flat, two-dimensional designs in which no single portion of the surface is more important than any other. By reducing the complexities of nature to these simplest of elements and posing them on his canvas in an equilibrium of opposites, nature's chaos is subdued to the canvas, and each component exists only as part of a relationship. Typically, the images on Mondrian's canvases run off the edge, into the space of the viewer, giving the appearance that every relationship is only a fragment of a larger whole: that of the canvas or that of the universe.

Mondrian's late works, painted in New York after the artist fled from Europe in 1940, are a celebration of the ideal patterns and energies of the city. The surface is not so much a street plan as it is a field of connecting energies, a divided field of twinkling intersections dissolving all discursive categorizations in a show of color and form that is completely modern, like the syncopated neon lights in Las Vegas or Los Angeles that have become the true reality in those cities.

Like the Futurists, Mondrian embraced dynamism, energy, everything absolutely new and liberating. The world was created anew but on the model of a geometry and rationality that had held Western thought in its grip since the seventeenth century. While seeming to step outside the boundaries of the conditions of objectivity, logical judgments, and discursive reason, these utopian artists actually reinforced these conditions of representation. Dynamism in the machine, energy in the total abstraction, remained subject to rationalism, and so to significational norms, that is, like the Kantian aesthetic, it remained useful, subverted to some purpose outside itself. The insights acclaimed on the canvas's surface by Vermeer, Hals, Friedrich, Malevich, Marc seem to have been lost. If the meaning of the sublime is to realize ideas, to make ideas real, this requires that art be ''de-humanized,'' freed of ''man,'' freed of the real. However, this era of abstract rationalism in modern painting remains entirely problematic insofar as, given its moral aims, it can be linked to the restoration of ''man'' as a center, to the unity of discourse or to the unity of the field of knowledge; while, given its sublime surfaces, it is often condemned for fragmenting all three.

Jean François Lyotard attempts to offer a solution to this dilemma. He claims that even though there is no intuition of what is absolutely great, there is the ''abyss,'' the fear and threat that in nature or in art, *nothing* will happen. Lyotard traces this interpretation back to Edmund Burke's *Philosophical Enquiry on the Sublime.* Says Lyotard, ''Terrors are linked to privations. . . . What is terrifying is that the 'It happens that' will not happen, that it will stop happening.''[26] For Burke, the sublime is the result of this terror mixed with pleasure, that is, it occurs where the terror-causing threat is suspended, distanced by art.

''Thanks to art, the soul is returned to the agitated zone between life and death, and this agitation is its health and its life. For Burke, the sublime was not a matter of elevation . . . but a matter of intensification,'' an intensification produced by the avoidance of representational and mimetic models and the shock this avoidance constitutes. Rather than subverting the sublime to moral ends, Lyotard would remain in the negative state of secondary privation (terror) where ''the spirit is deprived of the threat of being deprived of light, language, life.''[27] In this ''agitated zone'' between life and death, the spirit quests for the intensification of effects, and is continually "shocked" by the aesthetics of the sublime into the recognition that something is happening rather than nothing.

But does the notion of the threat of privation account for the "sublime" images of Vermeer, Hals, Friedrich, Malevich, Marc? Is our rapture in confronting these paintings nothing but a negative delight in not being subjected to privation, the privation of others, of language, of objects, of life? The question here is not so much about the reality of art but about the reality of philosophy. Is philosophy only effective at the borders, the margins of reality, because it must think in terms of concepts and generalities tied to the significational system or, at best, because it thinks in terms of their shocking but momentary rupture? Or can we not orient our thought about the sublime starting from the dissolution of the spatial and temporal discourse that dominated the canvas?

Looking at the work of contemporary artists like Robert Smithson, we may see either traces of the story, or we may attempt to reduce the work to the "lived experience" of the gallery or site visit. But this only evades the complexity of the work, the layerings of meanings it offers. Smithson's "Sites" and "Nonsites," huge works carved into the earth and earth brought into the gallery, involve not only stone, dirt, glass, water, and sand; but color, texture; the silent, broken, left-over; time breaking up into many times; the all-over image in which everything is equivalent to everything else; no figure, no ground; no before, now, or after. Smithson is experimenting with nature in its inhumanity and chaos. This is apparent in the work of other modern artists like Walter De La Maria, Michael Heizer, Nancy Holt, Andy Goldsworthy, and Christine Oatman. The work orients our thought about itself, and orients our thought about the world within which the work exists. And what is the significance of the work?

"It is meaning, insofar as it is sensually produced."[28] Textual analysis of the work of art places us in a situation of encounter, not with the subjective conditions of representation, nor with sublime rupture. Placing ourselves in front of the modern work of art may allow us to say of the work of art what Roland Barthes has said of the text; what we encounter is our individual body of bliss as an event: a complex process of biographical, historical, sociological, and neurotic elements that throws us back upon ourselves, upon the elements in our historical, cultural, and natural experience.

If the dominant mode of philosophical thinking about art has been founded upon what can be represented in the sensible, simply reversing this is no improvement, for, as Gilles Deleuze has shown in *Différence et répétition*, the reverse participates fully in its opposite. It is true that representation can be momentarily disrupted by shock, but, in artworks themselves, representation has been permanently distorted, altered, and torn from its position by a kind of movement.[29]

The representation has been "torn apart" by modern works of art insofar as each one calls for what Barthes refers to as a "science of the singular," and Deleuze calls a "science of the sensible," a "higher empiricism," wherein being is no longer found in the categorical identity of a being with other similar or analogous beings (that is, in the agreement of imagination and concepts) nor in its denial. Rather, it is found in the way in which each work of art leaves representation in order to assert the reality of the singular, sensible, and empirical. Each work of art is a point of view and not a re-presentation of the categorical or of its momentary lapse.

But this requires a thought spawned by the encounter, a thought nourished by divergence, disjunction, yet also by *affirmation*. We have come to recognize a vast area which our analyses cannot penetrate, which our words do not manipulate, which our thought will not dominate. This is not, however, nihilism—but a call for thought, a thought oriented by the work of art, and a responsibility on the part of thought to think the difference manifested by the work of art. Perhaps this may still be called the sublime.

VI

Foucault: Theory and the Destabilized Subject

15

Foucault and Theory: Genealogical Critiques of the Subject

David F. Gruber

Any suggestion that Foucault's work is theoretical—that it could produce more accurate theories, or that it could yield new and improved theories of familiar things and old concepts, or that it could generate theories of newly discovered entities and concepts, or even that it could rehabilitate or revitalize the activity of theorizing itself—facilely overlooks the structural connections and discursive isomorphism between a theoretical approach and modern forms of subjectivity. More importantly, such optimism misses the implications for theory of Foucault's genealogies of subjectivities. The subject and any inclination to theory are inextricably intertwined; theory would not escape a genealogical inquiry that interrogates the status and privilege of the subject. This unavoidable effect of Foucault's challenge to thinking unquestioningly from the subject can best be illustrated by examining the particular theoretical efforts that attempt to discover and produce the truth of subjectivity.

A useful initial caricature of the image that theory displays can divide that style of thinking into three functional components: the theory's object, its subject, and the relation it establishes between them. First, theoretical thinking presupposes an object with metaphysical privilege. That object has reality and truth as an ahistorical absolute or as the historical progress of an evolving and emerging potential, a progress that in its necessity itself transcends and escapes history, even if it fulfills history or occurs as history. In either case, theory's involvement with the object is limited and relatively safe. If the theory possesses a static object domain, it reports and represents its object either more or less accurately; its ultimate goal is comprehensive and final description. If there is a dynamic object, theory may also function as a catalyst which, by a gentle and appropriate nurturing, incites a lazy object to approach its potential. Here theory participates vicariously in the perfection and maturity of the object. At most, theory is an integral dimension of that development; it maintains a discreet separation from the object. However, whatever its role with regard to its object, theory only discovers the object or its potential; it does not invent or manufacture the object *ex nihilo*. The object is always there before theory begins its activity of representation or encouragement, even if the object is present only as occluded form or potential. Thus theory presents itself as secondary in every respect to its object, so that it portrays its activity as derivative and dependent on the priority of the object and its predetermined essence.

The initial character of the theoretical relation between subject and object is vision, the reassuring distance of observation without contact or influence. The structure of the relation places the subject apart from its object; sight is the sense historically preferred by the theoretical tradition, perhaps because it is the cleanest and the least responsible. Very little can happen in the thin ether between subject and object in which pure theoretical vision occurs; there is a qualitative difference between the primarily cognitive activity of the subject and the stasis or internal dynamic of the object.

Finally, the subject is the locus of theoretical activity, and theoretical activity reflects the object, basking in its light. The subject begins as the transparent ledger on which is written the knowledge attained through theoretical effort. Vision yields a reproduction of the object in the subject, a representation which is conceptual. The subject merely collects information about the object, synthesizing and reacting within its own limits. It does not create.

These simple elements—an independent object, a relatively passive object, and an innocent and minimal connection between them—evolve dramatically when theory turns its attention to the subject itself; suddenly the activities and duties of the theoretical subject become crucial. This is most familiar in the philosophical tradition of modern epistemology. First, the subject no longer simply repeats the object or mechanically collects and orders the elements that are cognized; the subject instead comes to contribute to the object so that the object as it is known bears the marks of the subject's activity. The subject carries responsibility for the character of the object. The functions and limitations of the subject's activity of reporting themselves become thematic. Thus theoretical attention must turn to the subject itself, to those structures and conditions that make objective experience possible. Next is the radical possibility that this subject might itself evolve and have stages of its maturity. Emphasis shifts from the subject's constant epistemic functions to the development of the subject as the site of individual, moral, political, and world-historical progress. Suddenly the burden of the subject shifts and increases: no longer is its duty merely to be aware of the character and progress of objects external to it, such as reason's march of enlightenment in the species; now the progress of reason over irrationality, the emergence of consciousness from opacity, the liberation of human potential from its historical bonds, emancipation to autonomy from heteronomy, the maturation of the individual and the species, all occur only to the extent that the individual and collective subject becomes self-conscious of its own dynamic process and drives that process forward. The subject's reflection on itself effects its own development. The progress of both individual and species happens precisely in the maturation of subjectivity. In this model, all critical thinking is theoretical thinking: intermediate stages of human existence which are inadequate to the truth of human potential are criticized and discarded on comparison with the regulative standard given by the theory of the subject. Critical thinking that is theoretical depends upon a discursive function of the truth of a subject; the as yet unattained subject comes to occupy the crucial place in the theoretical discourse.

However obvious this evolution of the subject might seem—after all, it is nothing more than the subject becoming aware first that it is an epistemic factor and second that it is a historical process—it constitutes a revolution in the values and operations of the theoretical discourse, a revolution obscured by theory.[1] This difference generates a tension between theory's original inclination to be reflective, separate, observational, and patient and this additional, self-imposed demand to be active, engaged, practical, and effective. Theory becomes responsible for the emergence of its object, which is in this case the individual and collective human subject. Theory becomes involved in the production of its object.

This difficult tension between theoretical thinking's observational and productive aspects, between its passivity and its activity, turns out to be fertile, not paradoxical. Theory utilizes mechanisms and an ideology of vision and perspective for the purpose of producing the subject. The first dimension serves the second. In the philosophical tradition this is so deeply embedded that it is veiled even when it is patently obvious. A natural light of reason penetrates the obscurities of dogmatic thinking or of unfortunate social and political developments to uncover and nurture the true potential of the individual and the species which lies safely below the false, the inadequate, the irrational, and the heteronomous. To accomplish this, light is thrown on the facade of the deficient, exposing its falsity, and then light searches out and lights up the hidden core of subjectivity that patiently waits to be found and drawn into actuality. Far less obvious, however, is a realization within theoretical thinking that this is a single, particular, distinctive style of analysis and action that has a history of its own. In ignoring its contingency and in taking itself as obvious, necessary, and automatic, theoretical thinking tends to ignore rather than to appreciate its implications and effects as an operation. It obscures its own role in manufacturing that which its seeks to educe and refine. The masking rhetoric of theory would offer the pretense that it merely discovers and elicits that which already exists in potential or that it only contributes in some small way to a process that must necessarily occur. Methods differing in details may compete to be the most efficient, but the essential objective of unearthing the truth of the subject remains unchanged throughout. Under the guise of mere observation or gentle suggestion, the second aspect of theory—its positivity as productivity—dominates. Theory accepts its credit in the progress of the subject, but not its complicity in the existence of that subject.

The function of a genealogical investigation into the emergence of the subject is to recover that which theory tends to forget about itself: that the production of subjectivities occurs in operations of construction and constitution, not in mere discovery or facilitation, that these are forceful operations that deploy distinctive patterns of thinking in coercive institutions and practices, and that they have very concrete, common, and far-reaching effects. Foucault accomplishes this by shaking the necessity and obviousness of our energetic pursuit of the subjective, reminding us that these are operations which erect that which they so vigorously seek. He deflects our gaze, which is fixed, mesmerized, on the spot where the ultimate subject should be growing. He distracts us from the ideology of our discourse of the single, unitary, true subject that would be the culmination of the human species and has us look instead at the diverse, dispersed, functional subjectivities that have been built in our institutions and practices. He redirects our attention from the difficult, ethereal, and global to the deceptively simple, concrete, and particular, from the historical discovery or enhancement of the ahistorical subject to the historical production of thoroughly historical subjects, from the monumental project of the transcendental, species, or world-historical subject to the empirical detail of existing subjects.[2] He interrupts the naive optimism addressed to the impressive if gradual perfection of the universal subject with the contrast of our attempts to treat the pathologies of stunted and deformed individual subjects. The effect of this hesitating redirection is an attention to the operations by which subjects are constituted rather than an exclusive, dogged determination to expend all the energy of critical thinking on the nurture of a pure subject. If we find the theoretical processes by which we construct pathological subjects in the process of healing them to be distasteful, perhaps there will also be room for concern about how we wish to make ourselves mature epistemological, moral, and political subjects.

Foucault finds in looking at the processes by which these specific historical forms of subjectivity are generated and directed that the metaphor of vision, distance, observation, and perspective, which structures and valorizes the theoretical discourse generally and specifically dominates the relevant philosophical and political discourse, is translated into concrete institutional and practical mechanisms. In the name of the discovery of the true potential of individual humans we have used architecture, lines of sight, observational perspectives, light itself, and structured conversations to produce a variety of subjects. Foucault looks to the practices that would instantiate and implement the theoretical mentality and finds not the diligent, patient, nonviolent search for the truth and potential of the human subject but instead the coercive production of a plethora of human subjects by instruments of search. The result of the deployment of theory is the use of perspective and vision to make the appropriate subjects and to make them fit circumstances and needs, not the unwinding of potential. *Discipline and Punish* is Foucault's account of how we have used the disciplinary monitoring of the slightest movements of bodies to effect subjects which docilely monitor their own bodily movements. From the extreme model of Bentham's correctional Panopticon to the mundane example of the spatial distribution of schoolchildren and factory workers, the metaphor of light is made literal and physical. For those who have deviated, light is the means by which they are corrected; for others, especially the young or those who are being trained for certain tasks, light precludes unacceptable behavior by its ubiquity. Fleeting visual observation is supplemented with written records maintained for each individual case; the same observation then can be repeated across time, with amendments and additions. The subjects created in these ways cannot escape illumination; these processes define and refine spatial subjects.

Among other things, Foucault's *The History of Sexuality* recounts how subjects who are expected to be able to tell their truth have been produced, subjects whose existence is the recitation of their truth. Just as there is a faith in the efficacy of light from without the subject, there is also a trust in speech from within the subject: both illuminate. The telling of the subject's dark truth of its sex would shatter the obstructions which bind it and finally set it free. These processes construct a talking subject, which is expected to tell its own truth, to display its truth through its speech.[3]

The point of these two genealogical accounts is not to show how these sets of practices have failed the potential of the subject and have, rather than fulfilling the emancipatory mission of the subject, once more obscured it. Instead, they shake the presumption of a faith that we could somehow finally reach that pure subject which must pre-exist all theoretical operations. Attention turns to the positivity of each set of practices to see just what subjects have been formed in the name of a true subjectivity.[4] However, this focus on the positivity of various theoretical approaches would not be possible within the theoretical mentality; theory is most effective when it is duplicitous, that is, when it hides its complicity with its object.[5] This deception is related to theory's stringent intolerance of any threat to its own status and to the metaphysical privilege of its object. The genealogical contrast between, on the one hand, our unquestioned reliance on the theoretical mentality as the sole means of access to the truth of the subject and, on the other, the use of the values and patterns of the theoretical discourse for practical applications which result in the constitution of pathological subjects challenges the security of that mentality. To borrow directly from Foucault, such a comparison puts the automatic tendency of historical-critical reflection to think from the theoretical perspective and in the name of the theoretical subject to the test of concrete practices—practices which are, in this case, consistent with, not structurally and discursively opposed to, theoretical thinking.[6] The inclination to assume that the critical thinking that would penetrate perverse forms of subjectivity to rescue the true subject is accomplished by theoretical thinking, is undermined by theory's role in the production of these subjects; we might need critical thinking in some form that does not rely so completely on the theoretical. Criticism of the present might need to include criticism of the theoretical, because the theoretical might turn out to be an essential factor in the present and its unsettling and unsatisfying limitations.

To retain the force of its exclusive grip on thinking, theory must maintain an image of totality: it must offer itself as the only possibility of understanding the subject or of luring the subject out of the shell of its potential. Theoretical thinking demands of itself that it should provide a comprehensive description and that it should perfect the subject. Theory's subject would have to be simple, singular, and discrete to retain its metaphysical force; theoretical thinking can tolerate neither a plurality of objects nor any ambiguity at the edges of this essential object. Behind the multiplicity of practices designed to eliminate pathology there must be but one subject and a variety of ways to discover, empower, and treat it. When a genealogical approach emphasizes a dispersion of the ideal subject and a plurality of concrete subjectivities, suggesting that no single subject can be captured but that several are produced, theoretical thinking might be led to question whether there is a single object waiting to be discovered. That, however, is not the response of theoretical thinking. Theory could not give up the function of identity that must underlie the surfaces of masks; that would admit the secret of the effectiveness of its operations.[7] Theoretical thinking instead redoubles its efforts to be comprehensive and final and to deflect the antagonism of its genealogical gadfly. It throws more light on the physical and institutional sites where the subject is supposed to emerge; it bores more deeply into the facades behind which the potential of the subject must lurk, insisting that the conversation go deeper and deeper, all in the search for what must exist. The intensification of theoretical efforts precludes any internal challenge to the dominance of theory. The more the subjective ideal eludes theory's totalizing grasp the more vigorously theory pursues its chimera, all the while leaving in its wake these fractured subjects, constituted from their origins as incomplete and in need of constant theoretical attention. Theoretical thinking can never pause to consider the possibility that the only subject that would exist would be precisely those finite, flawed subjects constructed in its efforts to find the true subject.

For genealogy, in contrast, what makes these particular subjects possible is not a unified and transcendentally empowering ideal in which they all participate and which they all resemble or approximate but is instead the practices and institutions that have produced them. They instantiate a practical and historical a priori founded in the implications of theoretical thinking, not a metaphysical or ontological a priori served by theoretical thinking. Genealogy resists the theoretical temptation to collapse particular analyses and practices or to substitute abstraction for specificity. It explodes the presumed unity of the theoretical object and undermines the privilege of theory's perspective. Genealogy's attention to fragmentation, disconnection, difference, diversity, and plurality is an intolerable assault on the unity and simplicity that theory requires of itself.[8]

Foucault's genealogies of the theoretical approach to the subject do not simply dismiss either the subject or theory; instead they perform their critical function by working through the theoretical perspective and its implications and products. They accuse theory with its effects and products, with its failures to procure that which it assumes must exist, and with its seemingly irresistible proclivity to generate the exact opposite of the healthy maturity it pursues. Specifically, genealogies of the theoretical perspective are effective in confronting theory's methodological imagery of emancipatory light with the concrete practices that theory establishes using light. Thus these genealogies parody theory, or, more aptly, they offer a different angle from which theory parodies itself. The coercive, violent reality of the practices of perspective mocks the calm, secure image that the theoretical standpoint projects. The historical reality of the uses of light exhausts theory's momentum, uses it up. The genealogical approach does not call theory to account by turning its back on theory; instead it lets theory turn against itself.

This is the moment of thinking that is transgressive of theory; it revokes both the privilege and naturalness of theory. The genealogical instant refuses to permit a subtle slide back into the dominance of the theoretical mentality.[9] Given the dominance of theoretical thinking in the present, this critique serves the genealogical function of finding the cracks in the facade of the present and wedging them open, so that it contributes to the strategy of liberty that motivates the genealogical enterprise. Thinking no longer works strictly within the regimen of theory but instead becomes capable of working at the limit of theory. Effort is redirected from the project of extracting the subject to the possibility of evaluating the acceptability and desirability of that process of excavation. We can think in the absence of theory and also in the absence of its primary object—the subject. Thinking without theory, indeed without the subject, suddenly seems possible and perhaps even desirable. Finally the implicit need for theory is suspended.[10] The grip of the theoretical is displaced. Hope no longer depends solely on the success of the project of uncovering or enabling the subject, and thus the theoretical gives up its necessity.[11]

— 16 —

Foucault's Move beyond the Theoretical

Ladelle McWhorter

Theory plays an important role in virtually every academic discipline currently vital. The specific functions of theory may differ from discipline to discipline, but it is difficult to think of any serious discipline that is able to dispense with it entirely; for theory, we usually assume, is quite simply the name of all instances of systematic speculation, all attempts at rational explication. Ordered mentation, most of us unwaveringly believe, is and must be theoretical. All that is not theoretical is either confused thinking— or, more positively, perhaps it is poetic—or it is not thinking at all, but rather a practice, object, or event. Thus the theoretical discloses itself to us as the essential nature of all our striving to make sense of ourselves and our world.

It is odd, then, that the word *theory* should be all but absent from the work of Michel Foucault. And yet absent it is, at every juncture where custom compels us to expect it to appear. When Foucault discourses at great length on knowledge, systems of knowledge, and various interpretations of what it is to know, we might expect him to offer us a new theory of knowledge, but he does not do that. Again, his detailed study of power (which appears in *La Volonté de savoir* and is referred to by many commentators as a theory) Foucault names not "theory" but "analytics";[1] and in an interview with Hubert Dreyfus and Paul Rabinow, he insists that his ideas on power "represent neither a theory nor a methodology."[2] His accounts of the development of subjectivities likewise yield not a theory of the subject— although, again, some commentators have called it that—but rather an odd collection of ordered insights that Foucault prefers to call, *á lá* Nietzsche, genealogies.

In light of this, one might suppose that Foucault simply harbors an irrational dislike of *theory* as a word. One might suppose that his works, though theoretical in nature, simply do not choose to announce themselves that way. Thus, commentators have either overlooked or disregarded Foucault's avoidance of the word *theory*; and some have simply supplied it in their studies of his work. Consequently, analyses of Foucault's social theories, political theories, and theories of language abound.

However, instead of assuming that Foucault's work—systematic, speculative, and explicative as it is—is, regardless of his sometimes perhaps rather eccentric terminology, theoretical, let us suppose for the moment that Foucault's avoidance of the word *theory* is indicative of a rejection of theoretical thought, of a conscious, intentional, premeditated dethroning of the theoretical gaze. Let us, in other words, take Foucault's vocabulary seriously and address directly the question that theory's absence raises. Why not theory? In what sense is theory at odds with the aims of Michel Foucault? That is the question this paper purposes to answer.

There are several points of entry into Foucault's discourse. One way to begin to engage his work—the way that I have chosen to begin here—is to situate it in opposition to transcendentality. Foucault is interested in thinking the world thoroughly historically, without reference to any metaphysical structure, without recourse to any transhistorical constant. In particular, Foucault is interested in understanding human subjectivities, human selfhoods, historically, as the ever-changeable products of traceable sets of historical forces.[3] Foucault takes Nietzsche at his word when Nietzsche speaks in *Beyond Good and Evil* of the "I" that occurs within thinking and that in its arrogance then posits itself as the cause of the very matrix—thinking—from which it arises.[4] Foucault's explicit task is to understand the processes that formed and subsequently inform this self-proclaimed agency, this "I," the self-conscious individual, the subject of knowledge, action, and moral responsibility.

But early in the attempt a problem arises. The "I" that posits itself as the cause of thought also traditionally has posited itself as the source and owner of force, of power. Therefore, reversing the traditional priority of subjectivity and power—which Foucault must do if he is to understand subjectivities as occurrences within history—will require a reconceptualization of power, one in which power operates without essential reference to human agency. It is this reconceptualization that Foucault christens "analytics."

But why is analytics not a theory? The answer is fairly simple, though the reasoning behind it is somewhat more complex. We must remember that with Foucault we are in a discourse that rejects transcendentality and refuses to grant privilege to subjectivity. These stances, as we shall see, entail opposition to theory, for theoretical thinking is intimately associated both with privileged observation and with transcendental truth.

Theory's alliance with privileged observation has been duly noted and fretted over at least since the end of the nineteenth century. Various remedies have been proposed with varying degrees of acceptance and success, but these debates will not concern us here. What has been problematized less often is theory's alliance with transcendental structure, the ahistoricity of its commitments and goals. We will examine this more carefully.

Theoretical work presupposes truth. One purpose, perhaps the main purpose, of theory is to render accessible—to capture in symbol, in language—the structure of the true. Whether the object in question is patterns of economic development, DNA replication, the sociology of warfare, or the creation of the world, theoretical discourse locates its target and attempts to seize it, to import it intact and alive into a linguistic structure that will display its complex order, its inner logic or form. To a very great extent, within theoretical discourse particular theories are measured against the reality that they purport to explicate. Theoretical discourses assume that there is a truth of DNA replication, that there is a truth of world creation. The theory that most adequately represents this truth is itself derivatively called true, or is at least tentatively treated as true until a "better" account presents itself. All other theories are held to be inferior to the one (or in some cases, the few) that most closely matches the reality with which it is concerned. The remaining untrue, or inferior, theories are usually discarded.[5] There is, then, so we are told, a kind of theoretic competition in which there are winners and losers, and, at the best of times—times unmarred by political maneuver or religious dogma—the judge in these games is truth, truth itself, the way things really are.

This is theoretical discourse's own account of itself. It understands itself to be a kind of game, albeit with a very serious purpose and very high stakes. If this self-portrait is accurate, then it would be reasonable to predict that theoretical discourse deprived of truth as both prize and judge would collapse into dramatic disarray. Without truth, theoretical thought would have no goal. It would be directionless or, what amounts to the same thing, multi-directional. Hence, competition among theories would be meaningless, for truth serves theory as its principle of valuational arrangement. In the absence of truth no theory could be disqualified from the field of play; no theory could be eliminated from consideration. Nor would any particular theory be able to command our assent. In theoretical discourse (to paraphrase Dostoevsky) without truth anything is possible. And the result is discursive chaos.

Before going on to link traditional conceptions of truth with ahistoricity, which is of course one of the objects of this paper, it is important to insert a slightly peripheral comment. There are those who contend that truth is not an essential element of theory for the simple reason that truth can never be attained. Our finitude hobbles us; truth is forever beyond our reach, and therefore it is external to theoretical discourse. Nevertheless, these thinkers would have us note that theoretical discourse is orderly, even in truth's absence. Theory deprived of truth simply proceeds according to the principle of approximation. Though we remain always at an unbridgeable distance from our goal, each of our theoretical improvements yields a "closer" approximation to truth.

This alternative account of theoretical thought, it is important to see, does not really dispense with truth. Like its more optimistic counterpart, it posits a truth, but a truth that it then projects—here using that word in a quasi-psychological sense—outside the theoretical domain. Nevertheless, truth still functions as the internal ordering principle of theoretical discourse. Theory still structures itself with reference to some truth, despite its insistence that this truth is "out there" rather than within the discourse itself. Hence, this second account does not differ from the more commonly accepted account in its description of theoretical discourse's internal structure, the aspect of the discourse of concern to us here. Like the first account, it describes theoretical endeavors as contests or games that are dependent upon the *concept*, though perhaps not the acknowledged and tangible presence, of truth. Therefore, what we might call the Peircean account of theory really differs from the other account only in its degree of pessimism regarding the ultimate agonistic outcome.

By its own account, then, theory takes its meaning from its presupposition of truth. As a result, the degree to which theory is bound up with transcendental thought depends upon the degree of transcendentality that we assign to truth. The question we now must ask is whether truth transcends history, whether history simply flows past an undisturbed and undisturbable truth.

In the Platonic tradition the answer is, of course, affirmative. The true is Being, never Becoming. Truth does not change; it is perfect, and its stasis is the hallmark of its perfection.

It was the Greeks who gave us theory, the Greeks with their emphasis upon seeing—as opposed to hearing, touching, tasting, smelling—the Greeks and their love affair with wisdom, their mania for rational contemplation conceived as a kind of nonphysical beholding of the changeless world beyond this realm of dancing shadows and decaying apparitions. In the tradition we might somewhat loosely term Socratic or Platonic, theory is profoundly ahistorical, for the truth it seeks is always understood as timeless.

But, surely, truth has matured since then. Some theorists would insist that truth has broken its infantile ties with transcendence and has historicized itself. In what may be loosely termed the Hegelian tradition, the true is precisely the historical itself; it is identified with the changing world. Consequently, these thinkers would assure us, Foucault the historical thinker need not be wary of theory in this tradition. And if he is, he simply has not been generous or thorough enough in his study of theory's transformations. He has failed to recognize theory in *its* historicity, in *its* changeableness. Foucault the self-proclaimed historical thinker has rejected theory only by overlooking its developmental nature in Hegelian thought. At this point, much to the delight of his critics, Foucault seems to be caught in a trap of his own making.

The accusation that Foucault is inconsistent on this point, however, is somewhat premature. For, upon closer examination, we see that it is not the case that theory in the Hegelian tradition breaks entirely with transcendence. It is not the case that Hegelian truth is subject to total change. Hegel does not after all leave Socrates so very far behind.

In *The Birth of Tragedy* Nietzsche locates the death of tragic art in the rise of Socratic cheerfulness, in the prevalence of the Socratic-Platonic conviction that everything ultimately is intelligible. For Socrates there is no positivity beyond the domain of intelligible arrangement. There is no Other, no Difference, nothing independent of the totalization of rationalistic order. It is above all this vision of absolute comprehension, of perfect and ultimately inviolable unity, that characterizes and undergirds the Socratic world.

Hegel does not challenge this vision. He simply renames it, identifies it, as a whole, with truth itself. The true now is, now means, that ultimately perfectly integrated whole, rather than simply the principles by which that whole orders itself. The true comprehends all change, all difference, all becoming. And all, *all,* is intelligible. Nothing effectively resists; nothing remains without. There is no chaos; there is no madness; there is no death. The true permanently excludes the very possibility of radical difference. Hence, the Hegelian comprehension of history is itself still beyond history, still partaking of transcendentality.

Theory, then, even within the Hegelian tradition, still orders itself according to an ahistorical truth. It still measures itself against a transcendental meter stick. Theoretical discourse still can be conceived as a competition in which transhistorical truth plays the part of both referee and goal.

With the thinking of history as his expressed purpose, Foucault cannot allow himself to slip into theoretical language; for to do so would be to risk the forgetfulness embedded in its terms and the arrogance inherent in its vision. The avoidance of theoretical terminology is, therefore, not simply a coincidence or the result of some semantic idiosyncrasy on Foucault's part. It is, on the contrary, an element in a very deliberate strategy aimed at the dismantling of transcendental thought.

Inevitably, a historical thinker runs headlong into truth. We may be able to let go of God, to historicize morality, to place the tenets of logic in question, to situate the knowing subject, but truth may still remain un-moved (its power directly proportionate to our inability to conceive of thought without its guidance; its strength of command precisely equivalent to our lack of imagination). As Nietzsche recognized, truth is the pillar of the temple of ahistorical intelligibility.

The thinker who would think history must interrogate truth. We must bring ourselves up short before the Nietzschean question: *"why not rather untruth? and uncertainty? even ignorance?"*[6] Is it the case, after all, that truth's position in our discourse, in our world, that truth's *value,* is inevitable? Are not other values, other systems of evaluation, equally imaginable, equally possible? It is the job of the historical thinker to articulate that question, to remember it, to nurture it. For in no other way will truth—will theory, will subjectivity or sexuality or power—ever be *transvalued.*

To undergo the question, "why not rather untruth?" is already to find oneself, if only for a brief interval, outside the discourses in which transcendental truth is an ordering principle. The transvaluational thinker must find ways to expand that interval, to make it possible to hear the silence beyond truth in its positivity, to allow the previously unthinkable to occur. And, if possible, one must speak from truth's boundary, truth's discursive limit, speak *of* that limit that theoretical discourse would deny. Foucault's discourse must transgress the discourse of truth in such a way as to make its transgressive movements audible, visible, *felt* within truth's own domain.

It is not overstatement to assert that every one of Foucault's works, the very event of Foucaultian discourse, constitutes an attempt to trangress, and thereby to transvalue, transhistorical truth. Historical thinking must occur as a violation of the transhistorical. And, accordingly, Foucault must refuse to employ any structure of articulation that cannot place in question the value of truth.

Theoretical thinking constitutes one such deficient structure of articulation. If Foucault were to think and speak theoretically, his discourse could not bring into question the value of truth as ultimate standard or final goal. If Foucault were to speak theoretically, he could not speak transgressively; he could not speak transvaluatively. To cast Foucault in the role of the theorist is to strip his discourse of the power it claims and exercises. It is to make nonsense of his entire enterprise. To understand Foucault's work as a collection of theories—of the subject, of power, of knowledge—is not to understand Foucault's work at all.

Serious attention to Foucault's work compels us to explore the possibilities opened up by his attempt to expand the transgressive interval, that moment at which the boundary, the limit, of transcendental thought becomes palpable, comes into view. However, before such exploration can occur, we must have some understanding of the structures of Foucault's discourse that en*able* the event that *is* that expanding interval, so that we do not inadvertently cover it over or cause it to contract.

One of the most significant and powerful of the transgressive structures that Foucault erects is his rigorous nontheory, which complements his insistence that theory be recognized for the ally of transcendentality that it is. Theory is one of Foucault's targets. If we are to be historical thinkers, theory must be one of our targets as well. And we must insist that the nontheoretical, anti-theoretical nature of Foucault's work be acknowledged and respected.

— 17 —

Local Theory

Peg Birmingham

Stressing Foucault's critique of transcendental subjectivity as well as his critique of ahistorical, objective truth, both Gruber and McWhorter conclude by pointing out the impossibility of understanding Foucault's thinking as remaining within the theoretical approach. Rejecting the possibility of theory, both essays emphasize the contingency, fragmentation, and discontinuity disclosed in Foucault's genealogical inquiries.

Although it is certainly the case that Foucault dismisses the possibility of theory (*if* by that is meant the search for absolute truth on the part of a transcendental subject), perhaps this understanding of theory is too narrow, addressing only one, albeit dominant, strand of the sense of theory in its long and complex history. This narrow understanding of theory and its consequent dismissal has its dangers, not the least being that it tends to obscure Foucault's continuous preoccupation with the danger of being merely a specific intellectual individual engaged only in local inquiry. Indeed, it is this preoccupation that prevents us from asserting that Foucault dismisses altogether the theoretical approach.

That Foucault retains a notion of theory can be seen in a lecture he delivered in 1976, wherein he states, "The main point to be gleaned from the events of the last fifteen years is the local character of criticism."[1] Cautioning his audience that he does not mean by that a naive empiricism nor a "soggy eclecticism" that devours every kind of theoretical approach, Foucault suggests that local criticism "indicates in reality an autonomous, non-centralised theoretical production, one that is to say whose validity is not dependent on the approval of the established regimes of thought." It is the possibility of a *noncentralized* theoretical production that needs to be examined in order to raise the question whether Foucault does retain a notion of theory in a broader sense. To examine this broader sense of theory, it is necessary to turn briefly to the history of this term.

The philosophical term *theory* emerges from the Greek word for spectators, *theatai*. Diogenes Laertius reports on this earliest sense of theory:

205

> Life is like a festival; just as some come to the festival to compete, some to
> ply their trade, but the best people come as spectators (*theatai*), so in life the
> slavish men go hunting for fame (*doxa*) or gain, the philosophers for truth.[2]

Hannah Arendt points out that the importance of this story lies in how we understand the nobility of the spectators. She writes, "What is stressed here as more noble than the competition for fame or gain is by no means a truth invisible and inaccessible to ordinary men; nor does the place the spectators withdraw to belong to any 'higher' realm. . . ."[3] Instead, the spectators are located at the festival, watching the actual event before them. The nobility of the spectators lies in their "active nonparticipation," allowing them to judge the actors involved in the competition.

Here Arendt's insight is again helpful. She points out that the concern for fame or opinion makes the actor in the event dependent upon the spectator's judgment, "for it is through the opinion of the audience and the judge that fame comes about."[4] The actor is not autonomous, since the final verdict concerning the event lies with the spectators. Moreover, it is important to note that the spectators are not solitary subjects. The judgment upon the event reflects the plurality of spectators, all contributing their views.[5] Therefore, if theory is that which is produced by the spectators, then the initial sense of theory (*theatai*) has to do with judgments upon events rather than an articulation of ahistorical truths.

In the emergence of *theoria* from *theatai*, the term continues to retain the significance of a judging spectator. Herodotus tells of the *theoroi* or sightseers who travel abroad to study the institutions and laws of other cultures. Specifically, he describes Solon's ten-year journey for the sake of *theoroi*. Solon's theoretical journey is not a turn away from specific regions and local events; rather, in the conversations with people abroad, he can determine which of his laws and institutions are good and which need improvement.[6] Furthermore, the theoretical journey served political expediency insofar as "he was on his travels at the time . . . in order to avoid the necessity of repealing any of the laws he had made."[7]

Plato takes up this sense of theory in the *Laws*. An important component of Plato's state are the *theoros* who go abroad to contemplate laws and institutions. After seeing the institutions of others, the delegation must return and report to the supreme council, whose domain is legislation and education and whose task is the improvement of both.[8] Again, these *theoros* are not solitary subjects contemplating ahistorical, objective truth. Plato is quite specific that the judgments of the *theoros* concern actual laws and events and, moreover, are subject to debate and criticism by other members of the council before transforming any of the state's practices. The judgments of the *theoros* are within the context of shared social practices;

the justifications of the judgments acquire their rationale only in the dynamic, political discourse.

Finally, perhaps it is Thucydides who best exemplifies this earliest understanding of theory in his attempts, as a historian, to take up an objective attitude toward the events of the Peloponnesian War. Thucydides suggests that the search for the truth (*theoria*) of this event is possible only by placing in a relation of contiguity several eyewitness accounts:

> In this history I have made use of set speeches some of which were delivered just before and others during the war. I have found it difficult to remember the precise words used in the speeches which I listened to myself . . . so my method has been, while keeping as closely as possible to the general sense of the words that were actually used, to make the speakers say what, in my opinion was called for by each situation.[9]

It is important to notice that Thucydides finds no contradiction between the search for the truth of the event (*theoria*) and the necessity of a judgment given by the spectator viewing the event.

Further, Thucydides makes each speaker say what he himself believes the situation demanded. Werner Jaeger points out the significance of this:

> His belief that, after considering the peculiar circumstances of each case, he could set down what was demanded by the situation (*ta deonta*) was based on his conviction that every standpoint in such a conflict has its own inevitable logic, and that a man who watched the conflict from above could develop that logic adequately.[10]

Again, the position of nobility, that of watching the conflict from above, is in no sense a position that escapes the historical event. Rather, the position of the spectator allows for the emergence of the *general sense* of the event.

Moreover, the general sense is not obtained by subsuming the particular situation under an a priori concept or universal principle. The profound sadness of Thucydides's final verdict lies in the recognition that such a principle could not be given in advance. In his search for truth (*theoria*) he recognizes that the truth of the event only emerges in the opinions of the spectators, the plurality of speakers, who give to the situation what is demanded of it. Here Jaeger's reading of Thucydides is again helpful:

> His purpose as a historian must be understood from his endeavor to achieve a dispassionate point of view towards the enormous event. . . . But Thucydides won his great intellectual victory by transferring that scientific attitude from timeless nature to the political struggle of his own age. . . .

> Thucydides, by transferring *historia* to the sphere of politics, gave a new and
> deeper sense to this ideal of the search for truth.[11]

Thucydides understands *theoria* as historical and political. Indeed, only by transferring *historia* to the sphere of politics is he able to grasp the demand of the situation. What is demanded or, more generally, what is the truth of this enormous event is political experience. Yet the event also demands that its general sense, its political experience, be grasped and preserved by its spectators.[12]

In the modern period this notion of *theoria* as the judging spectator is taken up by Immanuel Kant. In his essay, *The Conflict of the Faculties,* Kant writes, "This event is simply the mode of thinking of the *spectators* which reveals itself publicly in the game of great transformations. . . ."[13] The event, of course, is the French Revolution. According to Kant, this event is not composed of battles or deeds but, instead, emerges in the "wishful participation of the spectators who are not engaged in the game themselves."[14] And, Kant adds, it is a partial participation fraught with danger insofar as the validity of its speculations are not dependent on the approval of the established regime. Like the ancient actors who depend on the spectators in the stadium in order to have their fame, and, further, like the Peloponnesian War which depends on the opinion of Thucydides for its political experience, so, too, the event of the French Revolution, in order for its effects to transform institutions and practices, is dependent upon spectators (theorists) such as Immanuel Kant watching the conflict in Paris.

It is important to note that Kant is not interested here in universal statements about the nature of being human; rather, as a critical spectator he is, along with other fellow-spectators, responding to the events in his historical situation in such a way as to allow for the possibility of transformations.[15] Rather than being in a privileged situation, Kant is in a place of difference.

It is at this point that we can turn to Foucault insofar as he is also interested in the figure of Kant watching an event, in this case the event of the Enlightenment. Foucault suggests that in watching this event, Kant is raising the historical question of transformation and difference: "What dif-ference does today introduce with respect to yesterday?"[16] This question is one that Foucault greets with approval.

Moreover, this question, according to Foucault, gives us a specific philosophical attitude, that is, a way of relating to contemporary reality that marks the relation of belonging to an event while at the same time serves as a motive for a particular philosophical task of transgression (WI 39). He compares this philosophical attitude of both belonging and transgressing to what the Greeks call an *ethos*. Foucault further suggests that what connects us to the Enlightenment is this "permanent reactivation of an attitude—that is, of a philosophical ethos understood as a permanent critique of our historical era" (WI 42).

The philosophical attitude of belonging to and transgressing an ethos retains the notion of theory in its earliest form, that is, the judging spectator who, together with other spectators, transforms, through the judgment, the event. In other words, Foucault's notion of a limit-attitude within a philosophical ethos is precisely the place of a "noncentralized theoretical production." In order to clarify this, I shall examine Foucault's positive description of this limit-attitude in his essay, *What Is Enlightenment?*

In this essay, Foucault suggests that the limit-attitude reflects upon limits in a way that turns around the Kantian reflection concerning pure reason.[17] Rather than asking about the limits of rational knowledge, the limit-attitude asks, "In what is given to us as universal, necessary, obligatory, what place is occupied by whatever is singular, contingent, and the product of arbitrary constraints?" (WI 45). The limit-attitude asks about events, asking in such a way that the question takes the form of a possible transgression of limitation.

However, an event cannot be understood as a treaty, a battle, or a decision. Instead, Foucault understands an event as "a reversal of forces, the usurpation of power, the appropriation of a vocabulary turned against those who had once used it."[18] (Here one is again reminded of Kant watching the event of the French Revolution.) Events produce layers of effects. Therefore the limit-attitude within a philosophical ethos must proceed by way of genealogy.

It is impossible here to articulate completely Foucault's understanding of genealogy. Therefore I will simply point to those aspects of his genealogical approach that indicate that it does include a theoretical aspect. Certainly, Foucault is clear that genealogy is "a form of history which can account for the constitution of knowledges, discourses, domains of objects . . . without reference to a transcendental subject" (PK 117). Nonetheless, genealogy has an object. Foucault argues that it discloses the *intelligibility* of struggles, strategies, and tactics. Moreover he does not dismiss the contemplative, speculative aspect of genealogy. Instead, Foucault questions and inverts the relation between proximity and distance which, he suggests, is always included in the activity of contemplation. In other words, while the metaphysical gaze contemplates the highest forms, the greatest heights, genealogy "shortens its visions to those things nearest to it" (NGH 89). The genealogist within the limit-attitude studies what is closest, *"but in an abrupt dispossession so as to seize it at a distance"* (NGH 89, emphasis mine). In the abrupt and distancing dispossession, the genealogist is the active spectator who at a distance is critically involved.

Foucault also argues that genealogy affirms knowledge—however, knowledge understood as perspective. Located in a particular time and place, the genealogist deliberates, appraises, affirms, or negates. The genealogist reaches "the lingering and poisonous traces in order to prescribe the best antidote" (NGH 90). The genealogical inquiry allows the possibility of no longer being, doing, or thinking what we are, do, or think (WI 46). In still other words, the genealogist, as one of the active spectators belonging to the philosophical ethos, is involved in creating a space for *specific* transgressions of the limit.

Therefore Foucault suggests that the limit-attitude is one of experimentation. The work of genealogy not only opens up realms of historical inquiry but at the same time tests those places in contemporary reality where change is desirable and possible. Indeed, Foucault goes so far as to suggest that the genealogist must determine the form this change will take (WI 46). Again, one is reminded of the ancient *theoros* embarking on a sight-seeing journey in order to discern what specific institutions and practices need to be transformed.

Finally, although the limit-attitude within a philosophical ethos is itself always limited and determined, this does not mean that all is contingency and disorder (WI 47). Rather, the work of the limit-attitude "has its generality, its systematicity, its homogeneity and its stakes" (WI 47). This working of the limit-attitude can be seen in Foucault's attempt at articulating a genealogy of ethics.

Foucault suggests that a genealogy of ethics has as its object a homogeneous domain whose reference is the constitution of the individual as a moral subject. While the genealogical inquiry discloses that there are breaks, ruptures, and fundamental differences in the ways in which the moral subject has been constituted at different points in history (for example, the difference between the Greek ideal of an aesthetics of existence and the Christian ideal of purification), nonetheless Foucault insists that the overall question motivating a genealogy of ethics can be systematized: "How are we constituted as moral subjects of our own activities?"[19] This question interrogates a homogeneous domain that has four components: the ethical substance, the mode of subjection, the techniques used to achieve the specific ethical relation, and, finally, the telos of the activity, that is, the kind of being to which we aspire when we behave in a moral way (OGE 237–40).

Moreover, Foucault argues that the homogeneous domain, in this case the constitution of the moral subject, forms a practical system: a realm of practices and strategies as well as forms of rationality that organize the actual ways by which we carry out the ethical relation to ourselves. He further suggests that the practical system constitutive of the ethical relation is interconnected with two other practical systems: relations of control over things and relations of actions upon others. According to Foucault the genealogist as the active spectator must investigate these three axes of knowledge, power, and ethics, both in their specificity and in their interconnections.

Most importantly, the work of the limit-attitude can evoke generalities within the specific practical system. By evoking the necessity of generality, Foucault cautions against understanding this as a metahistorical continuity. Instead, he means to say that although the genealogy is concerned with specific bodies of practices and discourses, these practices and discourses have their generality insofar as the *problematics* of these practices continue to recur in our own time. For example, in the genealogical inquiry into the ethical relation, he suggests that one of the recurring general problematics that takes historically unique forms is the relation between acts, desire, and pleasure. (One is reminded of Thucydides's inquiry into the Peloponnesian War, which, in its analysis of a historically unique event, yields a general problematic in the sphere of political experience, namely, the relation between the state and power.)

Foucault emphasizes that through the general problematic the work of the limit-attitude is provided with its *theoretical coherence* (WI 50). This accounts for his interest in Kant. As noted above, Kant, watching enthusiastically the event of the French revolution, is not interested in proposing universal truths about the nature of human beings. (This is why Foucault argues that there must be a distinction between the notion of the Enlightenment and the notion of humanism.) Rather, Kant is interested in articulating a general problematic on the basis of this specific event. In *The Conflict of the Faculties*, Kant writes, "There must be some experience in the human race which, as an event, points to the disposition and capacity of the human race to be the cause of its own advance toward the better . . . (since this should be the act of a being endowed with freedom). . . ."[20] This not only articulates the Kantian general problematic as it emerges in the event of the French Revolution, but it reveals for Foucault the stakes of the limit- attitude in its genealogical inquiry, namely, the "undefined work of freedom" (WI 48).

In this analysis of Foucault's understanding of the work of the limit-attitude within a philosophical ethos, the point is that all is not disorder and contingency. Local, noncentralized theory is possible. The limit-attitude discloses specific grids of intelligibility that open up domains of historical understanding concerning the axes of knowledge, power, and ethics. Further, this attitude discloses those places where specific transformations are possible. Foucault insists that we intervene at dangerous moments. By retaining the sense of a local, noncentralized theory given in the genealogical inquiry, we need not intervene blindly. Moreover, this notion of a local, noncentralized theory unearths the ancient sense of theory. The limit-attitude, located in a particular philosophical ethos, participates in events as the active spectator, allowing these events to emerge as well as judging those places where specific transgressions are possible. These judgments indicate that we are able to say something general on the basis of our local events, thereby avoiding the danger of being merely local observers. To be sure, this opens up the problematic of judgment which must be taken up in a different time and place.

— 18 —

Postmortem Thought and the End of Man

Michael Clifford

> *Man is something that shall be overcome.*
> *What have you done to overcome him?*
>
> *—Thus Spoke Zarathustra*

Over a century has passed since Zarathustra descended from the mountaintop and in his gift-giving and untimely virtue spoke to us of our destiny. God is dead, the prophet told us, and in the wake of His wake must follow the death of metaphysics, of philosophy, of man—of all the otherworldly universals that separate us from ourselves. Or rather, more precisely and less didactically, in the wake of the discursive milieu in which the death of God is meaningful must follow the end of all the essentialist divisions in which 'separation from self' is pertinent and problematic. We know that God is dead, but what does it mean to say that man shall be overcome? Perhaps it means that the absoluteness of *man,* in all its tyrannical universality and categoriality, will give way to a new way of thinking in which man as such no longer informs and pervades the very discourse of our thought. What *have* we done to overcome man? To a great extent metaphysics still reigns, man still governs. Perhaps the best we have done is to place metaphysics in question, to cast man in doubt. Even those great torchbearers of the Nietzschean legacy—Heidegger, Foucault, Derrida—have as yet only placed the *question* of the end of man before us in stark relief. They force us to ask the question genuinely, even if they themselves have not, as yet, pushed it to completion.[1]

"In our day," says Foucault, "and once again Nietzsche indicated the turning-point from a long way off, it is not so much the absence or the death of God that is affirmed as the end of man."[2] The end of man, for Foucault, means the end of the "anthropologization" of the human sciences, under whose categories we have been forced to think. It means the end of the empirical-transcendental doublet in which man, as an object of knowledge and as a subject that knows, reflects and is reflected in the receding/advancement of reflected representation. It means the end of the analytic of finitude wherein man searches for his ever-receding origin. The end of man means the dispersion of the unity of man, as the governing epistemic positivity, to be replaced by the unity of language, in which the possibilities of human being would come to be understood in their discursive constitutiveness. In the posing of the question of language the disappearance of man is heralded. "In our day the fact that philosophy is still— and again—in the process of coming to an end and the fact that . . . the question of language is being posed, prove no doubt that man is in the process of disappearing" (OT 385). The end of man is tied to the end of philosophy in that philosophy is and has been permeated by an anthropological concern with man as an object of reflection. "Anthropology constitutes perhaps the fundamental arrangement that has governed and controlled the path of philosophical thought from Kant until our own day" (OT 342). Only when we have torn ourselves free from the "anthropological sleep" in which thought is always governed by the idea that it is man who is thinking, by a transcendental concern with man's essence, formed and informed by the discourse of anthropology, will it be "once more possible to think." Only then will a space unfold in which philosophy itself "can begin thinking again."

"It is no longer possible to think in our day other than in the void left by man's disappearance," says Foucault (OT 342). The end of man is almost synonymous with the death of God: where man ends, *thinking* begins. The possibility for such thought has been offered to us "as both a promise and task" by Nietzsche. What would it mean to free ourselves of the anthropologizing formalizing of the human sciences, of the transcendental universalizing of metaphysics? What would thought be then? This is the fundamental question of our day, says Foucault: "We know, in any case, that all efforts to think afresh are in fact directed at that obstacle. . ." (OT 386). Yet it remains, still, a question: "Ought we not rather to give up thinking of man?" But are not questions of the question of the disappearance of man themselves a response, a tentative heralding reply to the Nietzschean imperative? Perhaps so, but one that as yet awaits affirmation. To such questions it is as yet perhaps "not possible to reply; they must be left in suspense, where they pose themselves, only with the knowledge that the possibility of posing them *may well open the way to a future thought*" (OT 386, emphasis added).

To pose the question of the end of man, then, is to inquire concomitantly into the possibilities for thought following man's demise. If we trace genealogically the Foucaultian query we find standing at the threshold, as it were, and in some sense opening the space in which Foucault can even pose the question, Heidegger and the question of Being. Heidegger, who in posing the question of Being anticipates the end of metaphysics, is the bridge between Nietzsche and Foucault such that the death of God can be brought to fruition, completion, by the end of man. Although they are fundamentally the same question, the question of the end of metaphysics is in some sense prior to the question of the end of man. For what will disappear is man as a metaphysical issue. But whereas Foucault offers us the possibility that philosophy, philosophical thinking, can free itself from metaphysics, for Heidegger philosophy *is* metaphysics and must give way to *thinking* free of the Platonism and Aristotelianism of representational thought about Being.[3] "What characterizes metaphysical thinking," says Heidegger, "which grounds the ground for being is the fact that metaphysical thinking departs from what is present in its presence, and thus represents it in terms of its ground as something grounded" (EP 56). The end of philosophy means the "completion" of metaphysics, not in the sense of its perfection (as in Hegel), but rather in that it "is gathered in its most extreme possibility" (EP 57). The task of thinking will be to inquire into what was "unthought" in philosophy all along—namely, the question of being, which underlay and informed philosophical concern with Being, but which was and is never thought, never questioned. The task of thinking (as opposed to philosophy) will be to inquire into presence (being) as concealing unconcealment (*aletheia*), the opening of presence, the being of beings. "But philosophy knows nothing of the opening" (EP 66). And yet *aletheia* itself is still a question that thinking has to bring to thought in the form of a question. "Thinking must consider whether it can even raise this question at all as long as it thinks philosophically" (EP 69). But this raises the question of whether thinking can in fact free itself from philosophy, that is, whether it can think free of metaphysics. "To think Being without being means: to think Being without regard to metaphysics. Yet a regard for metaphysics still prevails even in the intention to overcome metaphysics."[4]

This is the crucial question regarding the end of man: if we are once again (for the first time?) to *think*, then man must disappear; but for man to disappear, it must be possible for us to think nonmetaphysically. Is this a real possibility? And again, what would thinking be like then? Is to abandon man to abandon *all* thinking about ourselves? Is being as such even thinkable? Or is the best we can do, or should want to do, to think with masks, to play, to dance, to be arbitrary?

For Heidegger, the end of man means the end of humanism. "Every humanism is either grounded in a metaphysics or is itself made to be the ground of one. . . . Accordingly, every humanism remains metaphysical."[5] In the "Letter on Humanism" Heidegger reiterates his primary criticism of metaphysics, that it fails to ask about the truth of Being itself, and inasmuch as humanism is metaphysical, it does not ask about the essence of man with regard to being. Humanism fails to see that the essence of man "lies in his *ek-sistence*," which is the real basis of his dignity, of his *humanitas* (LH 205). "In terms of content ek-sistence means standing out into the truth of Being. . . . As ek-sisting, man sustains Da-sein in that he takes the *Da*, the lighting of Being, into 'care'. But Da-sein itself occurs essentially as 'thrown'. It unfolds essentially in the throw of Being as the fateful sending" (LH 206–7). Humanism is "ensnared" in forgetfulness of ek-sistence as it is appropriated by the truth of Being. It is only as we think ek-sistence that we think the truth of the essence of man. When one thinks Being one thinks more primordially; one lets being be—prior to predication, to value, to ontic specification; in so doing, as the "shepherd of being," man realizes his dignity, which "consists in being called by Being itself into the preservation of Being's truth" (LH 221).

But this thinking, the thinking of the truth of Being, is, like Foucault's future thinking, as yet only *anticipated*. "*The thinking that is to come* is no longer philosophy, because it thinks more originally than metaphysics. . . ." "*Assuming that in the future* man will be able to think the truth of Being, he will think from ek-sistence." "Being is *still waiting for the time* when it will become thought-provoking to man" (LH 242, 216, and 203, respectively, emphasis added). The thinking that is to come still hides, still dances coyly on the horizon; and to the extent it is *here now* at all, it is only in the form of a question—a question that for most of us has yet to be even asked. Thinking now must be willing to risk the blind alley of its departure from metaphysics. At best, it can now only point toward the truth of Being. Now man is homeless to the extent that the question of the truth of Being eludes him. Only when thinking frees itself from metaphysics will man regain his home within—language, which is the "house of Being and the home of human beings" (LH 239). Can man free himself *from* the transcendental homelessness of metaphysics *for* his ek-sistence in the openness of Being? This is a question, says Heidegger, which itself must be "posed in the midst of metaphysics' domination. Indeed every inquiry into Being, even the one into the truth of Being, must at first introduce its inquiry as a 'metaphysical' one" (LH 202).

What assurance do we have that such inquiry can ever cease to be metaphysical?

Both Foucault and (the later) Heidegger indicate that the answer to the preceding question lies in language. It is in this house of Being that man *dwells,* says Heidegger. Foucault suggests that language and the unity of man are incompatible such that one cannot exist if the other holds dominance (not unlike the incompatibility of God and the *Übermensch*). It is Derrida who pushes this idea to its limits, to its margins, if you will, and questions even the question of the house of Being itself. In "The Ends of Man" Derrida traces the problem of the end of man from Kant through Hegel and Husserl, to Heidegger, and sees it as largely constitutive of modern thought about man. Like Heidegger, Derrida sees humanism as a metaphysics; like Foucault, he sees the attempt to describe the structures of human reality as philosophical anthropology. Thought about man remains substantive, onto-theological: *"The thinking of the end of man, therefore, is always prescribed in metaphysics, in the thinking of the truth of man."*[6] Derrida suggests that it would be difficult to think today of an end of man that would not be organized by the substantive, universal, transcendental language of absolute knowledge, of the unifying conceptualization of humanism, of the categorialism of anthropology, of metaphysics.

With Heidegger, says Derrida, the metaphysical preoccupation with man is "deconstructed" into the question of the *proper* of man—the question of man's *true* essence—which is "inseparable from the question of the truth of being" (EM 124). But with Heidegger it is not the end of man as such toward which the thought of Being moves, but the end of metaphysics. Man still remains:

> It remains that the thinking of Being, the thinking of the truth of Being, in the name of which Heidegger delimits humanism and metaphysics, remains as thinking *of* man. Man and the name of man are not displaced in the question of Being such as it is put to metaphysics. Even less do they disappear. On the contrary, at issue is a kind of reevaluation or reorganization of the essence and dignity of man. (EM 128)

There is, then, no end of man entailed by the thinking of Being. There is, however, the end of the subject/object dichotomous separation of man from Being. It is in this appropriation (*Ereignis*) of Being that man finds his true essence, his dignity, as the shepherd of Being within language as the house of being.

But is this truly as yet a liberation from metaphysics? Derrida contends that Heidegger deconstructs the domination of metaphysics only to replace it with "the presence of the present" (EM 131).[7] Being, as presence, is the nearest and yet the farthest; as such it is the most difficult thought. And yet it is the most essential, the most primordial; it is prior to, and the ground for, the possibility of valuation itself (valuation, on Heidegger's terms, is the possibility of objectification/subjectification by which we, qua subject, relate to the world of things, qua objects). Inasmuch as we *value* things, we conceal from ourselves both our being and the being of things. To think the truth of Being, on the other hand, is precisely to *let beings be*. It is not that Derrida denies the truth of the primordiality of the thought of Being; rather, he questions the genuine possibility of bringing such thought to language. "It remains that Being, which is nothing, is not a being, cannot be said, cannot say itself *except in the ontic metaphor*" (EM 131). The thinking of the truth of Being "can only metaphorize, by means of a profound necessity from which one cannot simply decide to escape, the language that it deconstructs" (EM 131).

Indeed, Heidegger would have us think, as he says, what is the nearest and yet the farthest: in this will consist "the thinking that is to come." But, as such, trying to think the truth of Being is rather like trying to *look at one's own face*.[8] The best we can do to know what we ourselves look like is to look in a mirror: yet our reflection in the clearest of mirrors cannot be what we really look like; mirrored reflection is always to some extent a *distortion*. Perhaps it is equally true that the best we can do to think Being is to think it in its reflection, however distorted, in things-in-the-world. Insofar as beings are thought at all they are *valued;* insofar as we bring thought of the being of beings to language, it is always, as Derrida says, in ontic metaphor. This is, it seems, a fundamental limitation we cannot overcome. I look for my face and I never find it; it is only within a cultural milieu, a discursive formation that forms and informs me, that I even discover I have a face—as, for example, when I am told of the mirror. It is likewise only perhaps through reflection in and reflection (thinking) upon beings that I come to understand even the notion of the thought of Being. But again, it is always beings as *valued*. But value means (here we recall Nietzsche and remember that the imposition of value is at once a violence, a destruction—and more) that I am valued (reflected) in the thing as much as it is valued (reflected) in me.[9] Of the thing in its being as reflected value I can speak; but the more primordial truth of the Being of beings, if there is such a thing, is and remains forever entombed in silence. If I think the truth of Being at all, it cannot be *in* language (as the home of being); it can only be reflection (in metaphor), which, if Heidegger is played out to his limits, would seem to mean that I cannot think the truth of Being at all; or perhaps it means that the truth of Being lies precisely in its being reflected. (Here we might recall—if unfortunately it did not call to mind the subject/object distinction— the mirroring mirror of *Las Meninas,* and we might admire the painter for his honesty in the affirmation that the king as *subject* of the painting is reflected doubly in the perpetual reflection of the mirror and of the painting itself.)

Letting beings be then would mean affirming, in a Nietzschean sense, the primordial inexpressibility of the being of beings. Such an affirmation would mean a letting-be in the sense of letting go—of forgetting. To the extent that Heideggerian thought about the truth of Being cannot voice this affirmation, in the sense that it still searches for the ontological language that might bring such thought to expression, Heidegger still has not freed himself from metaphysics. Says Derrida, "No doubt that Nietzsche called for an active forgetting of Being: it would not have the metaphysical form imputed to it by Heidegger. . . . Are we to take the question of the truth of Being as the last sleeping shudder of the superior man?'' (EM 136).

The death of God means the end of man. The end of man requires the end of metaphysics. The end of man heralds the possibility of a space in which it is once more possible to think. To think requires thought's liberation from metaphysics. Thinking requires a language that can speak ''outside of/free from'' the *arche* of a metaphysical discourse. If such thinking does not consist in thinking the truth of Being (and we have not ruled this out), then in what would such a thinking consist?

Perhaps it might, following Derrida, consist in the trace of *différance*. Unlike the presencing of being, the trace de-signifies itself in its signifying function. In the play of différance language is pushed to a space where the very idea of meaning collapses and is called into question. The mistaken *a* of différance gives trace to what cannot come to word; it differs and defers without presence. It is thinking without the primordiality of a metaphysical discourse; in fact, it undercuts, in its differing/deferring, the very idea of primordiality. Metaphysical discourse cannot think without positing the idea of a primordial essence, an essential truth, a faith in absolute knowledge, in *meaning;* it reaches for the universal that would ground all meaning. The trace functions as a deferral of meaning; it defers in a grouping of arbitrary signs that differ. ''*Différance* is the non-full, non-simple, structural and differentiating origin of differences.''[10] There is no continuity of meaning, no primordial process of ''gathering''—there is no ground. Différance is *not,* says Derrida; it has neither existence nor essence. It is not a category, nor does it fit into categories as such. It begins nowhere except in the arbitrary deferring of play. It anticipates its own dissolution in its ephemeral emergence. In its differing/deferring it brings to thought the very arbitrariness of language itself; and inasmuch as we are formed by language, inasmuch as our own subjectivity is a product of the arbitrary determination of a linguistic structure, it undercuts our own absoluteness. In the play of the trace the very formation of our sense of *meaning* and *truth* is seen to be optional.

Put very schematically, optionality and metaphysics are incompatible. Metaphysics is identical to absoluteness (and this is equally true of skepticism and positivism which try to make ''nonsense'' of metaphysics). But metaphysics qua language is revealed in its arbitrariness. Thus metaphysics is undermined (deferred) by its own optionality. Also, in the play of the trace, the end of man is anticipated. In the language of différance man *disappears.* What is called into question by the trace is the unity of language; in this, as Foucault observes, the unity of man as such apparently cannot even arise, except insofar as that unity is tied to language, to metaphysics qua language.

Like Derrida, Foucault recognizes a return to language as the key to dissolving the universality and essentiality of man. It is in the "counter-science" of linguistics that the concept of man is displaced by reflection on the unity of language. "From within language experienced and transversed as language, in the play of its possibilities extended to their farthest point, what emerges is that man has 'come to an end' . . ." (OT 383).[11] Unlike the human sciences, which try in vain to traverse the gap between an identical subject/object, linguistics "is constitutive of its very object" (OT 382). In it, to the extent we think man at all, we apprehend what underlies his being "trapped in the density of what he does not think" (OT 338). And what man does not think is that what he thinks is effected by language itself; indeed, that he himself is effected by the arbitrary determination of language. Linguistics reveals, says Saussure, that "language is not a function of the speaking subject."[12] To understand language, linguistics must abandon even the notion of a speaking subject, it must abandon the very concept of man. In linguistics the primacy of language displaces the primacy of a transcendental subject; the dominance of an a priori structure gives way to the dominance of gap, of fragmentation, of fissure, of a nexus of oppositions, of the arbitrary play of discrete *differences.*

In the "play of possibilities" we should hear, mediated by Saussure and Jakobson, who in some sense provide the "tools" of his departure from metaphysics, Derrida's notion of the playing trace of différance. "Such a play, *différance,* is thus no longer simply a concept, but rather the possibility of conceptuality, of a conceptual process and system in general."[13] With Derrida, what is apprehended in linguistics is carried forward and made in some sense a new mode of philosophical thinking that undercuts the very architectonic of metaphysics. In it, as in thinking the truth of Being, the "ontological difference" between being and beings is called into question.

But even here, and the same problem holds in principle for Foucault and for Heidegger, in spite of the "fact" that différance has no essence, that it erases itself in its trace, despite this, "For us, *différance* remains a metaphysical name, and all the names that it receives in our language are still, as names, metaphysical."[14] Thus, it is left for us to put "into question the name of the name." It turns out that "there is no name for it," but this is something which thought cannot yet think. Thinking still is unable to think the *unthought* of the unnamed and unnameable difference. To the extent that thinking must still *name* to think at all, it still thinks metaphysically.

Again we are pushed back to the question with which we began. What will thinking be like with the end of man? The possibility of such thinking requires, it seems, the capacity to think nonmetaphysically. And such a capacity is rooted in a genuine appropriation of the death of God. Yet all of postmodern philosophy, and indeed all contemporary thought to the extent that it calls man into question, is still pervaded by a general *preoccupation* with the metaphysical. This preoccupation is characterized by *opposition:* the metaphysical still stands as the point of departure in philosophy's attempt to move beyond the metaphysical; the metaphysical is still necessary to give philosophy's task its *significance*—and to that extent the metaphysical still forms and informs the discourse of contemporary thought about man.

But if the end of man is ever to become a reality, if the death of God is ever to be realized in its truth, then the metaphysical, the preoccupation with the metaphysical that still haunts contemporary thought, must *pass away.* This is not something that can be done immediately; it probably cannot be accomplished in a radical break; it perhaps has to be *played out*—and Foucault, Heidegger, and Derrida, each of them offers us a region, a surface, a *space,* in which to think man to an end. Man has been effected, produced, in the impact of language itself; and it will no doubt be in language that man is erased, displaced, dissolved. But it will not be in *a* language that this erasure will be accomplished. Rather, it will be in the *thinking* that emerges out of a language in which man is not the ground, foundation, or *telos* of philosophical reflection.

The lesson of postmodern thought—or rather, *postmortem* thought, in that it still lingers over the corpse of man—is that one ends badly by ending with conclusions, as if that were the end of thought, as if thinking had an end. Thus, let us end as Socrates met his end, with prophecy. There will come a time when all philosophy prior to Nietzsche will be looked upon as a deep nostalgia. All metaphysics from Plato to Hegel and beyond, to the extent it is remembered at all, will be viewed as grand mythology. Man will become a distant figure on the horizon, an echo of a thinking gone by. The great triad of God-Metaphyics-Man will be buried under the dancing feet of the *Übermensch*—his way of paying his respects.

Notes

From Intentionality to Responsibility:
On Levinas's Philosophy of Language

1. M. Heidegger, *Gesamtausgabe* (GA) 20. Certain elements of Levinas's critique of Husserl bear a striking resemblance to critical remarks made by Heidegger in the lecture of the summer of 1925 (GA 20: 61) and the summer of 1928 (GA 26: 169) on Husserl's privileging the *theoretical* intentionality and his tendency to describe the most fundamental intention as a form of knowledge. In his critique of Heidegger Levinas will pronounce a similar accusation not only about Husserl's work but also about Heidegger's thought of Being and Truth. See my "Phenomenology—Ontology—Metaphysics: Levinas' Perspective on Husserl and Heidegger," in *Man and World* 16 (1983): 113–27.

2. *Autrement qu'être; ou, Au-delà de l'essence* (The Hague: M. Nijhoff, 1974) (AE), pp. 39–76, 167–218; *Otherwise than Being; or, Beyond Essence,* trans. Alphonso Lingis (The Hague: M. Nijhoff, 1981) (OB), pp. 31–59, 131–71.

3. *En découvrant l'existence avec Husserl et Heidegger* (Paris: Vrin, 1967²) (ED), pp. 218–36; *Collected Papers,* trans. and intro. Alphonso Lingis (Dordrecht: M. Nijhoff, 1987) (CP), pp. 109–26.

4. *Ideen zu einer reinen Phänomenologie und phänomenologischen Philosophie I* (The Hague: M. Nijhoff, 1976), pp. 52–53 (my translation): vol. 3 of *Husserliana* (HU), published by Martinus Nijhoff.

5. Compare E. Husserl, *Zur Phänomenologie des inneren Zeitbewusstseins (1893–1917),* HU 10: 29ff.

6. Compare Heidegger, *Sein und Zeit* (Frankfurt: V. Klostermann, 1977) (SZ) §§ 31–34, especially pp. 198–200 (GA 2: 149–51). Levinas's analysis of identification can be compared to Heidegger's analysis in GA 20: 69–70. There, too, *intentionality* is interpreted as implying *identification,* and "evidence" is defined as "covering identification" (*deckende Identifizierung*), whereas *identification* is explained as "showing the meant or the intuited" (*Ausweisung des Vermeinten am Angeschauten*). Levinas himself refers, with some reservation, to Heidegger's analysis of the "as-structure," when he writes: " 'Quelque chose en tant que quelque chose'—la formule est heideggerienne. . ." (ED 219, CP 111).

7. The second meaning is close to the meaning of "vouloir dire," by which Jacques Derrida translated Husserl's *Meinen*. See "La forme et le vouloir-dire" in J. Derrida, *Marges de la Philosophie* (Paris: Minuit, 1972), pp. 185–207; "Form and Meaning: A Note on the Phenomenology of Language" in *Margins of Philosophy*, trans. Alan Bass (Chicago: Univ. of Chicago Press, 1982), pp. 155–73.

8. AE 44, 46, 54, 56, 73. Lingis translates "fable" as "tale"; see OB 34, 36, 42, 43, 56.

9. AE 45–46, OB 35–36. It is possible that Levinas, in using the words "narration," "récit," "epos," and "fable" (ED 217–18; CP 109–10; AE 46, 54; OB 34, 42) and also "kérygme" (*vide infra*), wants to allude to Heidegger's consideration of language as *Sage*. Compare Heidegger, "Der Ursprung des Kunstwerkes," in *Holzwege*, GA 5: 61 and *Vorträge und Aufsätze* (Pfullingen: Neske, 1959), pp. 212–18.

10. For the following, see AE 43–53, OB 34–41. In Heidegger's course of the summer semester 1925 (GA 20), cited in note 1, we find the same series of concepts: "identification" (69ff.), "proclamation" (*Kundgeben*, 75–76), and "denomination" (*Nennung, Nominalisierung*, defined as "the form in which we seize thematically a *Sachverhalt*," pp. 88–89).

11. SZ 218: "Imgleichen erfolgt die Gegenrede als Antwort zunächst direkt aus dem Verstehen des im Mitsein schon 'geteilten' Worüber der Rede."

12. "Der Ursprung des Kunstwerkes" in *Holzwege*, GA 5: 1–74.

13. "Die Sprache" in *Unterwegs zur Sprache*, GA 12:30: "Die Sprache spricht. Der Mensch spricht, insofern er der Sprache entspricht. Das Entsprechen ist Hören. Es hört, insofern es dem Geheiss der Stille gehört."

14. The idea of "unlimited responsibility," which I am explicating here, is constantly present in Levinas's work. See especially AE 12, 60, 172–74, OB 10, 47, 135–36.

15. Compare *Sein und Zeit*, GA 2: 71–84 (SZ 52–62), 116 (87), 152 (113), 174 (131), 182 (137), 202 (152), 240 (180–181), 241 (181), 245 (184), 253–54 (191), 256 (192), 260 (196). See also GA 26: 233, 234, 236, 237, 247, where Heidegger affirms very explicitly that totality (*Ganzheit*) is essential to "world."

16. In *Totalité et Infini* (The Hague: M. Nijhoff, 1961) (TI), see, for example, pp. xiv, xvi, xvii, 4, 10, 22, 33, 35, 37, 39; English translation, by Alphonso Lingis as *Totality and Infinity* (Pittsburgh: Duquesne Univ. Press, 1969[1]), pp. 26, 28, 30, 34, 39; Levinas uses the expressions "se produire," "épiphanie," and "révélation" to indicate the difference between the "invisible" face and the monstration or evidence of the phenomena.

17. AE 7–8, 193–98 (OB 6, 151–56). *Dédire* is already mentioned at the end of the preface of TI, p. xviii (English p. 30).

Rereading *Totality and Infinity*

The following abbreviations are used in references in the text and in the notes:

AQ Emmanuel Levinas, *Autrement qu'être; ou, Au-delà de l'essence*; see note 7.

DEE Emmanuel Levinas, *De l'existence à l'existant*; see note 9.

DVI Emmanuel Levinas, *De Dieu qui vient à l'idée*; see note 3.

ED Jacques Derrida, *L'écriture et la différence*; see note 4.

EE Emmanuel Levinas, *Existence and Existents*; see note 9.

FFL Richard Cohen, ed., *Face to Face with Levinas*; see note 6.

OB Emmanuel Levinas, *Otherwise than Being; or, Beyond Essence*; see note 7.

TeI Emmanuel Levinas, *Totalité et Infini*; see note 1.

TI Emmanuel Levinas, *Totality and Infinity*; see note 1.

WD Jacques Derrida, *Writing and Difference*; see note 4.

1. E. Levinas, *Totalité et Infini: essai sur l'extériorité* (The Hague: Martinus Nijhoff, 1961); trans. A. Lingis, *Totality and Infinity: An Essay on Exteriority* (Pittsburgh: Duquesne University Pr., 1969). Henceforth TeI and TI, respectively.

2. Although, like Levinas, I refer to the face-to-face as a relation, it should not be forgotten that he often qualifies this by employing the phrase "relation without relation"; see for example TI 295; TeI 271.

3. E. Levinas, *De Dieu qui vient à l'idée*, 2d ed. (Paris: Vrin, 1986), pp. 131–32 and 143. Henceforth DVI.

4. J. Derrida, "Violence et métaphysique," *L'écriture et la différence* (Paris: Seuil, 1967), pp. 117–228; trans. A. Bass, *Writing and Difference* (Chicago: University of Chicago Press, 1978), pp. 79–153. Henceforth ED and WD, respectively.

5. The phrase "ontological or transcendental oppression" refers to the last two sections of Derrida's own essay, "Of Transcendental Violence" and "Of Ontological Violence."

6. T. de Boer, "An Ethical Transcendental Philosophy," in Richard Cohen, ed., *Face to Face with Levinas* (Albany: State University of New York Press, 1986). Henceforth FFL.

7. E. Levinas, *Autrement qu'être; ou, Au-delà de l'essence* (The Hague: Martinus Nijhoff, 1974), p. 84; trans. A. Lingis, *Otherwise than Being; or, Beyond Essence* (The Hague: Martinus Nijhoff, 1981), p. 66. Henceforth AQ and OB, respectively.

8. E. Levinas, *Théorie de l'intuition dans la phénoménologie de Husserl* (Paris: Félix Alcan, 1930), p. 174; trans. André Orianne, *The Theory of Intuition in Husserl's Phenomenology* (Evanston: Northwestern University Press, 1973), p. 119.

9. E. Levinas, *De l'existence à l'existant* (Paris: Vrin, 1947), p. 56; trans. A. Lingis, *Existence and Existents* (The Hague: Martinus Nijhoff, 1978), p. 37. Henceforth DEE and EE, respectively.

10. See R. Bernasconi, "The Silent World of the Evil Genius" in *The Collegium Phaenomenologicum: The First Ten Years,* ed. Giuseppina Moneta, John Sallis, and Jacques Taminiaux (Dordrecht: Martinus Nijhoff, 1988).

11. M. Heidegger, *Sein und Zeit* (Tübingen: Max Niemeyer, 1949), pp. 57, 120, and 124; trans. John Macquarrie and Edward Robinson, *Being and Time* (Oxford: Basil Blackwell, 1967), pp. 83, 157, and 161. It should be recognized that there is a certain ambiguity in the last passage as to whether the indifference [*Gleichgültigkeit*] of passing another by is deficient or indifferent [*Indifferenz*]. The question of *Indifferenz* in *Sein und Zeit* needs further examination.

12. Levinas refers to cultural meaning as *signification,* which he distinguishes from *sens.* See, for example, "La signification et le sens" in *Humanisme de l'Autre Homme* (Montpellier: Fata Morgana, 1972), pp. 17–63; trans. A. Lingis, *Collected Philosophical Papers* (Dordrecht: Martinus Nijhoff, 1987), pp. 75–107. These are complex issues which need separate treatment, as Levinas's attempt to keep the ethical separate from the cultural threatens to recreate the problem he found in Heidegger. I will be giving a more thorough discussion of these questions in my forthcoming book *Between Levinas and Derrida.*

Absolute Positivity and Ultrapositivity: Husserl and Levinas

1. Edmund Husserl, *Ideas Pertaining to a Pure Phenomenology and to a Phenomenological Philosophy,* trans. F. Kersten (The Hague: Martinus Nijhoff, 1982), I: 39, 38.

2. Husserl, *Ideas,* I: 169, 167.

3. Alphonso Lingis, *Phenomenological Explanations* (Dordrecht: Martinus Nijhoff, 1986), pp. 1–2.

4. *The Presocratics,* ed. Philip Wheelwright (Indianapolis: Bobbs-Merrill, 1960), pp. 96–98.

5. See Edmund Husserl, *Formal and Transcendental Logic,* trans. D. Cairns (The Hague: Martinus Nijhoff, 1969).

6. George Heffernan, "Hermeneutical Remarks towards a Solution to the Problem of the Three-fold Structural Stratification of Formal Logic as Apophantical Analytics in the *FTL* of Edmund Husserl," in *Proceedings of the Husserl Circle,* 19th Meeting, Washington University, St. Louis, May 5–7, 1987, p. 114.

7. Since giving this paper in October 1987, I have come across a very beautiful and moving photograph (by Robert A. Hutchinson, *Smithsonian,* February 1988, p. 184) of Sunderlal Bahuguna, of India, hugging a pipal tree with tenderness and determination. I would say that this gesture, which is an integral part of Mr. Bahuguna's campaign to save the forests of northern India, exerts its positive effect not

just because it provides a unilateral protection for the tree, placing the physical and moral resources, the integrity, of a human life between chain saw and lumber, but also and more profoundly because it treats the tree as if it were another person, a person at the limits of vulnerability, without defenses, at the mercy of others.

Derrida and the Ethics of the Ear

1. See Fred R. Dallmayr, "Hermeneutics and Deconstruction: Gadamer and Derrida in Dialogue," in *Critical Encounters: Between Philosophy and Politics* (Notre Dame: University of Notre Dame Press, 1987), pp. 130–58. An abridged version of this essay, as well as a translation of Gadamer's response to it ("A Letter to Dallmayr") will be forthcoming in *Dialogue and Deconstruction: The Gadamer-Derrida Encounter,* ed. Diane Michelfelder and Richard Palmer (Albany: SUNY Press, forthcoming).

2. Gadamer makes this point both in his "Letter to Dallmayr" as well as in a lecture from 1986, *"Hermeneutik und Logozentrismus"* (the latter essay is also forthcoming in translation in *Dialogue and Deconstruction*).

3. Jacques Derrida, "Mnemosyne," trans. Cecile Lindsay, in *Mémoires: For Paul de Man* (New York: Columbia University Press, 1986), p. 3.

4. Dallmayr, p. 155.

5. Derrida, "The Ends of Man," in *Margins of Philosophy,* trans. Alan Bass (Chicago: University of Chicago Press, 1982), pp. 109–36; "The Laws of Reflection: Nelson Mandela, in Admiration," in *For Nelson Mandela,* ed. Jacques Derrida and Mustapha Tlili (New York: Seaver Books, 1987), pp. 13–42.

6. Jacques Derrida and Pierre-Jean Labarrière, *Alterités* (Paris: Editions Osiris, 1986), p. 70 (my translation).

7. Derrida, "Roundtable on Autobiography," trans. Peggy Kampf, in *The Ear of the Other,* ed. Christie V. McDonald (New York: Schlocken Books, 1985), p. 51.

8. "Ends of Man," p. 134.

9. Derrida, "Violence and Metaphysics: An Essay on the Thought of Emmanuel Levinas," in *Writing and Difference,* trans. Alan Bass (Chicago: University of Chicago Press, 1978), p. 80.

10. "Roundtable on Autobiography," p. 51.

11. "Hermeneutics and Logocentrism," trans. Richard Palmer and Diane Michelfelder, pp. 7, 8 (unpublished translation).

12. "Letter to Dallmayr," trans. Richard Palmer and Diane Michelfelder, p. 5 (unpublished translation).

13. Hans-Georg Gadamer, "Text and Interpretation," trans. Dennis Schmidt, in *Hermeneutics and Modern Philosophy*, ed. Brice Wachterhauser (Albany: State University of New York Press, 1986), p. 390.

14. *Mémoires: For Paul de Man*, p. 37.

15. Gadamer, "Text and Interpretation," p. 388.

16. Derrida, "The Principle of Reason: The University in the Eyes of Its Pupils," in *Diacritics* 13 (Fall 1983): 8.

17. "The Ends of Man," p. 135.

18. Derrida, "No Apocalypse, Not Now (full speed ahead, seven missiles, seven missives)," in *Diacritics* 14 (Summer 1984): 20–31.

19. Martin Heidegger, "Memorial Address," in *Discourse on Thinking*, trans. John M. Anderson and E. Hans Freund (New York: Harper and Row, 1966), pp. 43–57. The quote is from p. 56.

20. "No Apocalypse, Not Now," p. 31.

21. Gadamer, "*Destruktion* and Deconstruction," trans. Geoff Waite and Richard Palmer, p. 18 (unpublished translation, forthcoming in *Dialogue and Deconstruction*).

Disseminating Originary Ethics and the Ethics of Dissemination

*Permission to use parts of this paper, which were subsequently incorporated into my *Radical Hermeneutics: Repetition, Deconstruction, and the Hermeneutic Project* (Bloomington: Indiana University Press, 1987), ch. 9, "Toward an Ethics of Dissemination," is gratefully acknowledged.

1. In *Heidegger: Basic Writings*, ed. David Krell (New York: Harper & Row, 1975), pp. 193–242; see pp. 235ff.

2. Martin Heidegger, *What Is Called Thinking?*, trans. J. Glenn Gray and Frederick Wieck (New York: Harper & Row, 1968), p. 89.

3. See the threefold demarcation of the path of thought in Heidegger's *Vier Seminare* (Frankfurt: Klostermann, 1977), pp. 82–87.

4. Martin Heidegger, *Time and Being*, trans. Joan Stambaugh (New York: Harper & Row, 1972), p. 71. For more on this reading of Heidegger, see my *Radical Hermeneutics: Repetition, Deconstruction, and the Hermeneutic Project* (Bloomington: Indiana University Press, 1987), pp. 171–86.

5. Heidegger, *Der Satz vom Grund*, 3rd ed. (Pfullingen: Neske, 1965), pp. 185–88.

6. Martin Heidegger, *An Introduction to Metaphysics,* trans. Ralph Manheim (New York: Doubleday Anchor, 1961), p. 160.

7. See Derrida's critique of "onto-hermeneutics" and its search for the hermeneutic key in *Spurs: Nietzsche's Styles,* trans. Barbara Harlow (Chicago: University of Chicago Press, 1978). What follows is an attempt to give an ethical twist to Derrida's notion of dissemination. To get some idea of how Derrida himself puts his categories to a socio-political use, see "The Principle of Reason: The University in the Eyes of Its Pupils," trans. C. Porter and P. Lewis, *Diacritics* 13 (Fall 1983): 3–20; and "NO APOCALYPSE, NOT NOW (full speed ahead, seven missiles, seven missives)," trans. C. Porter and P. Lewis, *Diacritics* 14 (Summer 1984): 20–31; "Racism's Last Word," trans. P. Kampf, *Critical Inquiry* 12 (1985): 290–98; and Derrida's response to two critics of "Racism's Last Word" in *Critical Inquiry* 13 (1986): 140–70.

8. This expression from Saint Augustine's *Confessions* (Book X, c. 33) is cited frequently by Hannah Arendt; see e.g., *The Human Condition* (Chicago: University of Chicago Press, 1958), pp. 10–11, n. 2.

9. For a full account of *Gelassenheit* in Meister Eckhart, see my *The Mystical Element in Heidegger's Thought* (New York: Fordham University Press, 1986), ch. 3.

The Obligation to Will the Freedom of Others, According to Jean-Paul Sartre

1. *Cahiers pour une morale* (Paris: Gallimard, 1983) (hereafter cited as CM). Translations are my own.

2. *Being and Nothingness,* trans. Hazel Barnes (New York: Philosophical Library, 1956), p. 412 n. (hereafter cited as BN).

3. "Authenticity, Conversion, and the City of Ends in Sartre's *Notebooks for an Ethics,*" in *The Future of Continental Philosophy and the Politics of Difference,* ed. Hugh Silverman (Albany, N.Y.: SUNY Press, 1989).

4. CM 430, 515. Comprehension is discussed on pp. 285–303.

5. CM 17–18, 54–55, 95, 302, 421, 430, 434, 487, 515, 521–24.

6. *Existentialism and Humanism,* trans. P. Mairet (London: Eyre Methuen, 1973), p. 51 (hereafter cited as EH); *What Is Literature?,* trans. B. Frechtman (New York: Washington Square, 1966), pp. 108, 192; "Materialism and Revolution," in *Literary and Philosophical Essays,* trans. A. Michelson (New York: Collier, 1962), pp. 245, 253. Later works in which Sartre also proposes freedom as his ultimate goal are: "Self-Portrait at Seventy," interview with M. Contat in *Life/Situations,* trans. P. Auster and L. Davis (New York: Pantheon, 1977), p. 61; *Sartre by Himself,*

full text from a film produced by A. Astrure and M. Contat with the participation of S. de Beauvoir, J-L. Bost, A. Gorg, J. Povilon, trans. R. Seaver (New York: Urizen, 1978), pp. 42–43; "The Last Words of Jean-Paul Sartre," interview with B. Lévy, trans. A. Foulke, in *Dissent* 27 (Fall 1980): 398–400; "Conversations with Jean-Paul Sartre," dialogue with Simone de Beauvoir in *Adieux*, trans. P. O'Brien (New York: Pantheon, 1984), p. 439.

7. Joseph MacMahon in his review of my book, *The Foundation and Structure of Sartrean Ethics*, in *The French Review* 54 (May 1981): 879, claims that such demonstrations can be found in "*Saint-Genet, Le Diable et le Bon Dieu, Les Sequestres d'Altona*, and the essays on colonialism." While it is true that Sartre concretely describes and illustrates his moral ideal, individuals willing the freedom of others, in these and other works, description and illustration are not demonstration.

8. *Sartre by Himself*, 76–81; "L'Ecriture et la Publication," interview by M. Sicard in *Obliques*, nos. 18–19 (1979): 14–15.

9. EH 29–30. I have slightly modified Mairet's translation.

10. *The Foundation and Structure of Sartrean Ethics* (Lawrence, Kansas: Univ. of Kansas Pr., 1979), pp. 79–81. Chapter 4 of this book is devoted to the issue of this paper.

11. One recent author who maintains that universalization is a necessary condition for a moral judgment is Sander Lee, "The Central Role of Universalization in Sartrean Ethics," *Philosophy and Phenomenological Research* 46 (Sept. 1985): 59–72. As far as I can see, Lee offers no *argument* to support his position but rather assumes that the only morally relevant aspects of a situation are those that at least in principle can be duplicated.

12. EH 51.

13. In her review article of my book, *The Foundation and Structure*, in *Man and World* 14 (1981): 226.

14. In BN Sartre describes values as nonexistent ideals and says that to choose them is to choose to make them real; see Part I, Section III.

15. "Freedom as a Universal Notion in Sartre's Ethical Theory," *Revue Internationale de Philosophie* nos. 152–53 (1985): 146.

16. Thomas Flynn, *Sartre and Marxist Existentialism* (Chicago: U. of Chicago Pr., 1984), pp. 40–46. Flynn's book contains an extensive discussion of the issue this paper addresses.

17. "Materialism and Revolution," p. 255; see also CM 294, 487. However, in my opinion, Stone goes much too far in claiming "I just can't have the property [of freedom] at all in isolation from others," in "Freedom as Universal Notion in

Sartre's Ethical Theory," p. 145. Sartre himself states that "freedom as the definition of man" (EH 52), i.e., ontological freedom, does not depend on others. Also, whether others recognize it or not, I always have *some* free choices.

18. CM 287–99. *Search for a Method,* trans. H. Barnes (New York: Random House, 1963), pp. 152–56, 170–81, also discusses comprehension.

19. Of course Sartre believes that one is always prereflectively (implicitly) aware of one's freedom, CM 373, 401, 488. The issue under discussion is one's *explicit* recognition of it, and how this is dependent on the other.

20. "Comprehension implies in its structure the refusal to adopt as well as to transcend the end," CM 287–90. Sartre does say that the sympathetic union involved in comprehension naturally tends toward adoption, yet he insists that comprehension and adoption are separate acts.

21. CM 150–51, 294–95, 443–44, 515; "Materialism and Revolution," pp. 250, 254–55. Sartre suggests this argument, Simone de Beauvoir presents it in detail in *Pyrrhus et Cinéas* (Paris: Gallimard, 1944). Stone succinctly puts the point this way, "Only a free recognition will count in my own eyes," in "Freedom as a Universal Notion in Sartre's Ethical Theory," p. 146.

22. Lecture given in 1964 at the Gramsci Institute in Rome, pp. 97ff. This manuscript is now in the Bibliothéque Nationale, Paris. (I thank Professors Betsy Bowman and Robert Stone for sharing their copy with me.) In *Search for a Method,* pp. 91, 171, need is said to be the basis of *all* projects and goals.

On the Advantage and Disadvantage of Nietzsche for Women

1. See for example Nietzsche's "On the New Idol" in *Thus Spoke Zarathustra,* trans. Walter Kaufmann (New York: Penguin Books, 1954), pp. 48–51.

2. Jacques Derrida, *Spurs: Nietzsche's Styles* (Chicago: University of Chicago Press, 1979). Ofelia Schutte, *Beyond Nihilism: Nietzsche without Masks* (Chicago: University of Chicago Press, 1984). David Farrell Krell, *Postponements: Women, Sensuality, and Death in Nietzsche* (Bloomington: Indiana University Press, 1986).

3. *Postponements,* p. 80.

4. Julia Kristeva, "About Chinese Women," in *The Kristeva Reader,* ed. Toril Moi (New York: Columbia University Press, 1986), p. 155.

5. This discussion is further developed in Debra Bergoffen, "Sophocles' *Antigone* and Freud's *Civilization and Its Discontents,*" *American Imago* 43 (Summer 1986): 151–67.

6. Huanani-Kay Trask, *Eros and Power* (Philadelphia: University of Pennsylvania Press, 1986), p. 17.

7. Friedrich Nietzsche, *On the Advantage and Disadvantage of History for Life,* trans. Peter Preuss (Indianapolis: Hackett Publishing Co., 1980), p. 31.

8. For a discussion of the relationship between the woman as home centered and the subject of reproduction see Gayatri Chatravorty Spivak, "French Feminism in an International Frame," *Yale French Studies,* No. 62 (1981): 180–83.

9. Jane Gallop, *Reading Lacan* (Ithaca: Cornell University Press, 1985), p. 148.

10. *Eros and Power,* p. 30.

11. *Eros and Power,* p. 148.

12. For an extensive discussion of the proper cultivation of memory and forgetfulness see Nietzsche's *Advantage and Disadvantage of History.* See also Debra Bergoffen, "Seducing Historicism," *International Studies in Philosophy* 19:2 (1987): 85–98, for an analysis of the meaning of memory, forgetfulness, and history in Nietzsche's thought.

13. Nietzsche, "Upon the Blessed Isles," *Zarathustra,* pp. 85–88.

14. For a discussion of Nietzsche's inversion of the male-female roles in the couple see Derrida, *Spurs,* pp. 149, 150 n. 10.

15. See John T. Wilcox, "Zarathustra's Yes," *The Great Year of Zarathustra,* ed. David Goicoechea (Lanham: University Press of America, 1986), pp. 28–29 for a reflection on Zarathustra's imagery of mothering.

16. "French Feminism," pp. 180–81.

17. See Mary Beth Pringle, Judi M. Roller, Jennifer Smith, "Demystifying Feminist Criticism: A Response," *Antioch Review* 44 (Spring 1986): 231–41, for an overview of the history of feminist criticism.

An Ironic Mimesis

1. Luce Irigaray, *Speculum of the Other Woman,* trans. Gillian C. Gill (Ithaca: Cornell University Press, 1985), hereafter SO.

2. Maurice Merleau-Ponty, *The Visible and the Invisible,* ed. Claude LeFort, trans. John O'Neill (Evanston: Northwestern University Press, 1973), hereafter VI.

3. See Toril Moi, *Sexual/Textual Politics: Feminist Literary Theory* (New York: Methuen & Co., 1985), pp. 137–43.

4. For a full development of this question, see Kate Mehuron, "Metamorphoses: Thinking in the Crisis of the Speculative Tradition" (Ph.D. diss., Vanderbilt University, 1988), chap. 4.

5. The intrinsically languaged nature of carnal being needs exegetical support. For a full discussion, see "Metamorphoses," chap. 2.

6. More precisely, Merleau-Ponty states that "the flesh is an ultimate notion" (VI 140).

7. Relevant essays include "Indirect Language" in Maurice Merleau-Ponty, *The Prose of the World*, ed. Claude LeFort, trans. John O'Neill (Evanston: Northwestern University Press, 1973), pp. 9–46; "Eye and Mind" in *The Primacy of Perception*, ed. James M. Edie, trans. Carleton Dallery (Evanston: Northwestern University Press, 1964), pp. 159–90; "Cezanne's Doubt", in *Sense and Non-Sense*, trans. Hubert L. Dreyfus and Patricia A. Dreyfus (Evanston: Northwestern University Press, 1964), pp. 9–40.

8. Ferdinand de Saussure, *Course in General Linguistics*, ed. Charles Bally and Albert Sechehaye, trans. Wade Baskin (New York: The Philosophical Library, Inc., 1959). Saussure's influence is most obvious in Merleau-Ponty's essays "Eye and Mind" in *The Primacy of Perception*, "The Indirect Language" in *The Prose of the World*, and all of *The Visible and the Invisible*.

9. Maurice Merleau-Ponty, *Phenomenology of Perception*, trans. Colin Smith (London: Routledge & Kegan Paul, 1962; New York: Humanities Press, 1965).

10. Hugh Drummond, "The Ultimate Erector Set," *Mother Jones* 12 (1987): 9.

11. Shoshana Felman, "Women and Madness: The Critical Phallacy," *Diacritics* 5:4 (Winter 1975): 3.

12. With respect to the usage of irony and other indirect writing styles, I have in mind such exemplary figures as Socratic irony itself, the Platonic dialogues generally, and their counterpoint in Aristophanic parody. Also, I urge that we recall the philosophical prose of Soren Kierkegaard's pseudonymous works, and Friedrich Nietzsche's elaborate stylistic writing experiments that employ indirect styles ranging from hyperbole, prose essay, to dithyramb and aphorism. Nor should we ignore the thematic place occupied by irony and other indirect writing styles in systematic thinkers such as Friedrich Schlegel, Georg Wilhelm Friedrich Hegel, and, more recently, Jean-Paul Sartre.

13. Irigaray's texts should be read in conjunction with other feminist stylistic experiments produced in the United States and elsewhere. By doing so, our reading is more broadly informed by the comparative exchange with other exemplary, experimental texts such as Susan Griffin, *Women and Nature: The Roaring inside Her* (New York: Harper & Row, 1978), and Mary Daly, *Gyn/Ecology: The Metaethics of Radical Feminism* (Boston: Beacon Press, 1978) and *Pure Lust: Elemental Feminist Philosophy* (Boston: Beacon Press, 1984).

14. Luce Irigaray, *This Sex Which Is Not One*, trans. Catherine Porter and Carolyn Burke (Ithaca: Cornell University Press, 1985), hereafter SNO.

15. Irigaray's critique of phallocentrism is influenced by Jacques Derrida. The latter goes so far as to coin a neologism—phallogocentrism—with which to refer to the overriding ideology of the metaphysical tradition in general. For the usage of this term, see "Choreographies" in *Diacritics* 12 (1982): 66–76. This is a transcribed interview with Jacques Derrida, conducted by Christie V. McDonald.

16. My emphasis on the dialogicity and plurivocality of Irigaray's text is deeply influenced by the full development of these notions found in Mikhail Mikhailovich Bakhtin, *The Dialogic Imagination: Four Essays by M. M. Bakhtin*, ed. Michael Holquist, trans. Caryl Emerson and Michael Holquist (Austin, Texas: University of Texas Press, 1981).

17. Jane Gallop gives an insightful reading that is attentive to this issue, and carefully elaborates its implications for feminist readers. See Jane Gallop, "Quand Nos Levres S'Ecrivent: Irigaray's Body Politic," *Romantic Review* 74 (1983): 77–83.

Defusing the Canon: Feminist Rereading and Textual Politics

1. Jean Francois Lyotard, *Le Different* (Paris: Minuit, 1983).

2. Shelia Ruth, "Methodocracy, Misogyny and Bad Faith: Sexism in the Philosophic Establishment," *Metaphilosophy* 10:1 (1979): 49.

3. This determination is made on a quantitative analysis of the articles classified under "feminism" in *The Philosopher's Index* (1973–1986).

4. David Farrell Krell, *Postponements* (Bloomington: Indiana University Press, 1986), p. 10; see also p. 85.

5. For a discussion of the different strategies employed by feminists reading "against the grain," see Toril Moi, *Sexual/Textual Politics: Feminist Literary Theory* (London and New York: Methuen, 1985).

6. Luce Irigaray, *Speculum del'autre femme* (Paris: Mouton, 1974), p. 72.

7. I am indebted for this formulation to friend and colleague Kristina Straub, Department of English, Miami University, who offered it in the context of a reading of a draft of this paper, against the grain.

Alma Gonzalez: Otherness as Attending to the Other

1. Howard Schwartz and Jerry Jacobs, *Qualitative Sociology: A Method to the Madness* (New York: Free Press, 1979), pp. 250, 260, 262–64.

2. Jürgen Habermas, *The Theory of Communicative Action*, vol. 1, *Reason and the Rationalization of Society*, trans. Thomas McCarthy (Boston: Beacon Press, 1984), pp. 285-86.

3. Alfred Schutz, *Collected Papers*, vol. 1, *The Problem of Social Reality* ed. Maurice Natanson (The Hague: Martinus Nijhoff, 1962), pp. 21–22; Schutz, Collected Papers, vol. 2, *Studies in Social Theory*, ed. Arvid Brodersen (The Hague: Martinus Nijhoff, 1964), pp. 91–96, 175.

4. *Reason and the Rationalization of Society*, pp. 48, 52.

5. *The Problem of Social Reality*, pp. 209, 223; *Studies in Social Theory*, pp. 105, 223.

6. *Qualitative Sociology*, pp. 247–48, 264.

7. *Studies in Social Theory*, pp. 98–104.

8. Edmund Husserl, *Ideas: General Introduction to Pure Phenomenology*, trans. W. R. Boyce Gibson (New York: Collier Books, 1931), pp. 197–200; Husserl, *Erste Philosophie (1923/24)*, part 2, *Theorie der phänomenologischen Reduktion*, ed. Rudolf Boehm (The Hague: Martinus Nijhoff, 1959), p. 133; Husserl, *The Phenomenology of Internal Time-Consciousness*, ed. Martin Heidegger, trans. James S. Churchill (Bloomington, Ind.: Indiana University Pr., 1964), p. 159.

9. Jürgen Habermas, "Wahrheitstheorien," in *Vorstudien und Erganzungen zur Theorie des kommunikativen Handelns* (Frankfurt am Main: Suhrkamp, 1984), pp. 177–79.

10. *Reason and the Rationalization of Society*, p. 66.

11. *Reason and the Rationalization of Society*, pp. 51–52.

12. *The Problem of Social Reality*, p. 44.

Decentering the Self: Two Perspectives from Philosophical Anthropology

1. Heidegger, *What Is a Thing?*, trans. W. B. Barton, Jr. and Vera Deutsch (Chicago: Henry Regnery Company, 1967), p. 106.

2. Heidegger, *The Basic Problems of Phenomenology*, trans. Albert Hofstadter (Bloomington, Ind.: Indiana University Press, 1982), p. 123.

3. Heidegger, *The End of Philosophy*, trans. Joan Stambaugh (New York: Harper and Row, 1973), p. 98.

4. See Heidegger, *The Basic Problems of Phenomenology*, p. 127; *The End of Philosophy*, p. 88; and *The Question concerning Technology*, trans. William Lovitt (New York: Harper and Row, 1977), p. 127.

5. *The Question concerning Technology*, p. 150.

6. Derrida, *Writing and Difference*, trans. Alan Bass (Chicago: University of Chicago Press, 1978), p. 153.

7. *Writing and Difference,* p. 85.

8. Descartes, *Discourse on Method* (Indianapolis: Bobbs-Merrill, 1960), p. 18. I am grateful to Vincent di Norcia for this observation.

9. Michael Ryan, *Marxism and Deconstruction* (Baltimore: Johns Hopkins Univ. Press, 1982), p. 3.

10. *Writing and Difference,* p. 153.

11. Max Weber, *The Protestant Ethic and the Spirit of Capitalism,* trans. Talcott Parsons (New York: Charles Scribner's Sons, 1958), p. 107.

12. *The Protestant Ethic,* p. 122.

13. Hugh Silverman, *Inscriptions: Between Phenomenology and Structuralism* (London: Routledge and Kegan Paul, 1987), p. 304.

14. *Writing and Difference,* p. 38.

15. Derrida, *Margins of Philosophy* (Chicago: University of Chicago Press, 1982), p. 213.

16. Heidegger, *The Metaphysical Foundations of Logic* (Bloomington, Ind.: Indiana University Press, 1984), p. 137.

17. *Metaphysical Foundations of Logic,* p. 17.

18. *The Basic Problems of Phenomenology,* p. 155.

19. Adriaan Peperzak, "Phenomenology-Ontology-Metaphysics: Levinas' Perspective on Husserl and Heidegger," *Man and World* 16 (1983): 113–27.

20. Steven Gans, "Ethics or Ontology: Levinas and Heidegger," *Philosophy Today* 16 (1972): 117–21.

21. *Writing and Difference,* p. 82.

22. Derrida, *Positions,* trans. Alan Bass (Chicago: University of Chicago Press, 1981), p. 28.

23. Peperzak, p. 118.

24. See Peperzak's summary, p. 121.

25. See Kenneth Liberman, *Understanding Interaction in Central Australia: An Ethnomethodology of Australian Aboriginal People* (London: Routledge and Kegan Paul, 1985).

26. Fred Myers, *Pintupi Country, Pintupi Self* (Washington, D.C.: Smithsonian, 1986), p. 124.

27. *Understanding Interaction,* p. 38.

28. W. E. H. Stanner, *After the Dreaming* (Sydney: Australian Broadcasting Commission, 1969), p. 47.

29. Ed. Charles A. Moore, *The Status of the Individual in East and West* (Honolulu: University of Hawaii Press, 1968), pp. 6–9.

30. Trans. Robert Thurman, *Tsong Khapa's Speech of Gold in the Essence of True Eloquence: Reason and Enlightenment in the Central Philosophy of Tibet* (Princeton, N.J.: Princeton University Press, 1984), p. 67.

31. Langri T'angpa Dorje Senge, in G. Rabten and G. N. Dhargyey, "Thought Transformation in Eight Stanzas," *Advice from a Spiritual Friend* (New Delhi: Publications for Wisdom Culture, 1977), pp. 16–17.

32. See Kenneth Liberman, "The Tibetan Cultural Praxis: *Bodhicitta* Thought Training," in *Humboldt Journal of Social Relations* 13 (1987): 113–26.

33. Thurman, p. 67.

34. Thurman, p. 64.

35. Jeffrey Hopkins, *Meditation on Emptiness* (London: Wisdom Publications, 1983), p. 4.

36. Jeffrey Hopkins, *Emptiness Yoga* (Ithaca, N.Y.: Snow Lion Press, 1987), p. 275.

37. See *Emptiness Yoga*, p. 271.

38. *Emptiness Yoga*, p. 64.

39. Robert Magliola, *Derrida on the Mend* (West Lafayette, Ind.: Purdue University Press, 1984), p. 126.

40. Asanga, *Dbus-tha' rnam-'byed* (Dharamsala: Tibetan Cultural Printing Press, nd.). My translation.

41. See note 21.

42. *Writing and Difference*, p. 82.

43. Thurman, p. 95.

44. Jonathan Culler, *Theory and Criticism after Structuralism* (Ithaca, N.Y.: Cornell University Press, 1982), p. 132.

45. Nagarjuna, *The Philosophy of the Middle Way*, trans. Kenneth Inada (Tokyo: Hokuseido, 1970), p. 52. Compare Nagarjuna, *The Philosophy of the Middle Way*, trans. David Kalupahana (Albany: SUNY Press, 1986).

46. Nagarjuna (1970), p. 52.

47. *Margins of Philosophy*, p. 262.

48. Anonymous, "Around the Campfire," *Earth First!: The Radical Environmental Journal* 7 (1987): 2.

The Subjectivity of the Speaker

1. "Entretien avec Claude Francis," *Les Écrits de Simone de Beauvoir*, ed. Claude Francis and Fernande Gontier (Paris: Gallimard, 1979).

2. *Close to Home: A Materialist Analysis of Women's Oppression*, trans. and ed. Diana Leonard (Amherst: University of Massachusetts Press, 1984).

3. *La Révolution du langage poètique* (Paris: Aux Éditions du Seuil, 1974). *Revolution in Poetic Language*, trans. Margaret Waller (New York: Columbia University Press, 1984).

4. *Speculum: De l'Autre Femme* (Paris: Les Éditions de Minuit, 1974). *Speculum of the Other Woman*, trans. Gillian Gill (Ithaca: Cornell University Press, 1985).

5. *Parole de femme* (Paris: Grasset, 1974).

6. "Mon expérience d'écrivain," *Les Écrits de Simone de Beauvoir*, p. 456. This and other translations not otherwise credited are mine.

7. Trans. Patrick O'Brian (New York: G. P. Putnam's Sons, 1966), p. 42. *Une Mort Tres Douce* (Paris: Gallimard, 1965).

8. *Les belles images*, trans. Patrick O'Brian (London: Fontana Books, 1969), pp. 65–66. *Les belles images* (Paris: Gallimard, 1966). I expand this point in my "Simone de Beauvoir and Two Kinds of Ambivalence in Action," in *The Thinking Muse: Feminism and Modern French Philosophy*, ed. Jeffner Allen and Iris M. Young (Bloomington: Indiana University Press, 1989).

9. *Le texte du roman* (The Hague: Mouton, 1970), p. 93n.

10. "Pratique Signifiante et Mode de Production," in *La traversée des signes*, ed. Julia Kristeva *et al.* (Paris: Aux Éditions du Seuil, 1975), p. 17.

11. "Le sujét en procès," in *Polylogue* (Paris: Aux Éditions de Seuil, 1977).

12. "Stabat Mater," in *Histoires d'amour* (Paris: Denoël, 1983). "Stabat Mater," in *Tales of Love*, trans. Leon S. Roudiez (New York: Columbia University Press, 1987), pp. 234–63.

13. "L'éthique de linguistique," in *Polylogue;* "The Ethics of Linguistics," in *Desire in Language*, ed. Léon S. Roudiez, trans. Thomas Gora, Alice Jardine, and Léon S. Roudiez (New York: Columbia University Press, 1980). I develop this argument in my "Questions for Julia Kristeva's Ethics of Linguistics," in *The Thinking Muse*.

14. *Parler, ce n'est jamais neutre* (Paris: Les Éditions de Minuit, 1985), pp. 9–10.

15. *Le corps lesbien* (Paris: Les Éditions de Minuit, 1973). *The Lesbian Body,*

trans. David Le Vay (New York: Avon Books, 1976).

16. "The Mark of Gender," *Feminist Issues* 5 (1985): 11.

17. "The Mark of Gender," p. 5.

18. Zribi-Hertz, *Towards a Transformationally Expressed Explanation of Passive Verbal Morphology in French and English* (Bloomington: Indiana University Linguistics Club, 1981), pp. 10–14.

19. Zribi-Hertz, p. 24.

20. John L. Austin, "Other Minds," in *Philosophical Papers*, ed. J. O. Urmson and G. J. Warnock (Oxford: Clarendon Press, 1961), p. 115.

21. *Adieux*, trans. Patrick O'Brian (New York: Pantheon Books, 1984), p. 123. *La cérémonie des Adieux* (Paris: Gallimard, 1981).

22. Annie Cohen-Solal, *Sartre* (Paris: Gallimard, 1985), p. 493. See Cohen-Solal's discussion throughout, as well as Claude Francis and Fernande Gontier, *Simone de Beauvoir* (Paris: Librarie Académique Perrin, 1985).

23. Felman, *The Literary Speech Act: Don Juan with J. L. Austin; or, Seduction in Two Languages*, trans. Catherine Porter (Ithaca: Cornell University Press, 1983), p. 51. *La scandale du corps parlant: Don Juan avec J. L. Austin* (Paris: Denoël, 1980).

24. Felman, p. 51.

25. Leclerc, *Hommes et femmes* (Paris: Grasset, 1985), pp. 137–38.

26. Leclerc, p. 148.

27. Leclerc, p. 31.

28. "Pyrrhus et Cinéas," *Pour une morale de l'ambiguité, suivi de Pyrrhus et Cinéas* (Paris: Gallimard, 1944); "Entretien avec Claude Francis," "Entretien avec Simone de Beauvoir," in *Les Écrits de Simone de Beauvoir.* "Sur quelques problemes actuelles de la féminisme," *La revue d'en face* 9–10 (1981): 3–14; Alice Schwartzer, *Simone de Beauvoir aujourd'hui: six entretiens* (Paris: Mercure de France, 1984).

29. Luce Irigaray, *Parler, ce n'est jamais neutre*, pp. 9–10; *Éthique de la difference sexuelle* (Paris: Les Éditions de Minuit), pp. 100–111.

Lacan's Other and the Factions of Plato's Soul

1. It is only recently with the publication of J. Muller and W. Richardson, *Lacan and Language* (New York: International Universities Press, 1982) that an adequate interpretation of Lacan's work has become available for English readers.

This book, admirably clear and detailed, is indispensable for understanding Lacan's development. See also Ellie Ragland-Sullivan, *Jacques Lacan and the Philosophy of Psychoanalysis* (Urbana & Chicago: University of Illinois Press, 1986). William J. Richardson's "The Mirror Inside: The Problem of the Self," *Review of Existential Psychology and Psychiatry* 16:1–3 (1978–79): 95–112, provided the inspiration for this effort to retrieve Plato's thought on the factions of the soul.

2. There are, as we shall see, many "others" in Lacan's work. To distinguish this *Other* from all others we will both capitalize and italicize it.

3. William J. Richardson, *Heidegger: From Phenomenology to Thought* (The Hague: Martinus Nijhoff, 1967), p. 89.

4. Richardson, *Heidegger,* p. 93. I use Richardson's translation rather than that of James S. Churchill because it more clearly expresses the force and potential of retrieval. Compare Martin Heidegger, *Kant and the Problem of Metaphysics,* trans. James S. Churchill (Bloomington, Indiana: Indiana University Press, 1962), p. 211.

5. Jacques Lacan, *Ecrits: A Selection,* trans. Alan Sheridan (New York: Norton, 1977), p. 234. Page numbers in parentheses in the text refer to this work.

6. Sherry Turkle, *Psychoanalytic Politics: Freud's French Revolution* (New York: Basic Books, 1978), and Stuart Schneiderman, *Jacques Lacan: The Death of an Intellectual Hero* (Cambridge, Mass.: Harvard University Press, 1983), provide material for understanding some of the turmoil that swirled around Lacan during his lifetime.

7. The full text is to be found in "The Mirror Stage as Formative of Function of the I," *Ecrits,* pp. 1–7.

8. This is the saying numbered as 45 in Kathleen Freeman, *Ancilla to the Pre-Socratic Philosophers* (Cambridge, Mass.: Harvard University Press, 1948). I have altered the translation in order to stress both the theme of movement and the importance of *logos.*

9. In *Ecrits,* pp. 30–113.

10. For his understanding of linguistics Lacan draws heavily on the work of Saussure and Jakobson. Claude Levi-Strauss provided him with the anthropological significance of these linguistic discoveries. See Levi-Strauss, "Language and the Analysis of Social Laws," *Structural Anthropology,* trans. C. Jacobson and B. G. Schoepf (New York: Anchor, 1967), pp. 54–65.

11. Roman Jakobson and M. Halle, *Fundamentals of Language* (The Hague: Mouton, 1956).

12. Ferdinand de Saussure, *Course in General Linguistics,* ed. Bally and Sechehaye; trans. W. Baskin (New York: McGraw-Hill, 1966).

13. Jacques Lacan, *The Four Fundamental Concepts of Psychoanalysis,* trans. Alan Sheridan (New York: Norton, 1981), p. 208.

14. Sigmund Freud, *Beyond the Pleasure Principle,* in *The Standard Edition of the Complete Psychological Works of Sigmund Freud* (London: Hogarth Press, 1953), pp. 18, 99, 14–15.

15. See "Translator's Note" in *Ecrits,* p. x.

16. Lacan's reworking of the case of Judge Schreber provides compelling evidence of the interpretive power of his principles. See "On a Question Preliminary to Any Possible Treatment of Psychosis," *Ecrits,* pp. 177–225.

17. Richardson, "The Mirror Inside: The Problem of the Self," pp. 106–7.

18. The text (*Republic* Book IV, 434–445) by no means exhausts all that Plato has to say about the psyche. The *Symposium, Phaedo,* and *Phaedrus* contain significant additions and development. Still, for the sake of our task, these cryptic, undeveloped words contain the original possibilities—in Heidegger's sense—of the problem to be conserved and set free. See G. M. A. Grube, *Plato's Thought* (Boston: Beacon Press, 1958), pp. 120–49 for an overview of Plato's discussion of the psyche.

19. *Republic,* 439d–440a. The translation used is Allan Bloom, *The Republic of Plato* (New York: Basic Books, 1968). Bloom, unlike other translators, notes the ambiguity in the words used by Plato to discuss the ruling part of the soul. See his notes on page 457.

20. *Republic,* 440b. Bloom's translation demonstrates the profound ambiguity in the text. What he calls "the calculating part" later becomes "speech." I italicize the latter to underscore the ambiguity of the translation.

21. See *A Greek-English Lexicon,* ed. Liddell and Scott (Oxford: The Clarendon Press, 1889).

22. *Republic,* 440e.

23. *Republic,* 441b.

24. *Republic,* 440c-d; my emphasis.

25. Confer *A Greek-English Lexicon.*

26. This, of course, is Heidegger's point when he asks "What Are Poets For?" See *Poetry, Language, Thought,* trans. Albert Hofstadter (New York: Harper & Row, 1971), pp. 89–142.

27. Though Heidegger's later works abound with references to *logos,* a succinct account of his understanding of the Greek expression can be found in *Introduction to Metaphysics,* trans. Ralph Manheim (New Haven: Yale University Press, 1959), pp. 129–34. Also see Richardson's translation of the Marburg lectures of 1925–26 in "The Mirror Inside: The Problem of the Self," p. 10.

28. Martin Heidegger, *Being and Time,* trans. Macquarrie and Robinson (New York: Harper & Row, 1962), pp. 203–10.

29. Martin Heidegger, "Logos," in *Early Greek Thinking*, trans. Krell and Capuzzi (New York: Harper & Row, 1975), p. 64. It is important to know that Lacan translated this essay into French. "Logos," trans. J. Lacan, in *La Psychanalyse* 1 (1956): 59–76.

30. The phrases, of course, are taken from "The Letter on Humanism," trans. Edgar Lohner in *Philosophy in the Twentieth Century* (New York: Random House, 1962). See especially the identification of the essence of language with the dwelling of man's essence, p. 283.

31. Martin Heidegger, "Logos," p. 61.

32. Martin Heidegger, "Logos," p. 64.

33. *Mind Design* is the title of a recent collection of essays attempting to explain the psyche along the lines of a "semantic engine." See *Mind Design*, ed. John Haugeland (Cambridge, Mass.: M.I.T. Press, 1983), pp. 1–34.

34. Maurice Merleau-Ponty, *The Phenomenology of Perception*, trans. Colin Smith (New York: Routledge and Kegan Paul, 1962), p. 178.

35. T. S. Eliot, *The Waste Land* (New York: Harvest Books, 1934), p. 29.

36. T. S. Eliot, *The Waste Land*, p. 46.

37. *Lacan and Language*, p. 68. They are referring to the famous "Discourse at Rome," entitled "The Function and Field of Speech and Language in Psychoanalysis," *Ecrits*, pp. 30–113.

Space, Time, and the Sublime

1. Donald Kuspit, "Philosophy and Art: Elective Affinities in an Arranged Marriage," *Artforum* 94 (November 1984): 94.

2. Immanuel Kant, *The Critique of Judgment*, trans. J. N. Bernard (New York: Hafner Press, 1951), sect. 23.

3. André Malraux, *The Voices of Silence*, trans. Stuart Gilbert (Princeton: Princeton University Press, 1978), p. 470.

4. H. W. Janson, *History of Art* (New York: Harry N. Abrams, Inc., 1971), p. 36.

5. Michel Foucault, *The Order of Things: An Archaeology of Human Sciences* (New York: Vintage Books, 1974), p. 36.

6. David Summers, *Michelangelo and the Language of Art* (Princeton: Princeton University Press, 1981), p. 72.

7. *Order of Things*, p. 8.

8. *Michelangelo,* p. 73.

9. *Order of Things,* p. 53.

10. *Order of Things,* p. 64.

11. *Critique,* sect. 23. The agreement of imagination and concepts, the condition of objectivity, even though there is *no* concept, makes it possible for Kant to admit that reason is interested in nature containing in itself a ground for assuming a regular agreement of its products (or those of art) with our disinterested satisfactions. Thus, we cannot contemplate beauty without finding our interest in it akin to the moral. This interest is, in fact, the basis of good moral disposition (section 42).

12. *Critique,* sect. 23.

13. *Critique,* sect. 45.

14. *Critique,* sect. 27. From this we can see that, indeed, no sensible (intuited in accordance with the categories of space and time) form contains the sublime (section 23). In the apprehension of the sublime, the time series (and the spatial series) would be annihilated in intuition; intuition itself would suffer annihilation!

15. Jean François Lyotard, "What Is Postmodernism?," in *The Postmodern Condition: A Report on Knowledge,* trans. Geoff Bennington and Brian Massumi (Minneapolis: University of Minnesota Press, 1984), p. 81.

16. "What Is Postmodernism?," p. 79.

17. Robert Rosenblum, *Modern Painting and the Northern Romantic Tradition* (New York: Harper and Row, 1975), p. 12.

18. *Northern Romantic Tradition,* p. 13.

19. *Northern Romantic Tradition,* p. 50.

20. Paul Voght, *Expressionism, German Painting 1905–1920* (New York: Harry V. Abrams, 1978), p. 92.

21. Valerie J. Fletcher, *Dreams & Nightmares: Utopian Visions in Modern Art* (Washington D.C.: Smithsonian Institute Press, 1983), p. 49.

22. *Expressionism,* p. 92.

23. *Expressionism,* p. 94.

24. Jean François Lyotard, "The Sublime and the Avantgarde," trans. Lisa Liebmann, *Artforum* (April 1984): 40.

25. G. W. F. Hegel, *On Art, Religion, Philosophy,* ed. J. Glenn Gray (New York: Harper and Row, 1970), p. 87. In this and other statements Hegel aptly points out the serious limitations of the Kantian program. These include the division into subjective and objective, the subversion of all ends to the moral, and the "perverse idea" that asks, "What is the aim?" but means, "What is the use?" The advantage

of the Hegelian implication of consciousness in the development of the object is that we move beyond the spatial and temporal intuitions and so beyond the notion of substance.

26. "The Sublime," p. 40.

27. "The Sublime," p. 40.

28. Roland Barthes, *The Pleasure of the Text,* trans. Richard Miller (New York: Farrar Straus and Giroux, 1975), p. 61.

29. Gilles Deleuze, *Différence et répétition* (Paris: Presses Universitaires de France, 1968), p. 79.

Foucault and Theory: Genealogical Critiques of the Subject

1. This revolution, which extends the subject's emergence from cognitive passivity to epistemic activity, begins in Kant's work on history and politics. For Kant, it is the responsibility of the individual and the species to pursue enlightenment, which has as a motto *"Sapere aude,"* "dare to know." Remaining stuck in immaturity is a failure of courage and resolution. See Kant's "What Is Enlightenment?" in *Foundations of the Metaphysics of Morals,* trans. Lewis White Beck (Indianapolis: Bobbs-Merril Company, Inc., 1959), p. 85. However, this Kant, who is afire with enlightenment fervor, is also cautious if not conservative. In the same essay, enlightenment as the progress of reason is to occur in the scholarly realm of debate, not in the practical matters of organizing daily lives. In Kant's *The Contest of the Faculties,* theory as obsequious, separate observation again rears its head. For Kant the French Revolution several hundred miles away is a matter more of anthropological significance than of political importance. The success or failure of the event is relatively uninteresting; Kant's emphasis is the expression of a universal—if disinterested—sympathy with the revolution. The effectiveness of the revolution itself is not as promising as its evocation of a capacity and desire for progress and moral-political development inherent in the species. The theoretical promise of the eventual telos of the species is more pressing than particular efforts to attain that end. Kant's topic is a priori history, not political action. See *The Contest of the Faculties,* in *Kant's Political Writings,* ed. Hans Reiss, trans. H. B. Nisbet (Cambridge: Cambridge University Press, 1970), pp. 182–83.

2. According to Foucault, genealogy as effective history shortens its vision to what is nearest it, giving up the "contemplation of distances and heights." "Nietzsche, Genealogy, History," in *Language, Counter-memory, Practice,* ed. Donald F. Bouchard, trans. Donald F. Bouchard and Sherry Simon (Ithaca: Cornell University Press, 1977), pp. 155–56.

3. Of course, these few examples do not cover every subject produced in the effort to meet theoretical expectations. Although this short paper could certainly be filled out with more detail from Foucault's writings, its brevity is not an injustice to

Foucault's project. Once theory itself is called into question, its demand that an analytics develop into a general analytics has less force. According to Foucault, the designed fragmentation of genealogy does not aspire to mature into a new theory which would re-hierarchize and reorganize that which it has just made thematic. He makes this clear in "Two Lectures," trans. Kate Soper, in *Power/Knowledge: Selected Interviews and Other Writings, 1972–1977*, ed. Colin Gordon (New York: Pantheon Books, 1980), pp. 83–85.

4. On p. 73 of *The History of Sexuality: Volume I: An Introduction*, trans. Robert Hurley (New York: Vintage Books, 1980), Foucault stresses the need to challenge the assumption of pervasive sexual repression and to examine instead the positivity and power function of the idea of that which is repressed and the mechanisms and effects of that idea. For purposes of genealogical thinking, we need to shake the guilt of what we are supposed to know or to be.

5. Theory seems to have this in common with power, which, for Foucault, has a degree of success and effectiveness in proportion to its ability to hide its mechanisms. See *The History of Sexuality*, p. 86.

6. Foucault uses this language in "What Is Enlightenment?" trans. Catherine Porter, in *The Foucault Reader*, ed. Paul Rabinow (New York: Pantheon Books, 1984), p. 50.

7. In "Nietzsche, Genealogy, History," p. 142, Foucault disrupts the dialectic between the assumption of "the existence of immobile forms" and the "external world of accident and succession" inherent in the search for origin by suggesting that the real secret is not the potential waiting to be educed but is instead that there is no essence except perhaps that which is extrapolated from particular forms. Foucault here juxtaposes disparity to identity. On p. 161, he adds that the unity behind masks is in effect a parody of unity.

8. In "Intellectuals and Power," in *Language, Counter-memory, Practice*, pp. 204–9, Foucault and Deleuze do flirt with an experimental reformulation of theory as a partial and regional tool for struggle that multiplies itself and its effects rather than a totalizing, systematizing account that focuses and closes. Foucault considers the same sense of theory as a toolkit for specific investigations of relations of power in "Power and Strategies," trans. Colin Gordon, *Power/Knowledge*, p. 145. In "Two Lectures," p. 81, he offers the thought of a "non-centralised kind of theoretical production." However, Foucault's suspicion of theory's inherent connection to totality leads him to offer "analytics" as an alternative to "theory" in *The History of Sexuality* (p. 82) and in the interview "The Subject and Power" in Hubert L. Dreyfus and Paul Rabinow's *Michel Foucault: Beyond Structuralism and Hermeneutics* (Chicago: University of Chicago Press, 1982), pp. 208–9.

9. In one of his last essays, "What Is Enlightenment?" Foucault does speak of "theoretical coherence," but this is a continued displacing, not a renewed privileging, of the theoretical. Just as Foucault shifts the critical investigation of our limits from the transcendental, that is, from the search for the necessary, structural

limits that we may not transgress, to the archeological, that is, to the identification of the contingent, arbitrary, historical limits that have formed us and which now can be challenged, so also does he shift his use of the theoretical. See pp. 45–46. On p. 50, he says that the theoretical or archeological accounts of what we are do have a descriptive coherence in "the historically unique forms in which the generalities of our relations to things, to others, to ourselves, have been problematized." However, the theoretical and the archeological are instrumental in Foucault's project: his work occurs in the tension between the weight of a comprehensive description of the pervasion of the historical and the effort to shake the historical. At p. 50, that which is "archeological in its method" is "genealogical in its design." The theoretical does not regain its dominance: the critical ontology of ourselves is not to be "a theory, a doctrine, nor even . . . a permanent body of knowledge." See p. 50. The theoretical is developed and used in a genealogical context which explores the possibility of liberty and experiments with going beyond our limits. This is the shift from the accumulation of knowledge to a philosophical ethos of constant criticism of the present.

10. Foucault is perhaps as much concerned with our lazy and uncritical need for theory as he is with theory itself. See "Revolutionary Action: 'Until now',\u200b" in *Language, Counter-memory, Practice,* p. 231.

11. This paper has profited from discussions with my colleague Ladelle McWhorter and from comments by and conversations with Peg Birmingham.

Foucault's Move beyond the Theoretical

1. Foucault abjures the term *theory* in *La Volenté de savoir;* see English trans., *The History of Sexuality: Volume I: An Introduction,* trans. Robert Hurley (New York: Random House, 1978), p. 82.

2. Michel Foucault, "Afterword: The Subject and Power," in *Michel Foucault: Beyond Structuralism and Hermeneutics,* ed. Hubert L. Dreyfus and Paul Rabinow (Chicago: University of Chicago Press, 1983), p. 208. See also page 209.

3. Foucault makes this explicit in "Afterword," p. 208.

4. Friedrich Nietzsche, *Beyond Good and Evil,* trans. Walter Kaufmann (New York: Random House, 1966), p. 24 (section 17).

5. Of course there are exceptions. Sometimes theories that are known to be untrue are kept alive for political reasons. Examples can be found in Janet Sayers, *Biological Politics* (London: Tavistock Publications, 1982); and in Stephen Jay Gould, *The Mismeasure of Man* (New York: W. W. Norton and Co., Inc., 1981).

6. Nietzsche, *Beyond Good and Evil,* p. 9 (section 1); his emphasis.

Local Theory

1. Michel Foucault, "Two Lectures," in *Power/Knowledge*, ed. Colin Gordon (New York: Pantheon, 1972), p. 81; hereafter cited as PK.

2. Diogenes Laertius, VIII, 8, fragment 278, quoted in Hannah Arendt, *The Life of the Mind* (New York: Harcourt Brace Jovanovich, 1978, One Volume Edition), p. 93.

3. *Life of the Mind*, p. 93.

4. *Life of the Mind*, p. 94.

5. Ibid.

6. Werner Jaeger, *Paideia: The Ideals of Greek Culture*, trans. Gilbert Highet, 3 vols. (New York: Oxford University Press, 1939–1944), 3:259. Arendt also cites this journey by Solon in the context of the first appearance of the term *philosophy*. She points out that the term appears in Croesus's address to Solon: "Stranger, great word has come to us about you, your wisdom and your wandering about, namely that you have gone visiting many lands of the earth *philosophizing* with respect to the spectacles you saw." See *Life of the Mind*, p. 164.

7. Herodotus, *The Histories*, trans. Aubrey de Selincourt (Baltimore: Penguin Books, 1975), p. 51.

8. *Paideia*, 3:259.

9. Thucydides, *History of the Peloponnesian War*, trans. Rex Warner (New York: Penguin Books, 1977), p. 47.

10. *Paideia*, 1:389.

11. *Paideia*, 1:385.

12. *The Peloponnesian War*, p. 48. See also *Paideia*, 1:387.

13. Immanuel Kant, *Der Streit der Fakultäten*, *(The Conflict of the Faculties)*, bilingual edition trans. Mary J. Gregor (New York: Abaris Books, 1979), p. 153. I am deeply indebted to Arendt's analysis of Kant's political philosophy and the notion of the 'judging spectator'. See her *Lectures on Kant's Political Philosophy*, ed. Ronald Beiner (Chicago: University of Chicago Press, 1982).

14. *Der Streit der Fakultäten*, p. 153.

15. Thus, Foucault will argue that we must make a distinction between the Enlightenment and Humanism. See page 211 of this essay.

16. Michel Foucault, *What Is Enlightenment?*, trans. Catherine Porter in *The Foucault Reader*, ed. Paul Rabinow (New York: Patheon Books, 1984), p. 34; hereafter cited as WI.

17. Foucault's 'turning around' of the Kantian reflection is a turning around of the reflections found in the First Critique. As I suggested above, Kant's political reflections upon the event of the French Revolution raise similar questions to those raised by Foucault in *What Is Enlightenment?*.

18. Michel Foucault, *Nietzsche, Genealogy, History,* trans. Donald F. Bouchard and Sherry Simon in *The Foucault Reader,* p. 88; hereafter cited as NGH.

19. Michel Foucault, *On the Genealogy of Ethics: An Overview of Work in Progress,* in *Beyond Structuralism and Hermeneutics,* ed. Hubert L. Dreyfus and Paul Rabinow (Chicago: University of Chicago Press, 1983), p. 237; hereafter cited as OGE.

20. *Der Streit der Fakultäten,* p. 151.

Postmortem Thought and the End of Man

1. We have to ask what 'completion' would mean in the discourses of Heidegger, Foucault, and Derrida. It will certainly not mean fulfillment, actualization, or termination. There is a sense that a particular way of thinking of man is coming to a close. But this closure is also, perhaps paradoxically, an opening. A new way of thinking is made possible by the end of man, a thinking that resists closure, in fact. 'Completion' in this new sense is perhaps best thought in terms of fruition: the bearing of new fruit, but as the constant, ongoing enjoyment (*fruitio*) of the bearing rather than of the fruit. Compare: "To be the child who is newly born, the creator must also want to be the mother who gives birth and the pangs of the birth-giver." Nietzsche, *Thus Spoke Zarathustra,* trans. Walter Kaufmann (New York: Viking Press, 1966), p. 87.

2. Michel Foucault, *The Order of Things: An Archaeology of the Human Sciences* (New York: Vintage Books, 1973), p. 385; hereafter cited as OT.

3. Martin Heidegger, "The End of Philosophy and the Task of Thinking," in *On Time and Being,* trans. Joan Stambaugh (New York: Harper & Row, Inc., 1972), pp. 56–57; hereafter cited as EP.

4. Martin Heidegger, "Time and Being," in *On Time and Being,* p. 24.

5. Martin Heidegger, "Letter on Humanism," in *Basic Writings,* ed. David Krell (New York: Harper & Row, Inc., 1977), p. 202; hereafter cited as LH.

6. Jacques Derrida, "The Ends of Man," in *Margins of Philosophy,* trans. Alan Bass (Chicago: The University of Chicago Press, 1982), p. 121; hereafter cited as EM.

7. But perhaps Derrida forgets the *withdrawal* of presencing being.

8. This analogy should not be pushed too far. There is no suggestion here that

thinking the truth of Being is a matter of 'seeing' for Heidegger. The analogy is meant to convey the radical closeness of the face and yet the absolute impossibility of seeing it except indirectly through reflection. Similarly, as Heidegger says, being is the closest, but it is impossible to think it except through reflection.

9. Unfortunately, this may sound like a return to some sort of subject/object distinction. But, in fact, reflection, as I mean it here, refers to a discursive, non-subjectival *relation* between two previously undifferentiated ("un-valued") beings whose meanings are a function of the relation itself. That we call one being in the relation subject and the other object is an (optional) interpretation posterior to reflection.

10. Jacques Derrida, "Différance," in *Margins of Philosophy,* p. 11. But we must immediately cite its erasure as/of origin: "The trace is in fact the absolute origin of sense in general. Which amounts to saying once again that there is no absolute origin of sense in general"; Jacques Derrida, *Of Grammatology,* trans. Gayatri Chakravorty Spivak (Baltimore: Johns Hopkins University Press, 1976), p. 65; emphasis in the original.

11. Linguistics, psychoanalysis, and ethnology are "counter-sciences," in relation to the human sciences, in that they lead back to the epistemological bases, specifically life, labor, and language, that made the human sciences possible at all. But unlike the human sciences they neither posit nor operate from a general *concept* of man, "at no moment do they come near to isolating a quality in [man] that is specific, irreducible, and uniformly given to experience" (OT 381). To that extent they *dissolve* man, "they ceaselessly 'unmake' that very man who is creating and recreating his positivity in the human sciences" (OT 379).

12. Ferdinand de Saussure, *Course in General Linguistics,* quoted by Derrida in "Différance," p. 15.

13. "Différance," p. 11.

14. "Différance," pp. 26–27.

Index

Vermeer, Jan, 176–77, 183–84
Violence: in Futurist art, 182; of thought
   structures, 43, 60, 195, 225n5; of values,
   218; social, 58, 126

Ward, James, 180

Waste Land, The, 173–74
Weber, Max, 128
Wilcox, John T., 232n15
Wittig, Monique, 145–46, 148–49

Zribi-Hertz, Anne, 149